THE CHANGING AGENDA

World Politics
Since 1945

THE CHANGING AGENDA

*World Politics
Since 1945*

Sylvia Woodby
Martha L. Cottam

WESTVIEW PRESS
Boulder & London

This book was written while Sylvia Woodby was on the faculty at Goucher College in Towson, Maryland. The viewpoints expressed herein are those of the authors and do not necessarily reflect those of the Department of State.

Copyright © 1988 by Westview Press, Inc.

Published in 1988 in the United States of America by Westview Press, Inc.; Frederick A. Praeger, Publisher; 5500 Central Avenue, Boulder, Colorado 80301

Library of Congress Cataloging-in-Publication Data
Woodby, Sylvia.
  The changing agenda.
  Bibliography: p.
  Includes index.
  1. World politics—1945-   . I. Cottam, Martha L.
II. Title.
D843.C595 1988   327′.0904   87-13565
ISBN 0-8133-0412-1
ISBN 0-8133-0413-X (pbk.)

Printed and bound in the United States of America

(∞) The paper used in this publication meets the requirements of the American National Standard
     for Permanence of Paper for Printed Library Materials Z39.48-1984.

10   9   8   7   6   5   4   3   2

For Eric and Otto

CONTENTS

List of Illustrations   xi

Preface   xiii

Introduction   1

   The Three International Agendas, 2
   Chronological Perspective, 5
   Notes, 6

1   1945–1955/ Postwar Priorities   7

   THE GLOBAL AGENDA, 8
     Political Redesign and Institutions, 8
     Creating the International Economic System
      and Institutions, 12
   THE EAST-WEST AGENDA, 14
     Contention over the Political Future of Europe, 14
     Front-Burner Crises: Germany and Korea, 18
     Military Alliances and Security Needs, 20
   THE NORTH-SOUTH AGENDA, 24
     Decolonization, 24
     A New Issue: Forging a Southern Alliance, 30
     A Simmering Issue Heats Up: The South
      and the Cold War, 32
   Conclusions, 34
   Notes, 34

2   1955–1963/ Working Out the Rules   37

   THE GLOBAL AGENDA, 38
     Fear of War and Efforts to Control
      Nuclear Weaponry, 38
     Decolonization, 41
   THE EAST-WEST AGENDA, 44
     Control Problems on the Front Burner, 44

Crisis Diplomacy, 49
Arms Control: A Simmering Back-Burner Issue, 52
THE NORTH-SOUTH AGENDA, 54
Overview of the Issues, 54
Nonalignment: From Back to Front Burner, 57
Economic Issues Appear on the Agenda, 60
Conclusions, 61
Notes, 62

3 1964–1968/ The System Quakes:
   The Limits of Superpower   63

THE GLOBAL AGENDA, 64
Security and the Prevention of War, 65
Supranational Issues, 68
THE EAST-WEST AGENDA, 69
Weapons, War, and European Security, 69
On the Front Burner: The Limits of
   Superpower Strength and Influence, 72
THE NORTH-SOUTH AGENDA, 79
Economic Reform, 79
Nonalignment, 83
An Issue Leaves the Agenda:
   Afro-Asianism Fades, 84
Conclusions, 85
Notes, 85

4 1969–1975/ The Agenda Shifts:
   The Era of Détente   87

THE EAST-WEST AGENDA, 87
Détente: New Ideas About the
   East-West Relationship, 88
Détente: Reconstructing East-West
   Political Relationships, 92
Arms Control: The Top Issue for Détente, 93
The Documents of Détente, 96
Détente and the Dangers of East-West
   Competition in Regional Conflicts:
   A Hot Issue, 98
East-West Trade, 101
THE NORTH-SOUTH AGENDA, 102
International Economic Issues, 102
The New International Economic Order, 105

Simmering Issues: Nationalizations
and Producer Associations, 108
THE GLOBAL AGENDA, 110
Collapse of the Postwar Economic System, 110
Other Items, 111
Conclusions, 113
Notes, 114

5 1975–1980/ The Agenda Drifts Back:
Competitive Globalism   117

THE EAST-WEST AGENDA, 118
The Narrowing of Détente, 118
Arms Control on the Front Burner, 118
The Status and Value of Détente, 120
Superpower Crisis Diplomacy:
Condominium or Competition? 122
Third World Crises Leading to
a Mixture of the East-West and
North-South Agendas, 125
THE NORTH-SOUTH AGENDA, 131
Implementing NIEO, 132
OPEC as a North-South Issue, 136
Human Rights, 137
THE GLOBAL AGENDA, 138
Political Issues, 139
Economic Problems, 140
Food, 141
Conclusions, 142
Notes, 142

6 1980s/ Forward to the Past   145

THE EAST-WEST AGENDA, 146
Arms Control, 148
Competition for Influence and
the Use of Coercion, 154
THE NORTH-SOUTH AGENDA, 161
Economic Problems, 161
Trade, 164
Debt, 166
Revolution, 168

THE GLOBAL AGENDA, 171
   Disarray in the International
      Economic System Tops the Agenda, 171
   International Violence, 173
   Globalism as an Ideological Issue
      on the Agenda, 175
   Conclusions, 176
   Notes, 176

Conclusion   179

Illustrations   183
List of Acronyms   191
Chronology of Events Cited   193
Recommended Reading   197
Index   205

LIST OF ILLUSTRATIONS

Maps

3.1   Israel after the 1967 war   67

      The world   184

Figures

6.1   The impact of MIRV technology on the military balance   149

A.1   U.S.-Soviet strategic military balance: Total launchers,
      1963–1986   186

A.2   U.S.-Soviet strategic military balance: ICBMs, 1963–1986   187

A.3   U.S.-Soviet strategic military balance: SLBMs, 1963–1986   188

A.4   U.S.-Soviet strategic military balance: Bombers, 1963–1986   189

PREFACE

This book is the product of a set of frustrations. One resulted from our experience in attempting to teach various courses in international politics to students who had little preparation and time and who had so much to learn. We wanted to write a book that would not require students to memorize forty years of history and that would present international politics to them in a way they could understand and use to interpret international issues in the future, whether or not their careers take them into an international field. This complemented another frustration we have both experienced when confronted by students' search for *the* answer, *the* solution to world conflicts, and *the* good guys and bad guys. Therefore, we also wanted the students to learn that simple answers are rare and that conflicts frequently derive from differing perceptions of events and different judgments about what is right. We wanted to show students how differently those who made and make international politics see issues and perhaps in this way help students understand why conflict resolution is so difficult. Third, we both have spent much of our careers focusing on the policies of the superpowers but have each had a long-term interest in the Third World. We felt strongly that the Third World has often been neglected in books on international politics and that such a situation should be corrected.

We share equally responsibility for the material in this book. As in most coauthored projects, we began with a division of labor but by the end, with innumerable drafts, blends, and rewrites, it was impossible for either of us to tell who wrote what—which certainly did not help the annotation process. Woodby comes before Cottam as the authorship attribution in an effort to rectify the discrimination always suffered by those whose names are at the end of the alphabet.

Good critics and supportive friends and colleagues have been very important for us and this project. We especially appreciate the support of Miriam Gilbert and E. Thomas Rowe. Our thanks to Eric Fain for the graphs, Anne Meagher for graphics and maps, and Chih-yu Shih and Susie Hiss for research assistance. Otwin Marenin, Dr. Susan Stein, Rourke O'Flaherty, Dan Papp, and Marion Leighton supplied valuable comments on the manuscript.

The persistent curiosity of our students in North America has both inspired and rewarded us over the years. Martha Cottam's students at the University of Port Harcourt, Nigeria, provided a lesson in the strength and reality of the North-South agenda that we will never forget.

We extend special thanks to Eric Fain and Carolyn Cottam, who kept us going.

Sylvia Woodby
Martha L. Cottam

INTRODUCTION

Students of international relations confront an enormous and daunting task. Significant events and developments in world politics have come to involve so many actors and so many issues that mastering the subject seems impossible, and histories of world politics since 1945 easily assume unmanageable proportions. Yet detail is important: Without comprehensive knowledge of key events, the student may find theoretical treatments of international relations that offer analytical frameworks and organizing themes and concepts to be confusing.

In this book we attempt to supply such knowledge by providing an organized overview of the changing agenda of world politics. By *agenda* we mean those issues being addressed by world political actors that elicit significant action or attention. When we apply the concept of agenda to the study of any kind of politics, we assume that the subject matter is to some extent always in flux and that choices and judgments are made all the time about the problems, tasks, or circumstances on which action is desirable or necessary. Controversies over the proper definition and ranking of issues requiring action make up much of political life, and the list of issues under consideration at any given time will reveal much about the actors, values, and tension points in any political system. Over time, changes in the list of issues will reflect changes in political power as well as in perceptions, problems, and circumstances.

This general concept holds true for international politics as well; in fact, we believe that a focus on agenda is exceptionally useful for the study of international politics, where no central governing authority exists. Although states often collaborate and frequently agree, they all prize autonomy and claim the right to sovereignty—that is, the right to run their own affairs without interference from others and to decide for themselves what to do when conflicts occur. Thus, states have always spent much time and energy attempting to persuade other states to share their perceptions and ideas about what needs to be done—to forge agreement on what could be considered an international agenda. Much of the dialogue in world politics involves attempts to characterize events and situations in ways that attract the attention of other states, so as to justify or promote particular actions or to mobilize cooperative efforts. Frequently, these attempts concern the

[handwritten margin note: individual sovereignty key to conflict in International Relations]

1

ways in which the actions of single states are alleged or believed to represent problems for a larger community. At any given time the international political agenda may include issues that produce conflicts about acceptable behavior for states, issues that challenge states to work together to solve common problems, or issues that raise debates about what it is that states may properly do without any interference from others.

Although there may be many times when the issues of world politics seem self-evident, agendas are set by people: An issue receives international attention only when enough policymakers from enough countries believe that it should. In any period there are competing ideas, reflecting different interests and perspectives or different standards of state behavior, about what the international political issues are and about which issues are most important to which states. Issues arise because of new events or problems, new ways of thinking, or new definitions of the relevant group of actors. New issues can also arise because of effective demands to think about issues that were previously ignored.

The issues we have included in this book are those that the historical record shows are occupying the time and efforts of political leaders. Rather than cataloging all the sites of conflict or all the problems and projects that have occupied states since 1945, we have tried to highlight major events and to identify classes of issues. This presents some problems regarding selection, and we do not expect readers to agree with all of our choices. For instance, we have excluded many cases of regional and bilateral conflict that concerned only a few states, but we have included all major U.S.-Soviet conflicts. We have included economic and social issues where that seemed appropriate, even when little action was taken about them.

Just as selection of issues posed problems, so too did our decisions on levels of generality. We have tried as far as possible to discuss categories of issues that have been important for significant numbers of states or that seem to provide useful labels for recurrent episodes. Thus *peace* and *civil war* are too general to be useful issue labels, whereas *arms control*, *détente*, and *decolonization* do identify relatively distinct sets of related specific issues. (It may not be appropriate in all cases to provide general labels for specific issues. Such significant specific issues as the status of Berlin and Palestinian rights merit separate treatment.)

The Three International Agendas

In selecting the issues, we have tried to sort events in ways that are helpful to someone searching for general guidelines as a basis for later, more detailed study. One of our most important premises is that there are several agendas. World politics is so complex that reducing its issues to a single agenda will mean missing many important subsets of ideas, perspectives, and interactions. We see at least three international agendas: the East-West, the North-South, and the global. Multiple agendas will always coexist in world politics, but we believe that these three have been especially significant. Each of them represents a cluster of issues to which attention has been given by a significant group of states, on which action was urged or taken. We believe that our description of three competing but parallel agendas goes beyond most studies, which concentrate only on the affairs of the most powerful states. Some brief comments on each of these agendas will clarify the distinctions we are making.

The Global Agenda

The global agenda includes the issues viewed as important to the entire global community. These are not limited to what is discussed in international institutions such as the United Nations, although many global issues are debated in that forum. They are issues that most national leaders recognize as not only having consequences for all people but also as requiring a global solution—a course of action that is agreed to by the global community and that will be carried out by that community. The global agenda has included the need for new international political and economic systems and institutions, war prevention and conflict resolution, debt, population growth, food, and racism. The importance international actors have given to a global agenda has ebbed and flowed over the years. In the first decade after World War II a global agenda received considerable attention. By the late 1980s the very notion of the global agenda was rejected by important members of the international community.

The East-West Agenda

The East-West agenda items are those related to conflicts and relationships between the two major power blocs—the United States and its allies on the one hand, and the Soviet Union and its allies on the other. These matters are often described as bipolar politics. The Western alliance is most often thought of as including the United States, most of Western Europe, Canada, and Japan, with a few additional members from other regions (such as Israel, Australia, and New Zealand). The Eastern alliance includes the USSR, most Eastern European states, and various affiliated socialist states. The most powerful and industrially advanced states belong to these two groupings, and the states on either side tend to share with each other a number of political, economic, and military characteristics and concerns.[1] But it is important to note at the outset that relations within both alliances have often been contentious. Neither the United States nor the Soviet Union (the superpowers) has been able to take the support of its affiliated states for granted. In fact, the superpower control problem repeatedly occurs on this agenda—that is, the difficulty each has had in maintaining alliance cohesion and the repeated errors each has made in trying to preserve alliance unity.

There is little doubt that the East-West agenda has dominated world politics. In fact, for many, the Cold War, détente, and Soviet-American crises and summits have been the only important trends and events in world politics. Although the East-West agenda has included the concerns of the most active and powerful members of the international political system, it is an incomplete record. To trace only the rise and fall of superpower antagonisms would leave much of international politics unattended: There are serious and significant differences between this East-West agenda and both the global and North-South agendas.

The North-South Agenda

Whereas most students are familiar with the East-West dimension of international politics, they might find the North-South dimension more difficult to understand. First, it should be noted that in this book we use the terms *South* and *Third World* interchangeably. There are many different ways of defining the South, and geography alone does not determine membership in it. In terms of the North-South division, the South includes the countries in Asia, Africa, Latin America, the Middle East, and Oceania, with some exceptions. Israel, Japan, Australia, and New Zealand are usually considered Western states (and are therefore part of the North).

A great deal of thought has been devoted to the effort to determine exactly what characteristics are shared by the states of the South. In general, the countries of the Third World share a history in which "Western" forms of government have been imposed upon them and national boundaries have been set by outsiders. They also share characteristics of poverty and a level of industrialization generally below that of Europe (East and West), the United States, and Japan. They export natural resources and agricultural products and are heavily dependent upon foreign trade for national income.

There are numerous exceptions to these general characteristics. Some of the oil-producing states in the Middle East have become wealthy (Kuwait is a good example). Furthermore, some Third World states are much more heavily industrialized than others. Brazil, for example, has a much larger and much more industrialized economy than Mali. Some Third World states are troubled by internal disunity associated with artificial borders (Nigeria and Somalia are examples), whereas others are nations with histories of national grandeur and very strong national identities (such as Iran, Ethiopia, Egypt, and Vietnam).

It is equally difficult to find political characteristics common to all Third World states. (The term *Third World* contrasts with the "first" world, including Western Europe and North America, and the "second" world of the socialist bloc.) Many reject membership in either the Eastern or Western alliance and choose an international policy of nonalignment. Some are allied with one of the superpowers by formal treaty but consider themselves nonaligned politically. Finally, many Third World states are formally and politically aligned with one of the superpowers.

One political characteristic that is shared by most Third World states is a history of domination by some colonial power. This is closely related to another shared political characteristic, a current condition of weakness in ability to determine and influence international affairs. The Third World, as a whole, is on the periphery of the international system, in terms of its power and influence. Moreover, the political weakness of the Third World is not only international but also internal: Many Southern states suffer from chronic internal political and economic instability.

A final important political characteristic of the South is a shared identity and belief that its concerns and problems have their origins in North-South relations. This belief has inspired the South to try to raise the status of Southern issues and to shift international attention away from East-West conflicts and preoccupations.

South raises consciousness about self

Membership in the North is not so difficult to determine: For most people, the North includes the highly industrialized states in Western Europe plus the United States, Canada, Japan, Israel, Australia, and New Zealand. In this book we add Eastern Europe and the Soviet Union to the North despite the fact that these states have repeatedly argued that they are not part of the North because they were not colonial powers and thus not responsible for the condition of the South. Although this denial may be true historically, many members of the South believe that the East acts similarly to the West when it comes to resolving issues on the North-South agenda. Therefore, we include the East in the North but will often refer to the Western and Eastern portions of the North separately.

Chronological Perspective

Our survey of the three agendas proceeds by chronological periods. In defining these periods we have watched for points at which issues or the priorities assigned to issues have changed significantly. At the end of our study we will offer some observations about the shifts we have noted in the ways issues have been defined, the changing importance of certain key issues, and also in the relationships of the three agendas. We intend to show how issues have risen to prominence or fallen in importance, how the list of issues has expanded or contracted, and how competing or alternative agendas have interacted.

agendas are always dynamic

or are they?

It will become clear that for each of the agendas, some issues persistently appear. Yet the distinctions among the three agendas do not mean they are completely different. Some issues overlap, falling on different agendas at the same time. In such cases the distinctions are very useful, since issues that appear on different agendas are defined and evaluated differently, and the solutions recommended vary accordingly.

*   *   *

We have done our best to identify those issues that have made an impact on the public record. The reader is encouraged to use our themes as a guide and to revise them whenever and wherever more detailed study suggests a different account of the issues of world politics. It is our hope that the descriptions we present and the observations we offer will contribute to thoughtful study of world politics.

Notes

1. The North Atlantic Treaty Organization (NATO) includes the United States, Britain, France, Italy, Canada, Norway, Belgium, Denmark, the Netherlands, Luxembourg, Iceland, and Portugal. Greece and Turkey joined in 1952, the Federal Republic of Germany (FRG, or West Germany) in 1954, and Spain in 1982. Sweden, Austria, Finland, and Switzerland are neutral.

The Warsaw Treaty Organization (WTO) includes Bulgaria, Czechoslovakia, the German Democratic Republic (GDR, or East Germany), Hungary, Poland, Romania, and the USSR.

1945–1955

One / POSTWAR PRIORITIES

When World War II ended officially on September 2, 1945, entire regions across the world were left in political, economic, and social chaos. The war had touched nearly every state actively involved in world politics. It was clear at war's end that two major tasks that were global in scope and that seemed to require cooperative efforts faced the victors: restoring peace and redesigning world politics. What was not anticipated then was that by 1955, when two German states gained sovereignty, peace would be replaced by tension and world politics would be polarized into contending camps. In this chapter as in those that follow, we briefly summarize the agendas before turning to a detailed discussion.

• **GLOBAL AGENDA**   The global agenda and the cooperative framework for approaching its issues emerged while the fighting was still going on. As the victorious Allied powers—the United States, Britain, France,[1] and the USSR[2]—fought the war together, they also pledged to oversee the peace together so that a war of such magnitude would never happen again.

The first problem on the agenda was the fate of the aggressive regimes that had started the war—Germany, Italy, and Japan, known as the Axis. A corollary concern was to return to self-government and stability those territories that the Axis powers had conquered or commanded and to do so in ways that would contribute to a lasting peace. Although "liberation" was at first limited to the states occupied or colonized by the defeated Axis powers, significant movement toward self-government did begin in the colonies. The process of decolonization was uneven and marked with serious armed conflicts; nevertheless the establishment of new sovereign states began, a process that brought new interests and perspectives to the international stage.

Cooperative efforts to reform world politics were an important global agenda item. The United Nations was organized in 1944–1945 to monitor the peace, enforce collective sanctions against aggressor nations, and promote self-government and was also expected to serve as a forum for discussion of world problems and to coordinate efforts to solve them. Two other issues on the global agenda were cooperative reform of the international economic system and international control of atomic energy.

7

• **EAST-WEST AGENDA**   The extremely comprehensive global agenda of this period did not command a consensus for long. In fact, it was on issues where the Allied powers were working together most closely that cooperation was replaced by hostility and tension, and a new East-West agenda, based on conflicts of interest between two emerging camps, arose. The Soviet Union and a number of states in Eastern Europe and Asia formed an "Eastern" alliance in competition with a "Western" alliance that included the United States, the United Kingdom, France, Canada, Italy, Belgium, and the Netherlands. These East-West antagonisms produced the Cold War—a state of hostility just short of war—which quickly eclipsed the global agenda and raised fears of new armed conflicts. East-West issues included the nature of the political regimes in Europe, the status of Germany, and appropriate responses to political changes in Europe, the Middle East, and Asia.

• **NORTH-SOUTH AGENDA**   The pace and scope of decolonization was the most prominent issue on this agenda and a major motive for establishing vehicles for Southern unity. In the reformed international political system represented by the United Nations, the small states and newly independent former colonies were offered roles of dignity and equality. For many states of Africa, Asia, and Latin America (often referred to collectively as the South), the opportunities for self-assertion in postwar world politics brought evidence that the perspectives and interests of Southern states as a group would differ from those of the Northern states. The North-South agenda began to take shape in the first postwar decade as these distinctive interests and perspectives found collective expression.

THE GLOBAL AGENDA

Political Redesign and Institutions

Just as after World War I the victorious powers had sat down together at a peace conference to redraw the political maps of Europe and of many other areas where European powers had interests, so the scope of World War II made a similar redesign vital. This would include not just Europe, but also most of Asia, the Middle East, and parts of Africa. From the very beginning of World War II, the Allied powers made it clear that they blamed aggressive and militaristic regimes for starting the war. At a series of wartime conferences, the Allies outlined their intentions to prevent another catastrophe: They demanded an unconditional surrender and agreed to facilitate the "destruction of the philosophies in those countries which are based on conquest and the subjugation of other people."[3] The first step would be to demilitarize the enemy states and to destroy their war-making potential.[4] This would permit the next step: transformation of the governments, laws, economies, and social institutions of these states under Allied supervision. A transformation was thought to be necessary in order to render these countries more democratic and thus less warlike. The Allies also pledged to cooperate in designing an overall peace settlement and a "broad system of international cooperation and security" that would provide protection for all states against aggression.[5] However, distrust and suspicions existed among the Allies all along, and there were some problems in achieving real cooperation on all issues.

No Unity in allies

Formation of the United Nations

After World War I, the League of Nations had been established to maintain order and provide an antidote to international conflicts. For many reasons, this institution had not worked very well. Many believed that a stronger international body was needed—one that could control aggression, encourage cooperative relations among states, and promote political values that would assure peace. Accordingly, during World War II the Allies reviewed various proposals for global political institutions. The United Nations organization (known as the UN) was the final product of these deliberations. The term *United Nations* was first used officially in a declaration of the twenty-six nations that were allied against the Axis powers in 1942. Important details of organization, structure, and function were worked out in several wartime conferences. The United Nations Charter was formally signed by the representatives of 50 countries in San Francisco in June 1945.[6] The Charter's provisions reflected wartime preoccupations: Key operative sections outlined mechanisms for identifying potential threats to the peace and for mounting joint efforts by the most powerful states to deter aggressors. Although matters of "essentially domestic jurisdiction" were excluded, the Charter authorized a small group of major states to enforce the peace.[7] The UN Charter also declared its signatories' allegiance to some important political values: political equality, civil rights, and self-determination. All members pledged cooperative efforts to solve common problems.

UN formed in 1942

Finalized in 1946

Critics may be quick to point out that not all member states actually provided these rights within their own governments; however, the outline of ideals was an important statement of the underlying philosophy: The character of international relations reflects the character of government, and self-determination and responsible governments are effective antidotes to war and hostility among nations.

Implication that people are evil?

The United Nations and Decolonization

This philosophy was also reflected in the UN position that the era of colonialism had come to an end. The United Nations Declaration Regarding Non-Self-Governing Territories became a part of the UN Charter:

> Members of the United Nations which have or assume responsibilities for the administration of territories whose peoples have not yet attained a full measure of self-government . . . accept as a sacred trust the obligation to . . . develop self-government, to take due account of the political aspirations of the peoples, and to assist them in the progressive development of their free political institutions, according to the particular circumstances of each territory and its peoples and their varying stages of advancement.[8]

A trusteeship system was also set up for the colonies of the powers defeated in World War II. These arrangements gave the organized international community the right to monitor and evaluate the behavior of the "trustees." However, in neither provision did the Charter give explicit instructions concerning the course or pace of decolonization or the role of the subject peoples. In fact, many of the practical solutions suggested for independence struggles were collectivist ones: multilateral conferences, United Nations commissions, General Assembly debates, neutral arbitration, and investigations. All member states of the United Nations committed themselves to the ideal of full self-determination, although the colonial powers on the winning side (Britain, France, and the Netherlands) did not accept the imposition of any restrictions on their rights to govern their own colonies. Nonetheless each of these states did begin (not always voluntarily) to take some steps toward the conversion of colonies into independent states.

Limits to Implementation of Political Redesign

The creation of the United Nations was a symbol of the broad consensus in favor of globalist vision and a recognition of the need for mechanisms to articulate and resolve the global agenda in cooperative ways. The existence of the new institution helped to ensure that a global agenda would persist but did not guarantee that issues on the global agenda would attract the attention or commitments of resources necessary to solve them. Certainly the UN's existence did not guarantee that states would agree sufficiently in defining the issues as global ones. Conflicts that developed over the jurisdiction and proper scope of activities of the United Nations were one reflection of this.

Peacekeeping and decolonization issues revealed some limits of the global agenda. Unwillingness of interested states to permit UN involvement in their internal or international conflicts was the most obvious one. When the major states were in accord, disputes between small states could become global issues susceptible to cooperative international judgment and action within the UN framework or outside it. One example of UN intervention occurred in Palestine. In 1948, the UN attempted to devise a new system for the administration of Palestine (a territory the British had been governing under a League of Nations mandate). The UN plan suggested a partition of that territory between Arabs and Jews. After a war in 1948 established a different division of Palestine, the UN continued to be involved by providing truce observers and by attempting to maintain peace between the new state of Israel and its Arab neighbors. Another early intervention occurred in 1949, when the UN sent a military observer group to monitor a cease-fire in Kashmir, where India and Pakistan were disputing final disposition of that territory. In both the Arab-Israeli and the India-Pakistan cases, however, the stronger local parties effectively limited the global issue to peacekeeping and cease-fire supervision—not questions of title to territory.

[margin note: Wants U.N. to work in a selfish way]

United Nations enforcement mechanisms were used when war broke out on the Korean peninsula in June 1950 as a result of a North Korean invasion of South Korea. In this case, the United Nations authorized military action by member states against the North Koreans and later against the People's Republic of China. In a number of other situations, UN discussions treated enforcement of or adherence to agreements as global issues: for example, the withdrawal of Soviet troops from northern Iran (1946) and cease-fire violations by the Netherlands in Indonesia (1949). Actual UN involvement in decolonization disputes was limited: the UN became somewhat involved in the problem of Indonesian independence but not in other high-conflict independence cases such as Vietnam, India, and Egypt.

[margin note: UN power and action limited in decolonization]

These cases show that securing broad agreement to permit cooperative global action on issues where states were prepared to defend vital interests with force could be very difficult. There were other areas where global approaches were politically sensitive as well.

International Control of Atomic Energy

One of the trickiest issues brought up at the United Nations was international control of atomic energy. In 1946, the United States proposed a system of strict international regulation of nuclear weapons and nuclear fuel. The idea for an Atomic Development Authority was known as the Baruch Plan (after the U.S. delegate, Bernard Baruch, who introduced it). This body would have had a monopoly on weapons-related nuclear activities and would also have acted as an inspection agency to prevent any unauthorized nuclear facilities. The Eastern bloc states were enormously suspicious of this plan, which they rejected as an excessive infringement on national sovereignty—and specifically on the USSR's chances to pursue nuclear weapons programs of its own.

[margin note: Eastern block wants sovereignty over atomic energy]

Creating the International Economic
System and Institutions

Redesign of the international economic system was another major issue on the global agenda. When the quest for a new postwar economic system began, many Western leaders believed that both Eastern Europe and the Soviet Union would participate. However, the Eastern states chose to insulate their economies and left the international economic system in the hands of the states that eventually formed the Western alliance. These Western states, under strong leadership from the United States, agreed to cooperate to rebuild a strong international economy. Their goal was to construct a liberal international economic system to promote free trade, with several regulating institutions to keep the system functioning smoothly. They were particularly eager to prevent a return to the protectionist and "beggar thy neighbor" competitive economic policies that had existed before World War II. Because economic nationalism was widely blamed for the severe economic depression of the 1930s and thus also for World War II, economic cooperation was deemed crucial to international peace as well as prosperity.

Bretton Woods, the International
Monetary Fund, and the World Bank

Discussions to arrange the new international economic system began before the war was over. The most important of these discussions was held in Bretton Woods, New Hampshire, in July 1944, where forty-four states met to reform the postwar international monetary system. The United States had a particularly important voice in these discussions. As the postwar international economic system took shape and began to function, the United States quickly emerged as the dominant actor due to its economic (and therefore, political) power in comparison to Western Europe. The strength of the U.S. economy enabled the United States to provide crucial assistance for European postwar recovery in the form of loans, grants, and trade prospects. This gave the United States considerable political leverage in negotiations concerning the shape of the postwar economic system.

Bretton Woods produced the International Monetary Fund (IMF), established in December 1945. The IMF was supposed to stabilize exchange rates and alleviate balance-of-payments problems. The IMF would provide credit resources for states with temporary balance-of-payments problems and simultaneously impose certain corrective practices and policies for borrowers. To maintain exchange rate stability, members needed IMF approval before they could alter the value of their currencies more than 1 percent. Initially, the value of a currency was based on the value of gold. Members made contributions to the IMF reserves through a quota system that also determined voting power. In the early years the United States had 33 percent of the vote in the IMF, in accordance with the proportion of its contribution, and therefore had more than the 20 percent necessary to veto any action of the governing board.

A second institution designed to help regulate the international monetary system was the International Bank for Reconstruction and Development (also known as the World Bank), which began to operate in June 1946. The purpose of the World Bank initially was to provide assistance for countries rebuilding after World War II. Since the late 1950s, its role has been to provide technical and economic assistance for economic development, particularly to the Third World countries.

The Havana Charter and the
General Agreement on Tariffs and Trade

It was not long before it became clear that neither the IMF nor the World Bank could perform all its functions as constituted. European economies were desperately struggling to rebuild. They had incurred enormous debts, and the reserves of the new institutions were not large enough to provide the necessary relief. De facto acceptance of the U.S. dollar as the world's currency standard reflected the strength and reputation of U.S. economic performance and effective U.S. dominance of the international economy.

Plans for international trade organizations to parallel the monetary organizations also were proposed during World War II. Discussions that began in 1943 produced the Havana Charter, which proposed an International Trade Organization (ITO) to regulate tariffs, subsidies, commodity agreements, and other aspects of international trade. The ITO would have been the third major international institution for economic management. However, the prospective members of the ITO all had unique economic circumstances and trade requirements, and many with long-established trade practices designed to meet those needs were reluctant to change. Hence, these states objected to a centralized, multinational trade management body and insisted upon exemptions or exceptions designed to ensure protection of their own economies. In the end, the charter was so limited that it was useless.

The international trading system that eventually emerged was less comprehensive than that originally envisioned. In 1947 negotiations were completed on the General Agreement on Tariffs and Trade (GATT), which was initially designed as an interim agreement, pending the acceptance of the ITO. When the Havana Charter proved unacceptable to the U.S. Congress, GATT became and has remained the principal trade agreement (and institution) for the system. GATT was a multilateral compact designed to promote free and nondiscriminatory trade and has pursued these goals through regular multilateral negotiations to eliminate or reduce tariffs and duties. Members are assured "most favored nation" status, which requires that advantages given to one country must automatically be extended to others.

A word of caution is appropriate regarding the international economic system as a global agenda item. Originally, the aim of the planners was to create an international economy that would be global in scope. However, the Soviet Union and Eastern European states chose to remain outside it, partly because of a desire to avoid dependence on capitalist economies and partly because of incompatibilities between state-controlled socialist economies and the free-market economies of the West. Before long, the highly industrialized capitalist states found it in their interest to cooperate to impose special restrictions on trade with the Soviet Union and its allies. In addition, although many of the states in the South would eventually participate in this economic system, they did not play a role in creating it. They had to live by the rules established by the more powerful industrialized economies whose interests in many respects conflicted with those of the less-developed countries (LDCs). GATT afforded fewer opportunities for these states from the very beginning, since it generally favored industrial economies that exported manufactured goods, whereas the LDCs exported primary products and raw materials.

[handwritten margin note: International Economic Agenda was mainly western]

THE EAST-WEST AGENDA

Contention over the Political Future of Europe

Redrawing the Map

During World War II, the tide of battle turned against the Axis, and the extent of the challenge to redesign the map of the world became apparent. Most of continental Europe, Eastern and Western, had been under Axis occupation. Other areas had been the scenes of major battles (North Africa, Burma, and the Philippines) or had been occupied or fortified as a preventive measure (Iran, Palestine, and the Arabian peninsula). China had been partially occupied, and the Japanese had absorbed or conquered Korea, Burma, Malaya, and Indonesia. The end of the war brought a time of political fluidity to nearly every country touched by the conflict. In many instances, contending political or ethnic groups sought to take advantage of this fluidity to press for change or advantage, and the results were civil strife, insurrection, and political turmoil.

Joint Allied commissions were designed to coordinate operations in Axis-held territories, assign responsibility for accepting surrender of hostile troops, and set up occupation authorities, to be followed by planning for provisional governments. As might be expected, Europe was the focus of attention. A number of punitive schemes for Germany were proposed, including several that would have reduced it to a small, primarily agricultural state, "rewarding" Germany's victims with pieces of its territory. The most dramatic adjustment of this kind concerned Poland: The USSR wanted to keep the half of Poland that it had absorbed in 1939 as part of its nonaggression pact with Nazi Germany, claiming that this territory was vital to Soviet postwar security. As compensation to the Poles (a Polish government-in-exile in the United Kingdom eventually agreed to this), the USSR suggested that Poland be given a chunk of eastern Germany. In other words, Poland would be "moved west," leaving Germany smaller, Poland about the same size, and the USSR bigger. Germans living in the territory annexed by Poland would simply be evacuated. The Western Allies agreed to this in principle but expected to discuss all borders in a more definitive way at a peace conference.

As for political matters, the Allies agreed to "de-Nazify" the former Axis countries in Europe and to support everywhere a gradual transition to independent, democratic self-government. At a wartime summit conference in Yalta in February 1945, the Allies signed a declaration on liberated Europe in which they agreed that provisional governments should be "broadly representative of all democratic elements in the population" and promised to facilitate plans to hold "free elections of governments responsive to the will of the people."[9]

Yalta seemed to imply democracy for all of Europe

East-West Competition

Expectations of cooperative international interaction in pursuit of these common objectives were soon frustrated. Despite persistent professions of common purpose, disagreements among the Allies over postwar arrangements quickly reached a serious point. On more and more issues, there was a sharp split between the Eastern and Western groups on what was fair and what was in the interests of "peace" and "the people." Gradually, the competition between Western and Soviet purposes and plans became so intense that no general peace treaty to end World War II could be signed and an East-West agenda obscured and replaced the global one.

Conflicts in political ideology were key factors in this process. The USSR's Marxist-Leninist government, which has identified capitalist, free-market states as enemies, put forward the socialist systems as the only "true" democracies and believed that only those dedicated to a communist future could be safely entrusted with political power. This was in sharp contrast to the democracies, where an openly competitive political process presumes freedom for individuals is a necessary guarantee against abuses of power.

Political ideology caused Cold War

Political control of Eastern Europe was a major issue. The Western Allies objected to Soviet actions that had the effect of consolidating a socialist camp where the Red Army held territory. Many of these actions were decidedly coercive: Pro-Soviet individuals were favored, whereas potential opponents of the Soviet Union were harassed, arrested, or exiled; press and radio were under strict control; many political parties and groups were banned; Western representatives were restricted or barred from some Soviet-held areas; noncommunist parties were squeezed out of coalition governments or defeated in rigged elections; and "reliable" pro-Soviet leaders were installed and backed up with resident Soviet garrisons and an expanding network of "fraternal" Soviet-dominated institutions and organs of economic and political integration.[10]

Agitated Western protests to the effect that these actions violated the Yalta agreements were rebuffed as unwarranted or hostile. In response to complaints about the situation in Poland, Soviet leader Joseph Stalin argued that Soviet security needs absolutely required "friendly" governments on its borders. By definition, he said, a pro-Soviet government would be "representative" and "democratic": "Only people who have demonstrated by deeds their friendly attitude to the Soviet Union, who were willing, honestly and sincerely to cooperate with the Soviet state should be consulted on the formation of a future Polish government."[11]

Soviet representatives at Allied meetings had complaints too. The USSR was excluded from the peace negotiations with Italy and later from the occupation of Japan. The Soviet Union had been promised some Japanese and Chinese territory in return for joining in the war with Japan, but its requests for colonial trusteeships in North Africa and for pieces of adjoining territory in Turkey were rejected.

There were many disputes about Germany, where the shift to open conflict was acutely obvious. This country was under joint occupation—the United States, Britain, and the USSR were each responsible for a separate zone. The Soviets demanded half of all reparations that might be extracted from the defeated nation to compensate for losses they had suffered during the war (it is variously estimated that twelve to twenty million Soviets died; two-thirds of Soviet industrial areas were occupied and sustained heavy damage). They stripped factories of potentially useful machinery, objected to every Western proposal for reviving the German economy, and refused to give up any territory in order to make a zone for France (which was not originally treated as an occupying power). When U.S. authorities halted deliveries of reparations from West Germany to the USSR in 1946 and made plans to merge the Western zones economically, the Soviets protested that these moves violated Allied commitments.

Western Response to Soviet Actions

For the West, the issue was Soviet expansion, whether by force or by exploitation of social chaos. The apparent ease with which the Soviet Union was widening its control in Eastern Europe together with the fluidity of the political situation in many countries elsewhere generated a sense of uncertainty and real fear about how far the realignment of world actors would go. China was in the throes of revolution; Arab and Jewish armies were preparing to contest control of Palestine; procommunist nationalists had taken up arms in Iran and Greece. Enormous economic and political reconstruction tasks confronted all the European states too.

Many in the West believed that the United States could supply leadership to contain the threat of communism and maintain control by the West, although opinions differed about how best to achieve *containment*—which meant military or political actions to prevent the spread of communism. In 1947, U.S. President Harry Truman articulated this view of world politics in a speech on U.S. responsibilities. Although he was specifically defending a plan to provide economic and military aid to Greece and Turkey, his Truman Doctrine had a more general significance:

> At the present moment in world history nearly every nation must choose between alternate ways of life. The choice is too often not a free one. The seeds of totalitarian regimes are nurtured by misery and want. They spread and grow in the evil soil of poverty and strife. They reach their full growth when hope of a people for a better life has died. We must keep that hope alive. The free peoples of the world look to us for support in maintaining their freedoms. If we falter in our leadership we may endanger the peace of the world and we shall surely endanger the welfare of our own nation. Great responsibilities have been placed upon us by the swift movement of events.[12]

Shortly afterwards, the United States publicly committed itself to a massive economic aid program to finance European reconstruction—the Marshall Plan. This commitment to European economic recovery was an important expression of U.S. determination to keep the Western camp strong and united.

The Soviet Response

The Soviet side responded with its own redefinition of world politics. In 1943, in deference to its new wartime Western allies, Stalin had dissolved the Communist International—the international organization of the world's communist parties. But in 1947, the world's communist parties gathered to establish a new international grouping: the Communist Information Agency, or Cominform. The chief message of this meeting was a warning about

Soviets see Americans as expansionist

the "frankly expansionist course" of U.S. imperialism. The war was said to have left the international significance and prestige of the Soviet Union "immensely enhanced," but Soviet leaders claimed that the "imperialist and antidemocratic camp" led by the United States was "hatching a new war."[13]

By 1947, the euphoria about world peace that had surfaced at the defeat of Germany and Japan had faded. Collaborative redesign of the postwar world was replaced by the tense competition for control that became known as the Cold War.

Front-Burner Crises: Germany and Korea

Between 1948 and 1955 a series of nasty and dangerous East-West confrontations provoked a crystallization of alignments as each side sought to organize itself to defend against possible threats from the other.

Germany

The dispute over Germany seemed most menacing. Both sides paid lip service to cooperation but were unable to agree on any concrete proposals for uniting the occupation zones or transferring power to an all-German government. The framework set up for joint occupation accentuated and invited conflict. The situation in Berlin (the German capital) was especially troublesome, because although the city was under four-power occupation, it was located deep within the Soviet zone and therefore physically isolated and vulnerable. Western powers favored free elections throughout Germany so that the majority of the population would choose their own all-German government. The Soviets, who occupied about a third of German territory, insisted instead on various devices to ensure that the occupying powers would select a transitional government and unification based on equal representation of the Eastern and Western zones.

West wants democracy for all Germany

It became increasingly obvious that unification of Germany was not an attractive option for either side. Could a united Germany be neutral? With which camp would it affiliate? The fate of and the alignment of a united Germany was at best uncertain. Abnormal or not, the division of Germany gave each camp a piece. Each side rejected the unification proposals of the other and proceeded determinedly to shape the institutions of its zone in keeping with its own political values.

Allignment of unified Germany impossible

Berlin Blockade. When the Soviets rejected a British and U.S. proposal for a new German currency in 1948, the United States and Britain decided to introduce it in their zones anyway (including their parts of Berlin). This infuriated the Soviets, who protested by walking out of the Allied Control Commission, which governed the city and was supposed to coordinate policies of the four occupying powers. In May the Soviets began harassing

Western ground traffic traveling through the Soviet zone en route to Berlin. When all such traffic was halted in June 1948, it seemed that a military confrontation between East and West was inevitable. The Soviets may have meant the blockade of Berlin to force the Western powers to be more receptive toward Soviet ideas about Germany, but the West saw this action as proof of Soviet belligerence and as the beginning of an effort to drive the Western powers out of Berlin.

Berlin blockade forced strong alignment

Although the atmosphere was extremely tense for several months, no direct military confrontation occurred. A Western airlift was quickly organized to supply Berlin, and the Soviets did not challenge it, ending the blockade in April 1949. The net effect of the crisis was to accelerate Western rearmament and dramatically confirm the eclipse of the global agenda.

NATO and Two Germanies Emerge. Plans for a North Atlantic Treaty Organization (NATO) proceeded rapidly during the winter of the Berlin blockade. This was to be a mutual defense pact among the United States, Canada, Britain, France, Belgium, the Netherlands, and Luxembourg, with Norway, Denmark, Iceland, Italy, and Portugal invited to join. A constitution for a separate *West* German state was drawn up and elections announced. Conversion of Germany—or even a part of it—from an enemy into an ally was not easy, although organizing Western Europe against communism logically suggested it. The Federal Republic of Germany (FRG—West Germany) was formed in May 1949 and recognized by the noncommunist European states in September. The Soviets accordingly announced the formation of the German Democratic Republic (GDR—East Germany) in their zone three months later.

Nato - defense pact against Soviet aggression

two germanies form in 1949

Korea

The next East-West crisis occurred in Asia, which was the scene of a major communist gain. In October 1949, when the victorious Red Army swept to power on the Chinese mainland, leader Mao Zedong proclaimed that the new People's Republic of China would be a firm and fast ally of its fraternal socialist neighbor, the USSR.

The Division of Korea. Events in neighboring Korea presented a new challenge to Western positions in 1950. By prior agreement, the USSR had shared responsibility for accepting Japanese surrender in the northern half of the Korean peninsula at the end of the war.[14] Steps were to follow for a peaceful reunification of Korea under joint Allied auspices. However, cooperation proved impossible, and a de facto division of this country was beginning to look as permament as the one in Germany. Elections in the south had established the Republic of Korea (South Korea) in January 1948; two months later the Korean People's Democratic Republic (North Korea, widely viewed as a Soviet client) was proclaimed in the north.

Cooperation proves futile do always

Two Koreas formed in 1948

The Korean War. The stalemate did not hold. In June 1950, the North Korean army launched an invasion of the south. Demobilization of U.S. forces had proceeded swiftly in the Far East, and the United States was not prepared for a military encounter; nonetheless, President Truman and his advisers were determined to stop the invaders. As U.S. forces were rushed to Korea, U.S. representatives sought United Nations approval for the action as a legitimate exercise of defense against aggression. It happened that the Soviets were boycotting meetings of the Security Council at the time (in protest over refusals to seat a delegation from the People's Republic of China) and the U.S. proposal passed. Units from fifteen other countries eventually joined the U.S. and South Korean forces to fight under the UN flag.

Initially the fighting did not go well for South Korean and U.S. forces. Within two months the South Koreans had nearly been defeated and were struggling to hold two last small fronts. But in September, the UN forces under U.S. command began to overcome the North Koreans and drive them back toward their border. At this point, enthusiasm developed for an attempt to take control of the whole peninsula. Despite ominous warnings from the Chinese that such action would be considered a threat to China, the decision was made to invade and attempt to conquer North Korea at the beginning of October 1950. Confidence grew as the U.S. Commanding General Douglas MacArthur bragged that the troops would be home by Christmas.

Korean War ultimately achieved nothing

Instead, the UN forces suffered a humiliating rout as an estimated half-million Chinese soldiers began pouring into Korea in November. This soon reversed the tide of battle. Within a few months, the Chinese had not only "rescued" North Korea but driven the UN forces to a point thirty miles south of Seoul, the South Korean capital. It took many bitter battles before the Chinese and North Koreans were pushed back out of South Korea. By April 1951, the two sides had reestablished roughly the same division of Korea that had existed before the North Korean attack.

Military Alliances and Security Needs

U.S. Alliances and Actions

The effect of the Korean War on the U.S. commitment to global leadership was dramatic. A second phase of the Cold War opened from 1950–1955, during which time direct East-West diplomatic contacts and confrontations subsided and attention focused on Western efforts to institutionalize bipolarity. This was done, first, by rearming Germany and including it in NATO and, second, by supplementing the European alliance with a series of mutual defense pacts that would encircle the USSR. The imagery of a world at war was used to justify moving security needs and free world unity to the top of the agenda.

For the United States this entailed increased military expenditures, both to support military deployments and for aid to allies (for example, military assistance for French forces in Indochina was tripled after the Korean conflict began). Asia had a new, higher priority. In January 1950 the U.S. Seventh Fleet was committed to patrol the narrow waters between the Chinese mainland and the islands occupied by the forces of former mainland China leader Chiang Kai-shek. The United States signed bilateral defense pacts with former colony the Philippines and with former enemy state Japan. Envoys visited Middle Eastern capitals seeking to create a Middle Eastern security alliance even before the arrangements for independence there were complete.

Military expenditures increase

goal was to encircle USSR

Western concerns about communist expansion fueled efforts to prevent or contain unfavorable political change. In Iran, Prime Minister Muhammed Mossadeq allied with leftist forces to nationalize the British-controlled oil industry. Guided by the perception that nationalism was a threat to Western interests, the U.S. Central Intelligence Agency then helped organize a military coup in 1953 to remove Mossadeq and reinstate the monarch, Shah Reza Pahlavi, who had fled the country earlier that year. In the Middle East, the United States joined with Britain and France to declare their intention to keep local military forces in balance.

To stop communism or to create pseudo-colonies in disguise

Military developments added urgency to the attention to security needs, both in Europe and elsewhere. By 1949, the USSR had produced its own atomic weapon, four years behind the United States. Soviet scientists were only one year behind the major U.S. breakthrough in nuclear weaponry of 1951 that produced the hydrogen bomb, a more powerful atomic device based on principles of nuclear fusion. While both sides were working on rocketry, U.S. defense analysts who emphasized the value of airborne bombing capability argued that strategic positioning of "massive" retaliatory power at airfields around the world was essential to reinforce local defenses against aggression. Acquisition of airbases in important locations was a major U.S. goal during the 1950s.

Atomic and Nuclear weaponry important in cold war

Eastern Bloc Actions

For the Soviets during this time, Western European military unity was also a high priority issue, a unity they attempted to destroy by various tactics. Discarding openly confrontational policies, Soviets sought to disarm their critics and impede the movement toward German rearmament. In 1949 European communists launched a "peace movement" highlighting the dangers of U.S. "warmongering"—an approach that they contrasted with Soviet dedication to peaceful coexistence. The Soviets urged communists elsewhere to "become nationalists" and try to mobilize anti-American sentiments in Europe to increase popular opposition to NATO and frustrate European rearmament.

The Soviets also tried to get Allied cooperation and German reunification back on the East-West agenda. In November 1950 and again in November 1951, the USSR announced major new proposals on German unification, each with some concessions to Western positions. Each Soviet proposal would have kept Germany out of NATO or any other military alliance. In March 1954, the USSR actually indicated it might apply to join NATO itself—since Western states had insisted NATO was not an anti-Soviet pact, but a general mutual defense treaty.

In fact, renewal of diplomatic discussions among the wartime Allies did become a major issue in 1954 and 1955. There were several reasons for this. It was obvious that the prospect of a powerful Western military alliance that would include a rearmed West Germany was frightening to the socialist bloc. But many Western Europeans (particularly the French) were hostile to it also and uneasy about accepting the former enemy as military ally. It could easily be argued that any serious possibility for negotiations should be explored before hope was abandoned for peaceful German reunification— or for settlement of other outstanding issues.

Moreover, the communist states were offering to negotiate. After Soviet leader Joseph Stalin died in March 1953, his successors (Nikita Khrushchev quickly emerged as the dominant one) made a number of conciliatory gestures toward the West that were encouraging. The Chinese, too, presented a more accommodating posture than before. In the summer of 1953, after two years of rancorous negotiations, they suddenly agreed to sign an armistice in Korea. Soviet representatives also indicated a willingness to proceed with an Austrian peace treaty (Austria was still under joint occupation).

East-West Diplomatic Activities

A conference between the foreign ministers of the United States, the USSR, Britain, and France held in March 1954 made some progress on the Austrian question. Although no agreements were signed, this meeting cleared the way for a special conference at Geneva in May to discuss the situation in Asia. The People's Republic of China was invited to this meeting. The French were now eager to settle the war in Indochina, where local nationalist armies had been resisting the reimposition of French control for some years. The French forces had not done well against the Vietnamese army, which was led by communist Ho Chi Minh. A major French defeat at the fortress of Dien Bien Phu occurred during the Geneva conference and proved a significant stimulus to peacemaking efforts. Although a complete military victory appeared to be within their reach, the Vietnamese agreed (allegedly with Soviet urging) to a political settlement according to which Vietnam would be partitioned temporarily, but after a ceasefire and military disengagement, elections would be held to establish a government for all of Vietnam. Laos and Cambodia were recognized as separate independent states. The United States did not sign the agreements on Indochina and was suspicious of the plan for unification. In fact, the proposed all-Vietnamese elections and subsequent unification never took place.

The Stalemate on Germany

Despite all this diplomatic activity, no progress was made toward East-West agreement on the question of Germany and it was clear that the Western states were not interested in unifying the country. The NATO signatories ignored a Soviet-sponsored "all-European" security conference in November 1954 (to which both Germanies were invited) and a number of offers to discuss holding elections for an all-German government. Instead, the consolidation of an independent West Germany into NATO continued. Powerful anti-German sentiments (particularly in France) stalled this process for a while. In late 1954, a formula for a German military role that was politically acceptable to the French was finally worked out. In May 1955, the Western occupying authorities formally recognized the sovereignty of the Federal Republic of Germany, unilaterally ended the state of war with it, and admitted it into NATO. The Soviets quickly countered with their own Warsaw Treaty Organization (WTO, or the Warsaw Pact)—to which the GDR was admitted in January 1956.

[margin note: Soviets try to reunify Germany]

[margin note: French fearful of Germany]

Steps Leading to the Geneva Summit

Amidst all these moves it was difficult to see much progress in the reduction of Cold War tensions. Nonetheless, some dramatic new disarmament proposals helped to promote a renewed East-West dialogue in 1954. One result was a four-power conference in Geneva in July 1955—the first summit since the war. The mood on both sides was cautious.

[margin note: Geneva conference 1955]

As Eisenhower prepared to depart for Geneva, he warned of the dangerous spiral of "suspicion and distrust": "[My] purpose is to attempt to change the spirit that has characterized the intergovernmental relationships of the world within the past ten years. . . . I say to you, if we change the spirit in which these conferences are conducted we will have taken the greatest step toward peace, toward future prosperity and tranquility that has ever been taken in the history of mankind."[15] Eisenhower said that he welcomed the Soviets' interest in disarmament and proposed a radical confidence-building step: an exchange of military blueprints and open skies to permit mutual aerial inspection. The Soviets adamantly rejected this or any other form of surveillance of their territory. Although little was thus actually

No real but
success begins
dialogue begins

accomplished at Geneva, a process of discussion had begun, and it was agreed that the foreign ministers would gather later in the year to discuss concrete proposals reflecting the new agenda: reducing East-West tension.

The contest would continue in new and perhaps more dangerous ways. For the time being however, the "spirit of Geneva" said to have been generated by the conference meant that the rival camps were not afraid to talk with each other.

THE NORTH-SOUTH AGENDA

The first decade after World War II is the period in which the South began to establish itself as an entity of states with a particular political agenda. More than fifteen former colonies and trusteeships became independent during this period. It soon became apparent that these new states had their own ideas about the proper priorities for world politics. Tentatively at first these new states began to outline a Southern agenda, increasingly identified as a set of issues that cut across the East-West conflict axis. Decolonization was the major issue on this agenda, with Southern unity as a minor theme.

Decolonization

Background of Decolonization

From the standpoint of the global agenda, decolonization represented one aspect of the reform of world politics, both because independence for the colonies was an application of the principle of self-determination and because admission of these new states to the United Nations confirmed the equality of all states.

Yet decolonization was a complex phenomenon with very different meanings for all those involved. For the European states that had colonies and for some groups within the subject peoples, decolonization could be seen as a domestic political issue, not a matter of world political interest. The United States and the USSR supported decolonization in principle but came to approach it with East-West rivalry in mind. For the colonial peoples themselves, decolonization was an intensely local issue. However, as it became evident that the demise of colonialism was very definitely a general phenomenon, decolonization acquired definition as an issue between North and South—that is, an issue reflecting differences between the more powerful industrialized states and all small states.

industrial vs.
small states

The process of decolonization probably should have started after World War I. Certainly many colonial peoples thought so, especially those that had been promised independence or autonomy in return for cooperation with the imperial power's war effort. This was true, for instance, in the Middle East, where the British had made such promises to various Arab leaders. In Turkey, nationalist movements had taken advantage of political fluidity to oust monarchs or declare independence from foreign control. Delegations from many colonial and dependent territories appeared at the Paris Peace Conference of 1919 to lobby for independence or to argue about borders. None went away completely satisfied.

World War II reopened all these old questions. Once again the major states made a specific commitment to the principle of self-government, although once again this principle was applied only to territories of the losers (or to territories voluntarily designated as international trusteeships). When the war was over, it became clear that the imperial powers faced very serious opposition to continued control over their colonies.

Immediate Postwar Responses to Decolonization Demands

The demands for independence had emerged shortly after the end of the war. The response of the colonial powers to these demands varied greatly, as did the individual colonies' presentation of them. The colonial powers were not enthusiastic about the prospect of a general movement toward independence for all dependencies. Initially, there was a reluctance to part with colonies, which were seen as valuable sources of natural resources, strategic safeguards, and national prestige. Britain and France had promised political reforms and actually enacted some; in fact, important sectors of the French and British public favored colonial independence. But in general, Britain, France, the Netherlands, Belgium, and Portugal were determined to retain control over their colonies and protectorates and resented outside interference in what was regarded as a domestic issue. In a few cases extensive military operations were launched to reestablish European control and suppress nationalist revolts.

The superpowers initially agreed that colonialism should end. The United States honored its own commitment to grant independence to the Philippines and criticized Britain and France when they sought to rebuild their empires after the war. This anticolonial position of the United States was modified by the Cold War. Eventually the United States not only chose to support European colonial authorities in some cases but, as we shall see, also sought to establish U.S. dominance in the interest of an acceptable East-West power balance. Attempts to enlist new states (the case of Egypt is one example) into Western military alliances were the most graphic illustrations of this process.

Although to a certain extent the USSR and local Communist parties tried to win friends among rebellious colonial peoples on the strength of a common hostility to imperialism, the East was fairly suspicious of the independence rearrangements that were negotiated. Involvement by the socialist camp in decolonization was largely rhetorical even though opposition to colonialism has been a theme in communist ideology for a long time. According to Marxism-Leninism, communists should ally with anti-imperialist forces in the colonies in a common struggle against the industrialized capitalist states. Radical leftist groups in many colonies had accepted this logic, and in some places communists played an important role in independence struggles (in Vietnam, for example). By and large, however, most independence movements were not opposed to capitalist economic practices, and communists and nationalists were often at odds (for example, in India, the Philippines, Malaya, Indonesia, and Burma).

Obstacles to Decolonization

Overall, the movement toward decolonization was neither uniform nor universal, but this reflected the uneven and varied character of colonization. Each decolonization case had special features. Many colonies had experienced nationalistic movements well before World War II, but in others such movements came later. Nationalist movements faced a variety of obstacles including, in some cases, the absence of a national identity that could provide a political focus for an independence movement directed against the imperial power. In fact, the political order and administrative institutions established by the imperial powers did not always match natural or historical political boundaries. In some cases the European powers had actually created a political entity where none existed before, often with the aim of dividing and breaking the political power of local leaders. This meant that in some colonies there was very little national feeling and that after independence, the people often remained loyal to regional or ethnic (tribal) affiliations rather than the "new" central state government.

In many colonies a local elite had been permitted limited power, mostly in an administrative role. This elite often was educated in Europe and sometimes developed a vested interest in the continuance of imperial rule. The colonial economies of each imperial power also became closely integrated, making the economy of the individual colony little more than a link in a large imperial commercial circle, thus not able to be self-sustaining. The colonial economies themselves also had an inescapable vested interest in the colonial economic system. In addition, individuals who resisted the imperial power or demanded independence risked imprisonment or other punishment. The motivation for political change thus had to be quite strong for an independence movement to arise and in some cases that required a significant amount of time. Moreover, the prospect of independence could produce political unrest, and plans to transfer real political power often triggered bitter conflicts and rivalries within the subject peoples.

Nationalist Leaders

Despite all the obstacles, elements of the Western-educated elite who were attracted to European political institutions and ideas used them to forge nationalist movements of tremendous strength. Some of the most important national liberation movement leaders were Ho Chi Minh (Vietnam), Sékou Touré (Guinea), Kwame Nkrumah (Ghana), Mahatma Gandhi and Jawaharlal Nehru (India), Gamal Abdel Nasser (Egypt), and Sukarno (Indonesia).

Nationalists used European models

Several different kinds of situations occurred. Where the imperial power was ready and willing to negotiate and nationalist leaders were able to work together, the process could be fairly smooth. Where these conditions were absent, the transition to independence could be prolonged, tense and even violent.

Britain's Decolonization

Great Britain had played an active military role on many fronts against Germany, Italy, and Japan during the war. British forces accordingly took part in widely scattered mop-up operations and in several efforts to fortify Western presence in colonial territories that had been under enemy occupation. But by 1947 it was clear that the British would be trimming their empire and reducing their role in some key colonies. The most important reduction was the negotiated independence of India.

India. Anticolonial movements were well established in India, and their activities brought many concessions from the British who finally agreed to negotiate a transition to self-government. The nationalist movements were divided along communal lines, however, and eventually agreed to partition the colony into two parts: Pakistan would be set up as a predominantly Muslim state, while Hindus and other groups would dominate in India. The distribution of population did not make a neat territorial division possible, there were many disputes that inflamed Hindu-Muslim antagonisms, and the partition in 1947 was accompanied by considerable violence. Nonetheless, the transition to self-government for India had a dramatic effect on many nationalists elsewhere, who saw the negotiated independence arrangements as encouraging to their own prospects and as a sign that the old empires would indeed be crumbling. Yet the Indian case was also an example of the perils of political transitions.

religious conflict in liberation of India

Palestine. India was not the only place where prospects of independence brought communal conflict. Britain had been administering Palestine under a League of Nations mandate. Relationships between Arabs and Jews there were so intractable that Britain turned the problem of a transition to self-government over to the United Nations. In 1948, the United Nations plan to partition the territory was superseded by a war that resulted in a victory

independence invariably leads to communal conflict

for the state of Israel. The new state incorporated more territory than the UN plan had assigned, and the bulk of the remaining areas of Palestine were annexed by Jordan. The neighboring Arab governments refused to recognize the new state, which had been established by force of arms, and remained in a state of war with it. The Arab-Israeli dispute over control of Palestine has been a territorial issue ever since.

Other British Actions. Negotiations for independence were fairly smooth in Burma and Malaya, more difficult in Egypt. The Egyptian government was nominally independent but in fact had been under British protection. After the war the British were interested in withdrawing from Egypt but wanted to retain troops at the Suez Canal (which links the Mediterranean with the Red Sea). Nationalist resentments at the slow pace of the planned withdrawals helped to produce a military coup in Egypt in 1952 and a new government eventually led by Gamal Abdel Nasser.

Both British and Australian troops assisted the attempt of the Netherlands to return to Indonesia and dislodge the nationalist government that had been created there. In 1947, unable to win control of all the Indonesian archipelago, the Dutch agreed to a federation under Dutch sovereignty that would include the nationalist-controlled area. The United Nations Security Council became involved in 1949 when it became clear the Dutch were pressing ahead with their military efforts to gain complete political control. A republic was eventually accorded broad international recognition in 1950.

Elsewhere Britain moved forward slowly to give independence to its other colonies. In the process Britain attempted to control the direction of political developments and to oversee the formation of new independent governments by holding elections for national assemblies, negotiating constitutions (for example, in Nigeria), and repressing movements considered too radical (as in then British Guiana).[16] One of the greatest problems faced by the British came in determining the fate of the colonies (such as Kenya and Rhodesia) that had large white (European) settler populations. Ultimately, these colonies became embroiled in conflicts about the distribution of power between the European settlers and the indigenous majorities.

France's Decolonization

The response of other European colonial powers varied: France was unwilling to grant independence to its colonies or to acknowledge the legitimacy of their call for independence although it made some concessions. These conformed to the French notion that the colonial territories should remain associated with France but could gradually raise their status within that association. When a Vietnamese nationalist movement declared an independent state in 1945 in the wake of the Japanese withdrawal, the French chose to fight, and a long, bloody war ensued, until the French withdrew in 1954. Algeria was a special case: A large French population had settled there, and the territory had been annexed to France and considered an integral part of the republic. Algerian independence movements were thus regarded as subversive, and reprisals were harsh. In an effort to suppress an armed nationalist movement there, France became involved in a second long and costly colonial war in 1954.

Elsewhere in the French colonial territories, nationalist movements met a mix of concessions and repression. By steps, the colonies were given the right to elect representatives to the French National Assembly, and the prerogatives of their own legislatures were strengthened.

Neocolonialism and the United States

Achievement of formal independence did not end resentments against foreign control. The anticolonial issue did not disappear, but was transformed into a new issue: neocolonialism, which refers to political, economic, and military dominance—the kind of asymmetry that characterized relations between small and generally poor ex-colonies and the far more powerful European states.

The United States was not a major colonial power, but its emergence as a leader of the Western alliance ultimately caused the country to be accused by former colonies of neocolonial acts. U.S. opposition to colonialism in principle did not mean that the United States promoted complete independence for colonies. It opposed political transitions that threatened Western strategic positions and regarded with great suspicion hostile anti-Western independence movements. The United States was eager to resist independence movements led by communists, such as the case of Vietnam, where the United States replaced the French. The United States did not establish a colony there but did wield extraordinary political influence; it sought the transfer of power and influence in Vietnam not because it desired colonies but because of the intensification of the Cold War. This pattern is important because anticolonialism was the major issue on the North-South agenda through the first decade after World War II.

There are a number of ironies in the U.S. response to nationalist movements in the Third World. Philosophically, the United States has been anticolonialist. Distaste for European practices of colonial conquest has been strong; however, this disapproval of colonialism has traditionally been mixed with a sense of U.S. moral and political superiority. Its leaders expected that the United States would be hailed as a champion of democracy by anticolonial leaders and that the newly independent states would form governments friendly to the United States.

U.S. expectations were not realized. Moreover, political leaders found it difficult to understand the complexity of the forces that produced the new

Third World governments, which did not necessarily emulate the U.S. political or economic system and often insisted on the right to associate with either or both the United States and the USSR. These states in many cases came to see the United States not as the champion of democracy, but as an obstacle to change. For Third World nationalists, the United States has often been characterized as a country that was truly conservative, fairly intolerant of others' beliefs, and highly suspicious of revolution or rapid political change.

U.S. seen by many third world nations as destructive

The course of the conflicts over colonialism and neocolonialism drew attention to the special problems of the small states. Yet such attention was inhibited by imposition of East-West issues and priorities onto Third World terrain. The Eastern bloc was not an active competitor on the scene in the South at this time but did seek to capitalize on Third World resentment at being pressed to take sides. The net effect on East-West rivalry in the South was to raise new problems, as nationalist movements and regimes began to assert the priorities of their own agenda.

A New Issue: Forging a Southern Alliance

Decolonization was a fundamental expression of Southern interests. Efforts to promote these interests in specific ways produced a major issue on the North-South agenda in the first postwar decade: the effort to establish a Southern community of nations. The development of the Southern coalition proceeded sporadically but steadily during this period.

Early Moves Toward Southern Unity

Interest in Southern unity was hardly new: One of the most important early efforts to organize was the Congress of Oppressed Nationalities, held in Brussels in 1927. The conference was quite large, with 175 delegates from thirty-seven territories or countries in attendance. A number of regional unity movements were also organized during the prewar years. The Pan-Asian, Pan-African, and Pan-Arab movements reached their peak momentum during the 1920s.

The major goal of the political figures pursuing a Southern coalition—known after World War II as the "Afro-Asian" movement—was to gain strength through unity. Included under this geographic rubric were states from Southeast Asia across to the Arab states of the Middle East (considered West Asia) and into Africa, parts of the world that had been poorly represented at the United Nations in the years immediately after the founding of that organization. Of the fifty states represented at the founding of the UN in San Francisco in 1945, only twelve were from the Afro-Asian area and five of those were not interested in Southern unity. Many Southern leaders distrusted international institutions because of disappointing experiences with the League of Nations after World War I. Despite declarations in its charter about self-government, the initial steps taken by the United Nations toward decolonization did not satisfy all demands, such as those of the Arab states, which were particularly upset by the handling of the Palestine mandate.

The Cold War encouraged the search for Southern solidarity because the movement toward decolonization collided with Western efforts to organize defense alliances to contain communism. Pressure to join U.S. or British-sponsored military alliances followed on the heels of independence. The new states that resisted such pressures felt that they were protecting their independence against neocolonial domination.

Afro-Asian Conferences and Consultation

The first "unofficial" conference of representatives of the Afro-Asian states took place in India in 1947. It was organized by the Indian Council of World Affairs but was in fact the idea of Indian Prime Minister Nehru. The meeting—with participants primarily from South and Southeast Asia—focused on the anticolonial issue but reviewed Asian development problems and the prospects for Asian solidarity as well.

This conference demonstrated the potential for efforts to mobilize interest in Asian solidarity but also showed significant differences in interest and in needs of the various participants. Although an organization was formed, its executive council was torn by disagreements between independent states and the representatives of peoples still struggling for independence.[17] The degree of support for anticolonialism was the dominant issue.

By the time of a second, "official," Afro-Asian meeting (in New Delhi in 1949), a number of important events had occurred that complicated the political environment in the South and demonstrated how challenging decolonization could become. These included the wars in Palestine and Indochina, the fighting in Indonesia, and the communal conflict in India. Representatives were present from Afghanistan, Australia, Burma, Ceylon, Egypt, Ethiopia, India, Iran, Iraq, Lebanon, Pakistan, the Philippines, Saudi Arabia, Syria, and Yemen. Most Latin American countries had achieved independence by the 1820s and were not very interested in the decolonization problem. Instead, their concern focused on economic growth. They had been promised and expected economic assistance from the United States and therefore were not yet receptive to the growing call for Southern solidarity.

The meeting was specifically convened to discuss the Indonesian conflict, which provided a focus for shared anger about the way in which decolonization was being handled. The conference unanimously condemned Dutch actions

in Indonesia. Participants also discussed the possibility of creating an
institution for inter-Asian consultation. This goal was not achieved, but a
precedent was established for continued Afro-Asian consultation on major
issues on the emerging North-South agenda, leading many in Europe and
the United States to see this Afro-Asian gathering as the beginning of a
potential anti-Western bloc. But although the conference was critical of
the leading Western states, it was also affected by the Cold War. Communist
revolts in Southeast Asia (particularly an insurgency in Malaya) contributed
to bad relations between communists and nationalists in many places and
may have had some role in the decision not to invite either communist-
led Vietnam or the Soviet Asian republics to the Afro-Asian meeting.

It was five years before another major Afro-Asian conference was held.
There was a major effort by the Arab states to call a conference in 1952
on the colonial policies of the French in North Africa. Thirteen Arab and
African states brought the issue to the United Nations but could not even
get agreement on the formation of a three-member commission to study
the situation. They therefore called for a meeting in Cairo in December
1952 that would set up an international conference similar to the one
convened to discuss the Indonesian crisis.

A Simmering Issue Heats Up: The South and the Cold War

By 1954 when the Afro-Asian states again began the process of attempting
to establish an organization representing their interests and providing a
common meeting ground, the Cold War had penetrated the North-South
division. The process took a long time, however, and manifested itself in
a number of different ways. The newly independent states' varying positions
concerning the superpower conflict became an important issue.

The Southern states often resented efforts to convince them to take
sides on East-West issues and to join in Cold War alliances or military
pacts. Some Asian states became concerned about the course the Korean
War was taking, particularly the possibility of a U.S. attack on China.[18]
They expressed these concerns and in the process began to act more as a
bloc in the United Nations. They found that a neutral, united front was
viable and that nonalignment was a possible alternative to becoming engaged
in the Cold War.

At the same time, the early 1950s, the North became increasingly hostile
to the notion of neutrality. U.S. attempts to provide military aid and to
consolidate defense alliances in Asia and the Middle East met with varying
degrees of success. Some states, notably Burma, rejected U.S. military aid,
whereas others, such as Thailand, Pakistan, Iran, Iraq, and the Philippines
accepted it. The establishment of regional defense pacts proved divisive in
some regions: The Baghdad Pact, for example, included Britain, Turkey,

Pakistan, Iran, and Iraq, but neither India (Pakistan's rival) nor Egypt (Iraq's rival), both of which advocated a neutral, independent position, joined. Indonesia and Burma did not become members of the Southeast Asian Treaty Organization (SEATO), preferring to remain nonaligned.[19]

sporadic neutrality in South (handwritten margin note)

The Colombo Conference

The penetration of the Cold War conflict into the affairs of Third World states and the impact it made upon the issues on the North-South agenda during this period can be seen most strikingly in the 1954 conference held in Colombo, Ceylon. Both Indonesia and Ceylon were promoting this conference in late 1952. Indonesia had become increasingly interested in forming a regional neutralist bloc that would join together countries interested in anticolonialism,[20] but the final push for the conference came from Ceylon. The meeting included heads of state from Egypt, Pakistan, India, Burma, Ceylon, and Indonesia.

The Colombo Conference was extremely contentious. Pakistan and Ceylon proposed that the group condemn communist aggression. India opposed such a move as equivalent to aligning with the West and felt that approving such a resolution would violate its own policy of nonalignment and could threaten the pending Sino-Indian agreement on the status of Tibet.[21] Ultimately the participants compromised by agreeing to condemn intervention in the affairs of the small states by any external power, communist or anticommunist. The participants were also determined to express their views on other international and regional issues, specifically, the fact that China had been the only Asian state invited to the Geneva talks on Korea, Vietnam, and related problems. This was taken as an insult and an indication of the extent to which the North ignored the South.

conflict at Colombo conference (handwritten margin note)

North ignores South (handwritten margin note)

Planning for the Bandung Conference

During the Colombo Conference, a renewed effort to hold another large Afro-Asian meeting met considerable reluctance, but a preliminary planning meeting was held in Bogor, Indonesia, in 1954. By this time many changes had occurred in the Afro-Asian area. Of the newly independent states, some had taken sides in the Cold War; others had chosen varying kinds of neutrality. Egypt acquired an active leader when Gamal Abdel Nasser came into power in 1954; India had continued to acquire international prestige as a leader of the nonaligned. Because of these changes and the introduction of new issues onto the agenda, the question of who should be invited to a large Afro-Asian conference caused some debate, for example, whether or not invitations should go to China or Israel (the former was included, the latter was not) or African colonies still striving for independence

who should go to Bandung conference (handwritten margin note)

(African and Asian countries with independent governments were invited and even in some cases independence movements).

The conference took place in Bandung, Indonesia, in April and May 1955. The agreement to hold a general Afro-Asian conference in 1955 was a harbinger of the importance that Afro-Asian solidarity would acquire as decolonization produced more and more newly independent states in the South.

*   *   *

Conclusions

After 1945 the survivors of World War II were faced with tremendous political, economic, and social dislocations. The global agenda they hoped to pursue was supplanted by the gradual emergence of two other distinct agendas, the East-West and the North-South. Of these, the East-West was the more distinct and challenging. The North-South agenda picked up an issue originally on the global agenda—decolonization—and brought some attention to problems of special interest to the new states. Some progress was made in accomplishing global agenda goals. The United Nations was formed and the capitalist international economic system gained some order and a few central institutions. But in many other respects, especially with regard to peacekeeping and decolonization, the global agenda was over-shadowed by the East-West one.

Many factors account for the emergence of the two new agendas. Underlying philosophical differences resurfaced in conflicts over the character of postwar political regimes in Europe and in a struggle over the fate of Germany and related issues. Extensions of Soviet power in Central Europe, together with communist victories in Asia, generated fears in the West of further unfavorable changes and led to efforts to counter and contain the Eastern bloc.

At the same time, the crumbling of the Western empires brought many world order problems. The creation of new states was a natural source of new international issues, particularly when those new states had resentments against dominant states or against the prevailing international order. As succeeding chapters will show, the colonial legacy included the roots of many contentious issues that would find a place on the North-South agenda in the future.

Notes

1. France is considered as one of the Allies even though it was partially occupied by Germany in 1940 and the rest of the country, governed from Vichy, was officially

neutral. Until the end of the war, France was represented among the Allies by the National Liberation Committee under Charles de Gaulle.

2. The Soviet Union joined the Allies in 1941. It had signed a neutrality treaty with Japan in 1932 and a nonaggression pact with Germany in 1939. The USSR and Germany then promptly split Poland between them and carved out separate spheres of interest in Eastern Europe, an arrangement that freed Germany for a westward attack. The Soviet-German pact was broken when Germany attacked the Soviet Union in June 1941. That was the point at which the USSR entered the war in Europe. It did not enter the war against Japan until August 1945.

3. Franklin D. Roosevelt Press Conference, January 24, 1943, at the Casablanca Conference. Cited in Hans L. Trefousse, The Cold War: A Book of Documents (New York: G. P. Putnam's Sons, 1965), p. 6.

4. Protocol of the Crimea Conference, Yalta, February 4–11, 1945. Cited in Trefousse, The Cold War, pp. 24–25.

5. Communiqué of the Moscow foreign ministers conference, November 1, 1943. Cited in Trefousse, The Cold War, p. 7.

6. Poland was the fifty-first founding member of the United Nations but was not represented at the Charter signing ceremony.

7. Whereas all states have equal powers in the General Assembly, the major states have special powers in the United Nations Security Council. The United States, the United Kingdom, the USSR, France, and China are permanent members of the Security Council. According to the Charter, a majority vote of the council must include the votes of all permanent members. The practical effect of this rule is to give each of the permanent members a veto over Security Council actions. (In 1965 the Charter was amended to increase the size of the Security Council by the addition of four nonpermanent members, making the total membership fifteen.) The Republic of China, under Generalissimo Chiang Kai-shek, had been at war with Japan and was treated as an Allied power entitled to sit on the Security Council at the insistence of the United States and over the objections of the Soviet Union.

8. United Nations Charter, Chapter XI, Article 73.

9. Protocol of the Crimea Conference, February 4–11, 1945. Cited in Trefousse, The Cold War, pp. 21–22.

10. The USSR was not completely successful, however. In Yugoslavia, the Communists were a genuinely popular revolutionary movement that had come to power on its own. Heavy-handed Soviet efforts to control this country provoked Yugoslavian President Tito to rebel. When Tito secured Yugoslav independence by means of arrangements for aid and trade with the United States and Western European countries, the Soviets did not challenge him militarily, but they did launch a major campaign to quell any manifestations of nationalist defiance elsewhere.

11. Stalin, letter to Winston Churchill, May 1945. Cited in Trefousse, The Cold War, p. 47.

12. March 12, 1947. Cited in Trefousse, The Cold War, pp. 93–96.

13. Andrei Zhdanov, "The International Situation," Speech to the founding meeting of the Cominform, September 1947, For a Lasting Peace, For a Peoples Democracy, November 10, 1947, p. 2.

14. At first, the USSR was neutral in the Pacific, respecting its treaty with Japan. However, in 1943 the USSR did promise to break this neutrality treaty and join in the war against Japan three months after the end of the war in Europe—in return for some Japanese islands and a free hand in Mongolia.

15. *Public Papers of the Presidents: Dwight D. Eisenhower* (Washington, D.C.: Government Printing Office, 1955), pp. 702–703.

16. Christopher Clapham, *Third World Politics: An Introduction* (Madison: University of Wisconsin Press, 1985), p. 34.

17. The newly independent states offered only moral support. See G. H. Jansen, *Non-Alignment and the Afro-Asian States* (New York: Praeger, 1966), p. 56; and David Kimche, *The Afro-Asian Movement* (New York: Halstead Press, 1973), pp. 30–32.

18. Peter Lyon, *Neutralism* (Leicester, England: Leicester University Press, 1963), p. 37.

19. Critics called the U.S. drive to form or sponsor collective security treaties in the 1950s "pactomania." Not all of these have survived. The United States set up a collective defense pact with Australia and New Zealand (the ANZUS pact) in 1952 and a wider regional body called the Southeast Asia Treaty Organization (SEATO) in 1954, which included Britain, France, Australia, New Zealand, Pakistan, the Philippines, and Thailand. Pakistan withdrew from this treaty in 1973, and SEATO's organization was disbanded in 1975. The United States was not a formal member of a Middle East defense pact but encouraged Britain, Iraq, Turkey, Iran, and Pakistan to form the Middle East treaty organization known as the Baghdad Pact in 1955. The name changed to the Central Treaty Organization (CENTO) after Iraq withdrew in 1959, and the organization was disbanded in 1979.

20. Kimche, *The Afro-Asian Movement*, p. 42.

21. Jansen, *Non-Alignment*, p. 159.

Two / WORKING OUT THE RULES

The period from 1955 to 1963 was a tense and fearful era in which a series of crises in superpower relations clearly shook the international community. Growing nuclear arsenals meant that war between East and West would have catastrophic consequences. The crises of this period were a reminder that relatively minor conflicts could escalate into such a catastrophe. Thus any issue could be threatening if it implied a possibility of confrontation between the superpowers, either as direct adversaries or as rival patrons of smaller states.

• GLOBAL AGENDA   Two issues took a position on the global agenda: the fear of war and decolonization. The rising anxiety about war grew out of crises in Soviet-American relations that reflected changes in the nature of the "security dilemma" in the nuclear age. Decolonization became a matter of global attention because of dissatisfaction with the rate of progress toward independence and because of a specific crisis in the former Belgian Congo.

• EAST-WEST AGENDA   The East-West agenda was dominated by bipolar issues related to U.S.-Soviet conflict. These included crisis diplomacy and arms control. Efforts by each superpower to control its allies raised additional problems.

• NORTH-SOUTH AGENDA   The North-South agenda gained visibility in this period and was redefined in ways that made it both more distinct and more assertive. The concern with anticolonialism remained, but the more specific and positive movement for nonalignment rose to equal *nonalignment and economic development important* importance. As many of the new states sought ways to cooperate in pursuit of similar economic needs, economic development was added to the North-South agenda.

Clashes between the East-West and North-South agendas occurred in this period. Western efforts to contain the Eastern bloc by controlling foreign alignments of small states offended many nationalist leaders and regimes. This appeared to offer opportunities to the USSR, which became more active in the Third World, both politically and militarily. Despite rhetoric about common interests in "development" and "progress," both of the superpowers were suspicious of genuine nonalignment.

Consideration of the issues of this period will begin with the global agenda and a review of an important and dynamic contextual factor, the security dilemma in the nuclear age.

THE GLOBAL AGENDA

Fear of War and Efforts to Control Nuclear Weaponry

The Security Dilemma

The emergence of two hostile armed camps, each headed by a dominant power armed with nuclear weapons, provided a bipolar structure for world politics. The destructive power of these nuclear arsenals produced a situation in which the security dilemma brought special dangers of global importance.

What is the *security dilemma* and why is it important? It is a condition of international relations commonly said to derive from *international anarchy*, a term that refers to the fact that there is no international sovereign or world government capable of forcing states to behave according to accepted rules. (Although the United Nations has limited rule-enforcement functions, it is far from a true international government.) Hence all states must protect themselves or band together with other states to do so. This can produce a *security dilemma* wherein the actions that one state takes to protect itself may unintentionally have the effect of threatening the security of other states.

Where insecurity is pervasive, perceptions of common interests among states develop slowly. A state must make assumptions about the intentions of its opponent to decide whether the opponent's actions result from aggressive or defensive motives. The more mistrustful and hostile a relationship, the greater the tendency to perceive offensive intent. Events in international politics are often ambiguous, and policymakers tend to see what they expect to see. The accuracy of assumptions of hostility is not often tested, even where contrary evidence is present, when the risks of error are assumed to be very great.[1]

During the Cold War the United States and the Soviet Union have had "mirror images" of each other. Each sees itself as defensive in motivation, arming only to protect itself, while each sees the other as offensive in motivation, arming in hopes of waging war. The security dilemma inherent in international politics creates the conditions for this suspicion, and the advent of nuclear weapons technology makes the problem more severe.

Nuclear Dilemmas

Nuclear weapons are the most destructive forces humanity has ever created to use against itself. These weapons have not only raised the risks of war but have also challenged security policy in a number of ways. Installation of nuclear warheads on rockets has made it possible to launch these massively destructive weapons with very little warning time from friendly territory far from the target. Moreover, defense against these missiles is practically impossible. Because the consequences of decisions to use these weapons are weighty, accurate assessment of an adversary's intentions is extremely critical. Yet the weapons are most likely to be thought necessary at times of serious crisis, or as a last resort in a desperate situation.

Moreover, the nature of nuclear weapons makes assessments of the other side's intentions extremely difficult. Because nuclear weapons appear to be offensive, mere possession of them can intimidate other states. These weapons serve a defensive purpose if they deter undesired actions, and if they are hidden or protectively housed to survive an attack so that they can be used for retaliation, they can deter attack even by another nuclear power. The problem is of course that weapons with a deterrent mission can be used to take aggressive actions. Thus under any circumstances the distinction between offensive and defensive nuclear weapons is obscure, and an opponent state's intentions cannot be determined simply by examining the weapons it acquires. These uncertainties heighten the security dilemma.

Uncertainties about defensive and offensive armaments and about an opponent's intentions have generally produced arms races in the prenuclear age. In the nuclear era, the arms race is similarly driven by fear and anticipation of the actions of the other side. This arms race has technological and quantitative aspects: Both sides have sought to improve and enhance the capabilities of their weapons, and both sides have acquired greater numbers of increasingly diverse and changing arsenals.

The increasingly global scale of East-West competition has contributed to concern about the possibility that small conflicts can "escalate" to full-scale war, once the superpowers become involved. For all these reasons, the danger of war and the level of East-West tension became a major underlying issue on the international agenda. It is important to review the ways in which some of these weapons-related issues took shape at this time.

Development of Nuclear Stockpiles

It was in the period from 1955 to 1963 that construction of versatile, deadly strategic nuclear arsenals began and that the development of long-range intercontinental ballistic missiles (ICBMs) tipped with nuclear warheads occurred. At the beginning of this period, the United States clearly had nuclear weapons dominance. With U.S. long-range bombers and intermediate-range rockets based around the rim of the USSR, the members of the Western alliance could justly believe the Soviets would be very ill-advised to risk any major war. In the late 1950s, evidence that the USSR had acquired the rocketry needed to build large numbers of ICBMs meant not only that the United States had become vulnerable to sudden Soviet attack but that the aircraft assigned to carry nuclear bombs were also vulnerable. The fear was reciprocal, leading both sides to build and deploy ICBMs.

[handwritten margin note: Soviet success w/their own ICBM's accelerates arms race]

It is possible to argue that once both sides have substantial numbers of nuclear weapons with similar characteristics and destructive capabilities, the potential costs of war for both sides should create a stalemate—a balance of terror under which the entire world must live. Deliberate choice to start a war where both sides could employ nuclear weapons seems so nearly suicidal as to be improbable except in extreme cases. Yet the characteristics of the weapons could also lead a state to choose surprise or preemptive attack (a choice to precipitate a war to reap the advantages of striking first), given a changing or temporarily favorable balance. At the same time the finality of a decision to launch a global war does raise new worries about the dangers of accidental or irrational war.

[handwritten margin note: Is this really plausible?]

Realization that "weapons of last resort" were themselves logical targets produced a variety of new ideas and schemes in the 1960s: Plans were sought for weapons that could be effective against the other's weapons; ICBMs were put into underground launching silos fortified against attack; airplanes carrying nuclear bombs were dispersed or kept on alert; and missiles that could be fired from underwater were installed on submarines.

[handwritten margin note: U.S. spends time and money protecting weapons]

Paradoxically, states with large arsenals of nuclear weapons might be vulnerable to ambiguous, low-level, or indirect threats. That is, a state with few options other than full-scale nuclear attack might negotiate or concede rather than take the risk a small incident could escalate. Assuming long-range ballistic missiles and bombs would be reserved for strategic use against an adversary's homeland, some believed that small nuclear warheads could be used in armed conflicts of limited scope where the stakes were lower. In 1954, in fact, NATO had made a decision to deploy small tactical nuclear warheads for battlefield use in order to compensate for the relative weakness of NATO's European conventional (that is, nonnuclear) forces compared with the Soviet bloc armies.

These developments in weaponry suggested that superpower competition presented enormous risks for all states. The effect of nuclear weaponry on the security dilemma and the nature of war made it possible to argue that from a global point of view, the Cold War was dangerous. There was a general fear of war and a realization that superpower rivalry could bring war to all peoples, whether or not they were participants in the Cold War.

arms control a global issue

Thus tension reduction and arms control became issues of interest to the entire international community. These new items legitimately belonged on the global agenda, but how would they get there?

Arms Control Proposals

At the same time as the superpowers competed in efforts to display an interest in disarmament and "normal" international relations, both were actively exploring ways to increase their military capacities. Proposals for various forms of arms control did surface, however. One was a Polish proposal to create a nuclear-free zone in Europe (to keep nuclear weapons out of German control). In 1959 the Soviets suggested a revised version of this idea: a pair of nuclear-free zones that would link guarantees of a nonnuclear China with those of a nonnuclear Germany. Direct U.S.-Soviet discussions in 1960 produced an interesting document that laid out general principles for a complete disarmament program, but no practical steps emerged.

Ironic hypocrisy?!

people talk of peace but no practical steps taken

Concern about the dangers of radioactive fallout from atomic testing and the growing probability that more states would acquire nuclear weapons were important stimuli for multilateral meetings on disarmament. In 1961 the United States and the USSR agreed to cochair meetings of an Eighteen-Nation Disarmament Committee (ENDC) under UN auspices to consider specific proposals as they might emerge. This group, which included the ten nuclear or near-nuclear powers plus eight neutral states, did some useful work in clarifying the problems that seemed to require multilateral approaches. These discussions acknowledged the interests of the global community in the balance of terror and reflected a growing acceptance of the obligation of all states to manage their conflicts responsibly in the nuclear age.

why manage as opposed to avoid?

However, it was clear that concrete progress in arms control would require not just greater interest and motivation on the part of the superpowers, but some degree of mutual trust. It was also clear that the superpowers would not permit global organizations to determine their weapons policies. The issue of arms control thus inevitably shifted to the East-West agenda, where during this period it was of relatively low priority.

Mutual Trust is key

Decolonization

The issue of decolonization took a prominent and permanent position on the international agenda in the period 1955–1963. Although the importance of decolonization had been recognized in the United Nations Charter, colonial powers had generally retained control over the process of establishing independence in dependent territories. But by 1960 the membership of the United Nations had changed. Eighteen African countries became independent in the single year 1960. Altogether, Afro-Asian membership increased from twelve in 1946 to fifty-three by 1961. This changed the character of the General Assembly. Now Southern states could use their numerical importance to push issues such as decolonization onto the global agenda within the United Nations forum.

increased South could join together to exercise power

UN Involvement

By 1960 there was a growing sense that the decolonization process was not moving fast enough. One reflection of this was Resolution 1514, the Declaration on the Granting of Independence to Colonial Countries and Peoples, by the General Assembly in December 1960. The Declaration was designed to go beyond the Charter's rather vague endorsement of self-government by accelerating the process of decolonization:

Resolution 1514 ✳

> Recognizing that the people of the world ardently desire the end of colonialism in all its manifestations . . . [that] . . . the process of liberation is irresistible and irreversible and that, to avoid grave crises, it is necessary to put an end to colonialism and to the practices of segregation and discrimination that accompany it. . . . Convinced that all peoples have an inalienable right to complete freedom, the exercise of sovereignty and the integrity of their national territory . . . [the United Nations] . . . proclaims the necessity of putting an end rapidly and unconditionally to colonialism in all its forms and manifestations.[2]

Declaration was wide in scope

The Declaration was deliberately wide in scope. Its text treated racism, apartheid, economic exploitation, and coercive efforts to suppress anticolonial movements as manifestations of colonialism.

The UN's growing membership made it a more truly global institution and the UN agenda more reflective of global issues. Yet obvious disparities of power meant that the major states—and certainly the superpowers—could to some extent ignore issues raised within the UN General Assembly or violate principles enunciated there. The global agenda was tenuous: Issues important to the United States and the USSR could quickly move to the East-West agenda. Decolonization was an example of this.

The Congo Affair

Decisions by Great Britain and France to move toward granting full independence to most of their African colonies in this period raised the visibility of the remaining independence struggles. In 1960, Belgium precipitously granted independence to the Congo—a huge territory (now called Zaire) deeply divided by tribal and economic diversities. The new state almost immediately faced a mutiny in the security forces and a secession

by the richest province. The Congolese central government was weak and
divided, a coalition of political rivals. In May 1960, this government turned
to the United Nations for help in holding the new country together—a
novel approach that temporarily had the support of all the major states
and a multinational United Nations peacekeeping force went to the aid of
the shaky central government.

*Chaotic
Congo asks
U.N. to help
form peaceful
nation*

When one of the Congolese leaders, however, Patrice Lumumba, grew
dissatisfied with the UN operations and threatened to request Soviet assistance
in dealing with the internal problems, East-West rivalries became the dominant
feature of the crisis. While the Congolese political leadership split, with
each part seeking rival patrons, U.S. officials on the scene moved quickly
to cut off Soviet access to the Congo and pressed forward toward a political
outcome that would produce a pro-Western government. The Congolese
operations continued in this fashion under UN control despite strong
protests from the Soviet bloc, which angrily refused to pay its share of the
UN costs. The USSR also denounced the alleged partisanship of the UN
Secretary General, Dag Hammarskjold, who was personally directing UN
operations in the Congo.

*East-West
tension inhibits
global concerns*

Reassessment of the United Nations

In this instance, Western ability to influence the UN was an important
advantage. One aftereffect of the Congolese crisis was an unsuccessful Soviet
proposal to alter the UN structure to include a three-part ("troika") secretariat:
one Eastern, one Western, and one neutral secretary. This proposal failed,
and the Soviets grudgingly reaffirmed their support for the UN. Nonetheless
the experience in the Congo challenged expectations that the world organization could act effectively in support of a global consensus on decolonization—particularly if the superpowers were not part of that consensus.
The experiment of direct United Nations military involvement was not
repeated. One year later a special committee was established to try to
enforce Resolution 1514—which was still not being carried out by colonial
powers to the satisfaction of the majority of UN members.

*Western influence
over U.N.*

Whereas superpower enthusiasm for UN action on global issues waned,
consensus was possible even though this consensus was expressed symbolically. A 1963 decision by the Security Council to call for a voluntary
embargo on arms sales to South Africa because of its repressive official
racism (known as apartheid) is one example.

*1963
symbolic
denunciation
of Apartheid*

Both arms control and decolonization had a clear presence on the global
agenda during this period. Yet arms control also appeared on the East-West
agenda, while decolonization was also on the North-South agenda. As we
will point out, these issues took on different qualities and priorities on
different agendas.

THE EAST-WEST AGENDA

Control Problems on the Front Burner

Each superpower had to confront serious challenges to its supremacy within its own sphere. These challenges were of utmost importance to the superpowers. For the USSR the challenges were primarily inside the bloc and came in both Eastern Europe and Asia. Although the West experienced problems of cohesion within NATO, external challenges—to the credibility of Western power and to the value of the barriers that had been erected against an expansion of Soviet international activities—were regarded as more serious. Neither superpower was completely successful in reasserting control in its own sphere, and each endured major defections. These incidents helped to call attention to issues of intrabloc hierarchy, although at this point it was the outcomes of these alliance leadership crises that captured attention, not the legitimacy or character of superpower assertiveness itself.

USSR has internal problems (handwritten margin note)

U.S. has image problems (handwritten margin note)

Soviet Problems in Eastern Europe

Soviet control problems in East Europe first appeared after Stalin's death in 1953. Resentment against the Soviets and their political control was not new; poor economic performance of the satellite regimes intensified it. As the Soviets sought to reform their own political and economic policies, the prospect of change raised expectations in the satellite states and invigorated local critics of the ruling groups.

Denunciation of Stalin. In 1956, the new Soviet Party Secretary Nikita Khrushchev boldly denounced Stalin as a criminal guilty of all sorts of "illegality" and of violations of Leninist principles. This cleared the way for repudiation of Stalin's policies and institutions and replacement of his associates. Whereas Stalin had been associated with ruthlessly imposed uniformity, Khrushchev insisted that many paths to socialism were possible.

Khrushchev denounces Stalin (handwritten margin note)

Khrushchev may have assumed that his pledges to correct abuses and return to Leninist ideals would assure his own popularity and security. The impact of his critique of Stalin, however, proved enormously destabilizing in Eastern Europe, where the new socialist regimes were neither popular nor effective. Stalin had been so closely and personally identified with Soviet power that attacks on him legitimized attacks on the entire Soviet-style political system. Moreover, Khrushchev's sanction for diversity proved to be a stimulus for local innovation and dissent from Soviet recommendations. Long-pent-up demands for fundamental policy changes and eased controls were heard even within ruling party circles all over Eastern Europe, and strikes, demonstrations, and even riots erupted in East Germany and Poland.

Troubles in Eastern Europe. The situation became most critical in Hungary. In Hungary popular demands for relief from Soviet control, for better economic conditions, and for greater political freedoms were expressed in street violence that pressed the government into real change. A new Hungarian communist leadership group took a nationalist line, balked at Soviet efforts to direct them, and even hinted at withdrawal from the Warsaw Pact. In October 1956, the USSR sent in tanks and troops, and after several weeks the "counterrevolution" (to use Soviet terms) was subdued. The rebellious Hungarian communist leaders were imprisoned and a new Hungarian government installed.

[handwritten margin note: Hungarian Revolt shows internal strife in East]

The disturbances elsewhere in East Europe were handled without overt use of force. However, these events required the USSR to redefine the role and the future of its satellites. A series of international communist meetings in 1957 and 1960 sought to clarify some of the issues that had so disrupted the socialist camp and find ways in which the satellite governments could improve their performance and stabilize their political control.

Peaceful Coexistence. Khrushchev's bold attack on Stalin was not all that was new. He also appeared to reject a Marxist axiom about the inevitability of conflict between the communist states and their enemies. Picking up a theme once used by communist-inspired postwar peace movements, Khrushchev announced that war between East and West was no longer "fatally inevitable," that peaceful coexistence between East and West was possible. The Soviets accounted for this by bragging about increased Soviet strength and claiming that opposition to Western warmongers was creating a huge "zone of peace" that would oblige the West to coexist peacefully with the socialist camp. Nonetheless, warnings about the dangers of nuclear war suggested that the balance of terror was the real source of these new ideas. East-West struggle, the Soviets now said, would express itself in ideological fields and through economic competition. This aspect of Soviet policy produced a new issue: Soviet ideological authority within the world communist movement.

Sino-Soviet Split

The most important manifestation of the issue of Soviet authority was the public quarrel between the USSR and the People's Republic of China, known as the Sino-Soviet split, which involved issues of both policy and ideology. The Chinese communist leaders, who had many grievances against their Soviet allies, eventually charged that the new Soviet views on Marxism-Leninism were a virtual surrender to imperialism in foreign policy and an abandonment of Marxism's revolutionary mission domestically. By contrast, the Chinese claimed they were truer to Marx's ideas and were in fact

[handwritten margin note: Chinese accuse Soviets of denouncing the Cause]

leaping ahead to construct a communal society in their largely agrarian land. In practical matters, the Chinese resented Soviet arrogance, the low levels of Soviet economic aid they had received, and the USSR's reluctance to support Chinese interests in Asia. These grievances built up to a major break, which became widely publicized in 1960 when the Soviets withdrew their advisers from China.

The socialist camp was soon caught up in polemics and bitter political conflict over this rift. When the Chinese withdrew their ambassador from Moscow in 1962, the Albanians joined the Chinese in breaking with the USSR. While most foreign communist parties remained at least superficially loyal to Moscow, the ideological challenge was a major complication in Soviet efforts to retain political and economic control within its sphere.

The West's Problem Areas

NATO. Control problems for the West occurred in several areas. Although economic unification of Europe was proceeding relatively smoothly on a continental basis, uniting Europe in an alliance against the Soviet Union proved difficult in many respects. Despite the agreement to form NATO, implementation of practical military plans proved to be a problem. Once the Soviets had demonstrated an ability to build rocketry that could propel nuclear weapons to the continental United States, a debate raged on both sides of the Atlantic over the implications for European defense. Would the United States risk an attack on its own territory merely to protest Soviet behavior in Eastern Europe, to repel a Soviet threat to Berlin, or even to save Europe from invasion? As a response to this situation, the United States proposed stationing in Europe tactical nuclear weapons with small warheads and limited destructive capacity, intended for battlefield use. Questions about the control over such weapons then became a major controversy.

The French Initiative. The French took the lead in this period in challenging the United States within the alliance. General Charles DeGaulle, who had become president of France in 1958, was impatient with U.S. priorities. He rejected U.S. military plans, vowed to proceed with an independent French nuclear force (known as the *force de frappe*), and took steps to separate France from the military structure of NATO.

The Middle East

The Suez Crisis. Developments in the Middle East provided openings for the East and seriously disrupted Western power and influence. The most dramatic crisis involved Egypt. The nationalist government there had angrily resisted pressures to participate in any U.S.- or British-sponsored regional military alliance. Furthermore, Egypt announced in September 1955 that it had decided to purchase arms from Czechoslovakia. Nasser's main priority was independence and that meant dealing with both East and West, but his behavior was alarming to those for whom the East-West struggle was paramount. Regimes that might invite an Eastern bloc military presence earned enemy status in the eyes of the West very quickly.

Egyptian development plans had included an ambitious hydroelectric and water conservancy project on the Nile River at Aswan, for which Nasser had sought assistance. In the furor that developed in the West over Egypt's purchase of arms from the Soviet bloc, a U.S. offer to finance the Aswan project was publicly withdrawn. Nasser quickly responded with another defiant gesture: nationalization of the Suez Canal, the revenues henceforth targeted for Egypt's development needs. The canal had enormous symbolism for the British as the key link in its route to India and to the Persian Gulf oil fields. The United Kingdom and France shared an interest in the canal and had long cooperated in defending and administering it. Seizure of foreign property was also widely regarded in the West as intolerable. In summer 1956, the British, French, and Israelis produced a plan to recover the canal by force in an operation they hoped would weaken or remove Nasser's government. However, the United States was not consulted about these plans, and when the invasion of Egypt began in October 1956, President Eisenhower angrily denounced it as an unacceptable use of force. The Soviets saw a classic case of imperialist high-handedness, and—once it was clear that the British and French and Israeli forces would withdraw— the USSR boldly suggested that its rockets could protect states like Egypt.

Arab Nationalism. The Suez crisis made Nasser a hero and inflamed Arab nationalist passions against Israel and against those Arab regimes (mostly conservative monarchies) that were on friendly terms with the Western powers. The incident dramatically illustrated the ways in which assertive nationalism in pursuit of economic and military independence could produce conflicts parallel to the East-West conflict axis. Both the East and the West saw such behavior as pro-Eastern. The West sought to restrain it; the East sought to co-opt it.

Over the next few years, nationalist movements with pro-Nasser sentiments toppled or threatened to topple several governments in the region. In 1957 and 1958, the United States and Britain rushed troops and ships to the Middle East to forestall threats to the status quo in Lebanon and Jordan. Nonetheless, in 1958 the Iraqi monarchy fell to a radical nationalist military government, which took that country out of the Baghdad Pact in 1959 (thereafter, this alliance was referred to simply as CENTO, for the Central Treaty Organization). A coup in Syria produced a regime so enthusiastic about Nasser's brand of pan-Arab socialism that it agreed to a formal merger of the two states. (Internal political difficulties ruined that union, the United Arab Republic, eighteen months later.)

Two Threats to Bipolarity

The emergence of increasing numbers of assertive, professedly socialist, nationalist regimes raised questions about how global and all encompassing bipolar East-West issues might become. Two notable alignment crises occurred during this period. They involved Cuba, where an anti-American, pro-Soviet government came to power; and the Congo, where Western influence and control was retained.

Cuba. The Cuban revolution began as a small, leftist insurgency in 1956 led by Fidel Castro. In January 1959, Castro replaced Cuban dictator Fulgencio Batista and established a new government that was fiercely nationalistic and determined to reduce U.S. influence over the island state. Actions by the new government to change the terms of Cuba's relationship with outsiders, particularly U.S. business interests, quickly led to bitter disputes. Cuba's nationalizations of U.S.-owned property and its development of commercial ties with the USSR led to retaliatory moves by the United States, including a trade embargo supported by the Organization of American States (OAS) in 1960. The U.S. intelligence service had been working with anti-Castro Cuban emigrés to harass and subvert Castro's government, and in April 1961 a U.S.-sponsored invasion force landed at the Bay of Pigs. This poorly planned attempt to overthrow Castro failed and embarrassed the United States; the debacle encouraged defiant nationalists elsewhere.

Moreover, the failure of the Bay of Pigs invasion encouraged Castro to announce that he was a Marxist-Leninist (he had previously declared himself a socialist) and to seek a protective alignment with the Soviet Union. The Soviets responded with a trade treaty and a large long-term loan for Cuba. Suspended from the OAS in 1962, Cuba remained a defiant Soviet friend just ninety miles off the coast of Florida.

The Congo. In the case of the Congo (see above), civil war among competing nationalist groups within the politically fragile newly independent state created an unstable and dangerous situation. As we have seen, a United Nations force was sent to restore order at Congolese request; but when the Congolese government split, UN operations were used to help support a pro-Western group.

Competition for the Allegiance of the Third World

It was partly in response to frustration over Western actions against nationalists that Soviet leader Khrushchev in 1961 reaffirmed Soviet support for national liberation wars of oppressed peoples. His reminder that such wars were legitimate despite the perils of the nuclear age was undoubtedly intended to rebut Chinese criticism. Nonetheless, the West found reason to be worried about the growing Soviet role as political patron and donor of military and economic aid to Third World countries such as Egypt,

Indonesia, Algeria, Syria, and India. A competitive scramble to influence political change in the Third World was in evidence in a number of countries. In Indochina, the United States had been sending military and financial aid to anti-Communist Vietnamese. Partisan warfare had also erupted in neighboring Laos, where the United States, China, the USSR, and France all took an interest. Although a conference of fourteen interested nations in 1962 produced an agreement to respect a carefully "neutralized" Laotian coalition government, superpower aid to communist and anti-communist armed forces continued.

It was clear that both East and West were engaged in political activity that threatened to affect international alignments; however, it was not clear how far either side might be able to control such activity. Certainly both sides were taking care to avoid direct East-West confrontations. Instead, they were engaging in "war by proxy," which became a new form of competition and a dangerous manifestation of the way in which bipolarity could dominate not only international politics but also the domestic politics of small states.

Crisis Diplomacy

Brinkmanship

Crises dominated the East-West agenda from 1955 to 1963, a period during which the superpowers became involved in a number of efforts to test each other's strength and resolve in Europe and elsewhere. The struggle to retain control in their respective spheres and to manage the complexities of advances in military technology made direct East-West relations dominate world politics. This direct diplomacy was fraught with tension as crisis succeeded crisis. It was in this period that the term *brinkmanship* (appearing to threaten a nuclear attack) entered popular usage. The crisis diplomacy of this period constituted a frightening chapter in the Cold War as each superpower implicitly or explicitly threatened to use nuclear weapons to end a conflict.

Rocket Rattling. In a series of crises that all fell short of war, one side or the other could and often did claim that a willingness to threaten war had secured an advantage or prevented a loss. In the cycles of threat and counterthreat, it was difficult to be sure. Soviet rocket rattling was a frightening technique that illustrated both the appeal and the limits of the bluff in a nuclear bipoplar world where no one wanted to risk an East-West war. After the Suez crisis, for example, the Soviets offered their rockets to defend Nasser, and in 1957, Khrushchev warned that Soviet rockets might be used against Turkey in the event of any U.S.-backed interference in increasingly anti-Western Syria.

U.S. used similar tactics in Far East

For its part, the United States employed similar diplomatic tactics. In late 1955 the People's Republic of China (PRC) began shelling offshore islands (Quemoy and Matsu) held by the forces of Chiang Kai-shek. Fearful that the Communists might be contemplating an invasion, U.S. leaders publicly suggested that atomic weapons might be used should war break out in Asia. When the Chinese resumed attacks on the offshore islands, the United States first declared its intent to prevent a communist victory in this vulnerable spot, then denied such a position after Khrushchev warned that an attack on the PRC would be regarded as an attack on the USSR.

Crisis over Berlin. The most serious war-threatening crises were two involving Berlin. In November 1958, Khrushchev attempted to revive the issue of Germany's political future with a novel threat: Unless a summit conference were called within six months to discuss Germany's situation, he declared, the USSR would hand over its zone of occupied Berlin to the East Germans, unilaterally ending the wartime arrangements for joint occupation. Khrushchev did not threaten to use force but warned that any *Soviets border on forcing Berlin issue. Brinksmanship* Western attack on East Germany could mean war. Britain, France, and the United States refused to budge, insisting they would not use force, but neither would they recognize a transfer of Soviet authority in Berlin to the GDR. Together the Western Allies consulted about the steps they might have to take to meet the new situation. Since the East Germans were not interested in continued Allied control of Berlin, some Western officials worried that the Soviet threat could have the effect of forcing the Western Allies to choose between fighting the East Germans for access to the city or conceding the capital to the Soviets. However, the Soviets did not call their bluff, but decided to withdraw the deadline and ask for a summit conference instead. The Western powers would not agree to this, but tensions were greatly reduced by an agreement for Khrushchev and U.S. President Eisenhower to exchange bilateral visits.

The U-2 Mission. Khrushchev traveled to the United States in September 1959. The apparent friendliness of this visit cleared the way for a four-power summit planned for Paris in May 1960, to be followed by Eisenhower's *U2 incident destroys possibility for summit* return visit to the USSR. However, the summit never officially opened. When representatives assembled in Paris, Khrushchev revealed that the Soviets had brought down a U.S. U-2 aircraft engaged in a photo reconnaissance mission over Soviet territory. It was an embarrassing confrontation because Eisenhower had earlier denied that any such overflights were taking place. When Eisenhower nonetheless defended the practice in public and took responsibility for these flights, Khrushchev walked out of the summit.

Tensions in Germany. Tensions concerning East Germany and Berlin continued when President Eisenhower left office and was succeeded by President John F. Kennedy. Khrushchev and Kennedy met in June 1961 in

Vienna just two months after the failure of a U.S.-backed effort to invade Cuba at the Bay of Pigs. It was an acrimonious meeting. When it was over, Khrushchev announced a new six-month deadline on the question of Germany's status: If no agreement were reached by December 1961, a separate Soviet–East German treaty would be signed.

Khrushchev removed the December deadline at a party congress in November, but the intervening months were full of tensions. First the Soviet Union and then the United States announced increases in defense spending and troop strengths and engaged in mutual accusations of provocation. Small-scale U.S.-Soviet confrontations occurred over access routes to Berlin. On August 13, 1961, the Soviets and East Germans hastily erected ✱ a barrier (the Berlin Wall) to close off access to their zone of Berlin, thus halting what had become a flood of refugees fleeing westward through Berlin. Shortly afterwards the USSR announced resumption of nuclear *USSR increases Nuclear testing* testing—a series of tests of unprecedented explosive power. The Western states did not challenge the wall directly but reaffirmed their determination to stay in Berlin and defiantly reinforced their garrisons there.

The Cuban Missile Crisis

War had been avoided over Berlin. But an even closer brush with the possibility of a nuclear exchange came with the third major crisis of this period, the Cuban Missile Crisis. This crisis made the possibility of a nuclear exchange seem very real and pressed home to both sides the need for alternatives to a nuclear exchange.

In October 1962, U.S. intelligence agencies discovered the presence in Cuba of missile sites for Soviet missiles, which the United States interpreted as an escalation of the Soviet presence in Cuba. Worse, U.S. officials regarded the missile sites as an unacceptable change in the strategic status quo, a change that immediately increased the offensive Soviet threat to U.S. territory—and to U.S. nuclear weapons forces. President Kennedy was under *missile threat to America* considerable pressure to respond. After deliberating over several policy options with a group of advisers known as the ExCom (Executive Committee), Kennedy decided on a partial naval blockade to keep Soviet missile cargoes from reaching the island and demanded that the Soviets dismantle all existing missile launchers. No negotiation was suggested: The demand was made and the Soviets were given time to think about their response. Eventually the Soviets conceded: They agreed to remove their missiles if the United States would promise not to invade Cuba. It was a tense and frightening two weeks of maneuver, threat, and countermove. Yet it was also quite clear that conventional military superiority around Cuba had made it possible for the United States to find a way short of direct conflict to secure a desired action.

The crisis was a warning about how close the superpowers could come to war where issues of pride and spheres of influence were involved. For many, it was a clear signal that bipolarity could easily get out of hand—and that it was urgent to find ways to moderate the competition between the two superpowers. Thus the crisis was a spur to arms control negotiations and to efforts to improve superpower relations. However since the Cuban Missile Crisis was in many respects a humiliation for the USSR, the encounter was also clearly a spur to the Soviets to increase their own military capacities in order to reduce or eliminate the U.S. advantage.

results of Cuban Missile Crisis are noted

Arms Control: A Simmering Back-Burner Issue

Arms Buildup

Arms control issues did receive new attention on the East-West agenda in the period between 1955 and 1963; unfortunately, so did a competitive arms buildup. Khrushchev's talk about peaceful coexistence notwithstanding, the Soviet Union's efforts to increase its own military strength were impressive and served as a powerful incentive to the United States to keep ahead. In October 1957, the Soviets launched Sputnik, a small earth-orbiting satellite. This caused considerable concern in the United States not only because the Soviets were the first to launch such a satellite, but also because of the impressive rocketry required to accomplish this feat. Advances in Soviet rocket power signaled the imminent demise of U.S. invulnerability to nuclear attack. Although it soon became clear that the Soviet Union was not so far ahead of the United States in rocketry as had been first believed, the race was on.

Soviet space program eclipses our own

The United States was clearly dominant in numbers of nuclear weapons and in delivery systems. It also had a geographical advantage in that the United States had military bases in Europe and Asia close to Soviet territory, while the Soviets did not have an equivalent geographical threat. In brief, during these years, the United States still had "first-strike" capacity (that is, the ability to attack the Soviets so destructively that they could not respond with unacceptable levels of damage to the United States). But the ability of U.S. forces to survive an attack by the USSR became a serious concern during these years as that country improved its nuclear forces. One step taken by the United States to protect its nuclear weapons was diversification. Nuclear forces were distributed on land, at sea, and in the air as a triad of submarine-launched ballistic missiles (SLBMs), land-based missiles (intercontinental ballistic missiles, ICBMs), and long-range bombers. This distribution was thought to ensure that a sufficient number of weapons could survive an attack to permit a devastating retaliation. Such a "second-strike" capacity would provide security by deterring the Soviets from attacking in the first place.

Cooperation Between East and West

Test Ban Treaty. Partly because of the new U.S. vulnerability and partly because of the fear of nuclear war aroused by the Cuban Missile Crisis, arms control issues attracted more attention, but it was the dangers of testing nuclear weapons, not reduction of weapons, that produced the first significant arms control agreement. Everyone agreed that nuclear tests in the atmosphere were dangerous because of the radioactive fallout they produced, but many feared that a state that stopped testing might suffer a disadvantage in weapons development. Thus a test ban was highly symbolic of the benefits to be gained by arms control agreements between the blocs, provided trust could be established. Although at various points both the United States and the USSR had halted their own nuclear tests and expressed interest in banning all such tests, negotiations on this subject had made little headway. All this changed after the Cuban Missile Crisis. Three-power talks (including the United States, the USSR, and Great Britain) worked out the Partial Nuclear Test Ban Treaty in June 1963, which was initialed on July 25, 1963. One hundred and eight countries eventually signed this treaty, which prohibited tests in the atmosphere, in space, and under water. (Subterranean tests could continue.)

Hot-Line Agreement. At about the same time, Soviet-U.S. negotiations within the Eighteen Nation Disarmament Committee produced what became known as the hot-line agreement, an arrangement between the superpowers for a direct telegraph link, which could facilitate communication in times of crisis. Coming in the wake of the Cuban Missile Crisis, both of these agreements were reassuring symbolic demonstrations of responsible behavior by nuclear nations.

Types of Nuclear Strategy

Flexible Response. It should be noted that in the United States during the early 1960s there was a high-level debate concerning nuclear strategy that would affect U.S. conduct of future arms control negotiations. For the United States to threaten nuclear weapons (since the Soviets had the ability to respond in kind) was regarded as too dangerous and lacking in credibility for all but the most extremely threatening situations. The advocates of the strategic option known as Flexible Response maintained that the United States should develop the ability to fight any kind of war at any level of violence, ranging from guerrilla warfare to tactical nuclear war to a thermonuclear exchange with the Soviets. An ability to fight at any level of violence could help prevent a resort to nuclear weapons. This strategic orientation required that initial targets of U.S. nuclear forces be Soviet military installations, but cities would eventually become targets as the conflict escalated.

Mutual Assured Destruction. Others found the Flexible Response approach dangerous and foolhardy and doubted that use of nuclear weapons could be avoided once any kind of warfare began. For some, nuclear weapons offered security through deterrence; these people argued that a Soviet nuclear attack was unlikely if the United States could survive such an attack with enough nuclear weapons left to "assure" the "destruction" of 25 to 30 percent of the Soviet population and 50 to 75 percent of the Soviet industrial capacity. As both sides began to protect and disperse their weapons, the possibility of a mutual standoff emerged. Security through possession of a second-strike capacity is known as Mutual Assured Destruction, or MAD. This strategy implied that U.S. nuclear forces should be aimed at Soviet cities.

Nuclear weapons offer deterrence?

U.S. Strategic Options. Until 1962 the United States followed the Flexible Response approach as both declared (official) policy and actual policy. By the mid-1960s the declared policy was Mutual Assured Destruction but there actually was a military targeting strategy reflecting the Flexible Response approach.[3]

U.S. supports Flexible Response and MAD while increasing arsenals

Strategic thinking evolved along with weapons technology, and patterns of weapons acquisition and deployment in the nuclear nations have been carefully studied for clues to intentions and long-range war plans. By the mid-1960s it was clear that the United States had a more diversified strategic arsenal than the Soviet Union, although there were signs that the latter was seeking to catch up, particularly in submarines. Assessments of the relative status of the superpower weapons arsenals and projections of potential new weapons developments have greatly affected the level of interest in arms control and have also defined its issues.

THE NORTH-SOUTH AGENDA

Overview of the Issues

The 1955–1963 period was marked by efforts to assert a distinctive, more positive Southern agenda and also by efforts to organize to pursue this agenda. Anticolonialism was still a key issue, but nonalignment became almost as important in this period. Economic development was the third major item on this agenda. In many ways the Southern agenda was a protest against the domination of world politics by the East-West agenda and a call for new priorities more like those of the postwar global agenda, which emphasized a democratic and tolerant international political community.

The Bandung Conference

The Bandung Conference of April–May 1955 was an important early landmark in these attempts to find organizational expression for Southern concerns. A joint initiative of Indian and Indonesian leaders, the conference gathered Afro-Asian states in order to discuss common problems and find ways in which Afro-Asian peoples might contribute to world peace. India's Premier Jawaharlal Nehru had already outlined the kind of peaceful co-existence he recommended in his Five Principles of Peaceful Coexistence:

1. Respect for each other's territorial integrity and sovereignty;
2. Mutual non-aggression;
3. Mutual non-interference in each other's affairs;
4. Equity and mutual benefit;
5. Peaceful coexistence.[4]

An effort by ex-colonial states to co-opt the egalitarian and communitarian aspects of the global agenda made sense. Certainly Nehru's themes, like key themes in the United Nations Charter, would protect small states from domination by larger ones. These principles envisage a cooperative international community, not one polarized by ideological and political rivalry.

Nehru worked with other nationalist leaders in an attempt to pull together a conference that would organize Southern states around these ideals; however, their efforts encountered many difficulties. The United States, for example, was very suspicious of the conference at first and tried unsuccessfully to pressure its allies not to attend the meeting. After Thailand, Turkey, Iran, the Philippines, and Lebanon had accepted their invitations, the United States backed off. Apparently the British also contributed to the change in the U.S. position by advocating that the latter take a more moderate and tolerant position on the meeting.[5]

The conference discussed a number of important issues. It is hardly surprising that both the East-West and the North-South issues were discussed, including communism (the pro-Western countries wanted to condemn it), colonialism, economic cooperation, cultural cooperation, self-determination, human rights, and world peace. Nehru and other leaders appealed for a clear statement that Asia and Africa would not join either East or West in making war. They argued that this principled position could do much to help reduce international tension. However, the composition of the conference made this a contentious appeal.

The Invited and the Uninvited Countries. The Bandung Conference was an imperfect Afro-Asian meeting. States were to be included in this conference on the basis of geography and statehood, that is, they had to be Afro-Asian and independent. However, these criteria were not strictly adhered to. China was invited, but not Australia or New Zealand. Specific objections *do the countries really want world peace? If so, how could they justify uniting old Southern controls?*

by some participants led to the exclusion of South Africa, South Korea, Israel (because the Arab states would not attend with Israel present), and the Republic of China (because the People's Republic of China would not attend with the Taiwan government present). Delegations from twenty-seven states and two liberation movements attended. Conference participants were divided along East-West lines; a majority were pro-Western, a smaller group were neutrals, and a few were Soviet allies.[6]

Military Alliances and Coexistence. The pro-Western majority criticized the USSR while defending military alliances. This point of view was reflected in the final communiqué, which justified membership of Afro-Asian nations in alliances like SEATO and CENTO and encouraged small states to seek Western economic aid. Nonetheless the conference did agree on ten principles of coexistence that satisfied all participants. Among the principles were

* result of the Bandung Conference

> respect for fundamental human rights and for the purposes and principles of the Charter of the United Nations; respect for the sovereignty and territorial integrity of all nations; recognition of the equality of all races and of the equality of all nations large and small; abstentions from intervention or interference in the international affairs of another country; respect for the right of each nation to defend itself singly or collectively, in conformity with the Charter of the United Nations; abstentions from the use of arrangements of collective defence to serve the particular interests of any of the big powers, and abstentions by any country from exerting pressure on other countries; refraining from acts or threats of aggression or the use of force against territorial integrity or political independence of any country; settlement of all international disputes by peaceful means.[7]

The Spirit of Bandung. The Bandung conference was a meeting with extensive debate on international issues. Despite the disputatious nature of the conference, the deliberations produced what is commonly referred to as the "spirit of Bandung." At a minimum, this spirit reflected excitement about the potential importance of political cooperation among the Southern states. Certainly nonalignment achieved new prominence as a leading item on the Southern agenda.

Nonalignment

The failure to mobilize a complete consensus on nonalignment actually encouraged those who believed such a movement was desirable, particularly as a collective protest of the priority of the East-West agenda. Nonalignment proved to be a welcome alternative to transplanting East-West rivalries into the Third World. But since it was the West (not the East) that had colonies and dependencies in the Third World and since it was also the West that was attempting to organize military alliances in the service of containment, *nonalignment movement was against West.* (margin note)

a nonaligned movement was most visibly directed against the West. Western suspicion of Southern nonalignment was increased by the willingness of leading states in the Southern solidarity movement like Egypt and India to accept Soviet military aid.

Soviet efforts to coopt nonalignment by sponsoring explicitly anti-Western groupings added to this hostility. Specifically, the USSR and China joined the Afro-Asian People's Solidarity Organization (AAPSO), which formed in 1957. The AAPSO was clearly anti-Western and partisan in its approach; its purpose was to promote the continued growth of Afro-Asian solidarity, and to do so it sponsored several Afro-Asian meetings from 1957 to 1965. Although the AAPSO helped maintain Afro-Asian solidarity, it was not an organization likely to last long or succeed. Disputes of various kinds plagued the organization: Soviet-allied communist groups and leftist neutrals had many disagreements about control and direction of the organization; moreover, before long the organization became a forum for Sino-Soviet debates. These disputes were severe enough to paralyze its activities, and the AAPSO basically died in 1965 when a major conference failed to convene.

communist interface cause problems (margin note)

Nonalignment: From Back to Front Burner

The most interesting and important aspect of the remainder of the period from 1961 to 1963 is the transition of nonalignment from the back to front burner and its merger with anticolonialism. This merger drew new attention to a back-burner issue that ultimately dominated much of the North-South debate of the 1960s and 1970s: the problem of Third World economic development. Three heads of state, Tito of Yugoslavia, Nasser of Egypt, and Nehru of India, took special interest in nonalignment and helped to make it a major issue.[8]

Third World economic development was important (margin note)

Leaders in the Nonaligned Movement

Yugoslavia and Tito are new names in the discussion of the North-South agenda thus far. Yugoslavia was ruled by an indigenous Communist party that had come to power without Soviet assistance and had successfully defied both Soviet control and Soviet ideological authority. Postwar Yugoslavia even received Western economic and military aid. In the mid-1950s Yugoslavia's leader Tito came to the conclusion that a reduction of Cold War hostilities would serve his country's best interests and accordingly became an advocate first of peaceful coexistence, then (in 1961) of nonalignment.

Yugoslavia was not an Afro-Asian state, but Tito had long held an interest in expanding Yugoslavia's foreign relations to include close ties to the Afro-Asian states, arguing that Third World solidarity and Third World interests were not and should not be thought of as limited by Afro-Asian parameters.

Moreover, the Yugoslav record was of interest to other Third World states since Tito's regime had protected its independence by playing the USSR and the United States against each other and accepting economic aid from both.[9]

Nasser strives for progressive future

Nasser of Egypt also had grand visions, seeking changes that would permit Arabs everywhere to unite and pursue independent development toward a progressive future that could recall past greatness. Nasser's major foreign policy positions all served this goal: support to nationalist Arab political movements in neighboring countries, support to the Algerian rebels and their government-in-exile, rejection of Western-sponsored military pacts, purchase of arms from the Soviet bloc, and nationalization of the Suez Canal. Solidarity with other Third World states appealed to Nasser as an effective way to defend the rights of small countries and deter interventions by larger states. Cooperative nonalignment, if effective, could offer genuine foreign policy independence and freedom for small states to pursue their own agendas.

Finally, the nonaligned issue is associated with India and Nehru. Nehru was more skeptical about the prospects for Third World unity after the Bandung Conference. India had practiced nonalignment in its foreign policy before nonalignment became a popular policy position. India, although it refused to side with either the Soviet Union or the United States in the Cold War, was not pacifist in its foreign policy and did not forswear the use of force. Moreover, caution regarding the two superpowers should not obscure Nehru's ambitions for India: He saw India's role as one of a world leader, a moral and political force, a great power.[10]

Nehru believed India would one day be a great power

Constructing the Nonaligned Movement

Tito was the first of the three to make a concerted effort to construct a nonaligned coalition. He began his efforts in 1959 by calling for yet another conference. His strategy was to use the United Nations as a forum for promoting a meeting of the nonaligned. Those efforts ended in little more than a restatement of Afro-Asian opposition to colonialism.

In April 1961, Tito and Nasser met in Cairo to launch a nonaligned summit organized independently of the UN. This time they were successful, planning a conference with a specific political rather than geographic basis.

Criteria for Nonalignment. A preparatory meeting of nineteen states in Cairo agreed on a definition of nonalignment, which they used for invitations to the major conference in Belgrade in September 1961. Their criteria for nonalignment were as follows:

criteria for non-alignment

- an independent policy based upon peaceful coexistence with other states or "trends" in that direction;

- support for popular liberation movements, that is, anti-colonial movements;
- no membership in military alliances that were a result of the superpower conflict;
- no bilateral treaties with a regional defense bloc if that implied involvement in the East-West conflict;
- no foreign military bases on the state's territory with that state's consent.[11]

[handwritten margin notes: "weren't most of these criteria broken by participants"; "Is this really nonalignment?"]

Despite the apparent clarity of this definition of nonalignment, there was considerable debate concerning who should be invited to a conference of nonaligned states. Latin American states were invited even though they were members of a defense pact with the United States. However, since Cuba would be at the conference, the Latin American states were not interested anyway. Several other states that were invited did have military alliances but they were alliances not particularly important to the Cold War.[12] Finally, it is important to note that anticolonialism was a requirement for nonaligned membership—an indication that the two issues had begun to merge.

Interest in the Conference. A number of factors help explain the interest other states demonstrated in a nonaligned conference. By the late 1950s the international environment had changed in many ways that made nonalignment more attractive to many states: The shift in numerical balance to Third World states in the UN meant that cooperation could convey control—at least over General Assembly resolutions. Moreover, the conflicts in Suez, the Congo, Cuba, and Indochina had made many states wary about the penetration of East-West rivalries into the South and more interested in exploring collective local solutions because the Cold War threatened the security of Southern states. In addition, relations between the South and the Soviet Union had deteriorated (the Soviets had criticized Tito and Nasser for their advocacy of nonalignment), the Sino-Soviet split was adding to world tensions, and India and China were on the verge of a border war. In these circumstances, nonalignment meant more than a simple refusal to join military alliances—it could be presented as a highly moral philosophy of foreign policy that promoted peace.

The Belgrade Conference

The nonaligned conference that finally convened at Belgrade, Yugoslavia, in September 1961 represented quite a different group compared with Bandung in 1955. With a few exceptions, the states attending were not aligned with either the United States or the USSR.[13]

The Issues. Anticolonialism was expressed through denunciations of oppression and demands for full independence for all dependent peoples

[handwritten margin note: "conference denounces Anti-colonialism"]

who still lacked self-government. Attendees expressed their concern with world peace through criticisms of the policies and actions of both East and West. In fact, the conference specifically complained about the USSR's resumption of atmospheric testing of nuclear weapons on the day before the conference began. The advocates of nonalignment viewed the international status quo as harmful to the interests of Third World states. The participants at the conference disagreed as to whether colonialist imperialism or the Cold War posed the greater threat, but ultimately they focused on the Cold War conflict between the United States and the Soviet Union.

The conference ended with a statement concerning the dangers of war and the need to preserve peace and issued an appeal to the United States and the Soviet Union to enter into some form of bilateral contacts. Conferees prepared a twenty-seven-point declaration that emphasized the need for decolonization, disarmament, a moratorium on nuclear weapons tests, and peaceful coexistence. Thus, in the end anticolonialism and international conflict were both emphasized and the problems of economic development that were also on the agenda were overshadowed by political concerns in this time of international tension.

The Significance of the Conference. Belgrade began the process of constructing a clearly distinct Third World identity and issue agenda. The concept of nonalignment became crucial for Third World solidarity, and it set the foundation for future issues on the North-South agenda. The Belgrade meeting also marked the beginning of a number of further attempts by Southern countries to stage nonaligned, Afro-Asian conferences designed to explore their needs and to act on resolving some of their economic problems. After Belgrade the South undertook a major effort to set the groundwork for a UN conference on economic issues. (The first of these was held three years later, in 1964.)

Economic Issues Appear on the Agenda

Two months after Belgrade, Tito, Nasser, and Nehru met to discuss the possibility of a conference on economic problems in the South. Nehru was again reluctant, but Nasser and Tito arranged for an economic conference in Cairo in July 1962. Most of the states that sent representatives to Cairo were nonaligned. This conference drew more states from Latin America (Bolivia, Brazil, Chile, Ecuador, Mexico, Uruguay, and Venezuela), in part because of an increasing recognition by Latin American states that their economic problems were produced by the same characteristics of the international economic system that affected other Third World economies.[14]

Cairo set the stage for the next chapter and the next period in North-South relations. Several points should be made in conclusion of the discussion of the North-South agenda. During this period the agenda was transformed, as Afro-Asian issues moved from top priority and were replaced by non-alignment. Anticolonialism did not disappear but became tightly intertwined with the concept of nonalignment. Nonalignment, in turn, was redefined politically, without geographical limitation. This established the foundation for a broader Third World coalition. The emphasis on nonalignment also encouraged the Third World to set forth its own positions on the Cold War and to identify its own interests in disarmament, arms control, and particular superpower disputes. Finally, by the close of the period, economic *Economic* development had moved from the back burner to a more prominent position. *Development became important again*

The response of the North to these developments is interesting. In general there was a Western concern that the South would form an anti-Western bloc. Many in the West maintained that true nonalignment was impossible; indeed, heads of Third World states ran the risk of being associated with the USSR if they chose the nonaligned path. By the time of the Belgrade conference, the position of the United States was still wary but slightly less hostile. In the 1950s Secretary of State John Foster Dulles had regarded neutrality as "immoral"; by contrast, the Kennedy administration hoped to woo the nonaligned over to the Western camp, in part through economic aid programs that were designed to diminish the appeal of socialism to poverty-stricken people of the Third World. Suspicions of the nonaligned remained, however, as is indicated by the reaction of the Western press to Belgrade: They accused the nonaligned of criticizing the West, but not the East.

The position of the Soviet Union, also part of the North, was similar to that of the United States in some ways. This part of the North had begun the period in good stead with the South, and its reputation was fairly good when the Suez crisis occurred; after that crisis it was even better, since the USSR was seen as a champion of small states against Western imperialism. But by the time of the Belgrade conference the reputation of the Soviet Union had deteriorated in the South. The Soviets were fairly hostile to the Belgrade gathering and were identified as adversaries by many of the states that attended. The North-South agenda with respect to both political and economic issues was thus much clearer by the end of this period.

*   *   *

Conclusions

Bipolarity was key

Bipolarity was a dominant theme of the East-West agenda in world politics during the 1955–1963 period—both because the nuclear standoff made East-West crises a threat to all peoples and because East-West rivalry reached into so many areas of the globe. It was also clear from the events

[handwritten margin note: East West overrides all concerns]

[handwritten margin note: Third World begins to bind together]

of this period that issues of global interest and attention could be caught up in East-West conflicts. Nevertheless, the nonaligned movement and the effort of small states to organize themselves outside of existing diplomatic frameworks testified to the persistence of alternate ways of formulating outstanding issues of world politics.

Notes

1. For a sophisticated discussion of perceptions and the security dilemma see Robert Jervis, *Perception and Misperception in International Politics* (Princeton: Princeton University Press, 1976).

2. *Yearbook of the United Nations, 1960* (New York: United Nations Office of Public Information, 1961), p. 49.

3. For details on the development of U.S. strategic doctrines and policies see Fred Kaplan, *The Wizards of Armageddon* (New York: Simon and Schuster, 1983).

4. G. H. Jansen, *Non-alignment and the Afro-Asian States* (New York: Praeger, 1966), p. 127.

5. Ibid., p. 185.

6. The participants were Afghanistan, Burma, Cambodia, China, Egypt, Ethiopia, Ghana, India, Indonesia, Iran, Iraq, Japan, Jordan, Laos, Lebanon, Liberia, Libya, Nepal, North Vietnam, Pakistan, Philippines, Saudi Arabia, South Vietnam, Sri Lanka, Sudan, Syria, Thailand, Turkey, and Yemen. See Robert Mortimer, *The Third World Coalition in International Politics*, 2d updated ed. (Boulder, Colo.: Westview Press, 1984), pp. 6–7.

7. Gwyneth Williams, *Third World Political Organizations: A Review of Developments* (Montclair, N.J.: Allanheld, Osmun and Co., 1981), p. 50.

8. For the details of the formation of the Southern coalition and the important roles played by Nasser, Tito, and Nehru in promoting nonalignment, see Mortimer, *The Third World Coalition*, chapter 2.

9. David Kimche, *The Afro-Asian Movement* (New York: Halstead Press, 1973), p. 84.

10. Nehru is quoted in Peter Willets, *The Non-Aligned Movement* (London: Frances Pinter, 1978), p. 6.

11. Peter Lyon, *Neutralism* (Leicester, England: Leicester University Press, 1963), p. 181.

12. According to Willets, *The Non-Aligned Movement*, the most important of these were Morocco, Ceylon, and Cuba. The United States still had a base on Cuba, Guantanamo, despite the hostility that had developed between the two countries by 1961. Cuba was not excluded from the nonaligned group because the Castro government did not consent to the presence of that base. See p. 22.

13. Mortimer, *The Third World Coalition*, pp. 12–15. Participants at Belgrade were Afghanistan, Burma, Cambodia, Cuba, Cyprus, Ethiopia, Ghana, Guinea, India, Indonesia, Iraq, Lebanon, Mali, Morocco, Nepal, Saudi Arabia, Somalia, Sri Lanka, Sudan, Tunisia, the United Arab Republic (Egypt and Syria), Yemen, Yugoslavia, Zaire, and the Algerian independence movement.

14. Ibid., p. 16.

1964–1968

Three / THE SYSTEM QUAKES: THE LIMITS OF SUPERPOWER

The period from 1964 through 1968 witnessed conflict and war and was a time in which the entire international arena experienced major instabilities. There were no direct superpower confrontations during this period, but many indirect ones. Numerous challenges to order and the status quo occurred, causing crises that appeared on all international agendas. Whereas the nuclear stalemate made the United States and the USSR cautious in their mutual relations, each became actively involved in a number of conflicts. Yet what was striking about these involvements was what they showed about the limits of superpower influence. Neither superpower was very successful in efforts to manage crises and conflicts to its advantage. The inability of the larger states to control world political developments encouraged contention about the agenda.

The distinction among agendas blurred with regard to some issues during this period. Each crisis could be defined as presenting different issues. We have seen before that the definition of issues is important, since that definition to a certain extent indicates appropriate actors, rules, and applicable principles. The way in which an issue is defined also suggests appropriate forums wherein that issue may best be debated or resolved. The fact that several issues were present on all three agendas, albeit in quite different form, reflects the fading strength of bipolar East-West imagery and the energy and persistence of competing concepts.

This overlap is well illustrated by controversy over the proper definition of the issues in the two major conflicts of this period, the war in Vietnam and the Six-Day War in the Middle East. These were variously considered to reflect episodes of the Cold War, examples of decolonization problems, or illustrations of disrespect for international agreements and legal principles. If a superpower could be associated with aggression or provocation, the conflict would appear on the East-West agenda. The same conflict would appear on the North-South agenda as a result of neocolonialism, when national liberation aspirations were recognized as a cause of the conflict. When the conflict was related to the need for more effective conflict resolution procedures to resolve territorial disputes or provide secure borders, it became a global agenda item.

On some issues, the label and treatment of the problem could be effectively controlled; in others, disputes over labels also brought multiple and competing responses. Thus, some issues were more clearly associated with one agenda or the other.

• **GLOBAL AGENDA**   The global agenda included arms control, an item also on the East-West agenda, as part of a general interest in reducing the risks of war. Conflict resolution problems related to demands for action against illegitimate uses of force were an important global agenda item. Cooperative actions on behalf of global community interests were a back-burner issue.

• **EAST-WEST AGENDA**   The East-West agenda included arms control, with increased emphasis on superpower talks on arms limitations. Reduction of tensions was a minor theme during this period.

• **NORTH-SOUTH AGENDA**   Economic matters and coalition-strengthening issues dominated the North-South agenda. The United Nations' Conferences on Trade and Development were an important step toward revision of GATT.

Thus the agendas themselves continued to remain distinct although some issues made their boundaries rather obscure.

THE GLOBAL AGENDA

It proved difficult to establish a consensus about global issues. To some extent this was the result of strenuous efforts by strong states to keep issues off the global agenda. However, the lack of consensus also reflected real discord and some deep partisan divisions. In every case, the conflicts that arose in this period apparently violated accepted notions about the legitimate uses of force. But aggression could be a matter of perception, since almost any use of force—even a surprise attack on a neighbor—could be claimed to serve essentially defensive purposes. Invasion, attack, insurgency, or rebellion could all be described as just struggles for national liberation. Widespread partisanship with regard to the armed conflicts of this period frustrated efforts to apply general principles of peaceful conflict resolution. For these reasons, much discussion about the business of the global community—within the United Nations and elsewhere—became caught up with negative issues and clarification of those cases in which global concern or judgment about uses of force was *not* valid (such as self-defense and national liberation).

Security and the Prevention of War

The one issue that clearly remained on the global agenda was community security and war prevention. The United States and the USSR had already outlined some key principles for making the nuclear world safer. The United Nations became an active sponsor of resolutions and recommendations for agreements to make these principles effective, including nuclear-free zones, nonproliferation of nuclear weapons, and test bans. Yet in almost every case, the consensus resolutions produced at the United Nations were only a prelude to regional or bilateral agreements that worked out details. A process developed that set a pattern during this period: first a declaration of a general principle; then bilateral U.S.-USSR negotiations or NATO–Warsaw Pact negotiations; then a draft treaty for the United Nations General Assembly (UNGA), then a final treaty that might incorporate suggestions made in the larger multinational forum. Apparent global initiatives thus were really ratifications of bilateral East-West understandings or specific regional deals. This pattern could be seen in several notable arms control agreements of the 1964–1968 period.

Arms Control Treaties

The Treaty of Tlateloco making Latin America a nuclear-free zone was worked out regionally, and the treaty was submitted to the United Nations in 1967. The Organization of African Unity (OAU) adopted a similar resolution for a nonnuclear Africa in 1964. Again, this resolution was endorsed and welcomed within the United Nations. In 1963, the USSR had announced its willingness to consider a ban on nuclear weapons in outer space. The United States responded positively, the General Assembly passed a supportive resolution on the subject, bilateral negotiations on rival draft treaties took place, and a final draft treaty reached the UNGA in 1966. In 1965 the United States and the Soviet Union exchanged drafts of a treaty to control the spread of nuclear weapons (the Nonproliferation Treaty, or NPT). A final draft was submitted to multilateral negotiation and eventually submitted to the United Nations General Assembly in summer 1968. A similar process began in 1967 for a treaty to ban nuclear weapons from the seabed (which was eventually signed in 1971).

All of these issues had been identified as arms control problems before and had been discussed for some time as part of comprehensive disarmament schemes. The willingness of the United States and Soviet Union to consider them separately made it easier to reach agreements and indicated a conscious choice of collaboration. Whether or not these agreements represented true gains for the priority of global interests in reducing the risks of war, the series of real negotiating achievements had an enormous impact on the level of international tension. The content and subject of the agreements were primarily symbolic: No arms reductions were involved. Rather, these agreements dealt with sensible restraints that reflected interests of both sides and could be packaged as responsive to the general interest in peace, to the need for a more relaxed international political atmosphere, and to UN ideals.

UN Actions in Support of the Charter

Local Conflicts. Indications of the weakness of the global agenda during these years can be seen in other types of conflict and conflict resolution. International peacekeeping efforts by the United Nations suffered a general loss of credibility as that body failed to be effective in preventing or resolving several violent international confrontations. UN forces in Egypt were asked to stand aside for the war there in 1967. The UN was bypassed completely in regard to Vietnam, where the major conflict of this period involved neither the United Nations nor the secretary general.

The UN often did serve as a forum for arguments about unacceptable uses of force. The UN Security Council urged independence for Portuguese colonial territories in Africa as a way to end increasingly violent warfare between the Portuguese military and nationalist forces in Africa. UN bodies also criticized Portugal for supporting military interference in Guinea, Senegal, and Zambia.

Human Rights and Political Violence. Various UN organs sometimes acted to investigate disputes (as in the Dominican Republic in 1965 and the Congo [Brazzaville] in 1967) or to facilitate humanitarian assistance (as in the aftermath of the Nigerian civil war, 1967–1968). The General Assembly recommended a number of measures to demonstrate disapproval of South Africa's system of apartheid, including a call for a ban on international aid (1965) and a voluntary ban on cultural, educational, and sports exchanges (1968).

The Six-Day War. The United Nations did take action in an attempt to settle the Arab-Israeli conflict, but without impact. In June 1967, Israel struck preemptively against Egypt, Jordan, and Syria, which had been preparing an attack against Israel. In only six days of fighting, Israeli forces not only defeated the Arab forces but also occupied large areas of neighboring territories. Following this "Six-Day War," painstaking negotiations at the United Nations produced a carefully phrased formula for peace (Security Council Resolution 242). The Israelis had taken control of all of Jerusalem, the entire West Bank (won from Jordan), the Sinai desert and the Gaza Strip (won from Egypt), and the Golan heights (a strategic escarpment on the border with Syria) (see Map 3.1). Accordingly, the United Nations resolution proposed that Israel return "territories of recent conflict" in

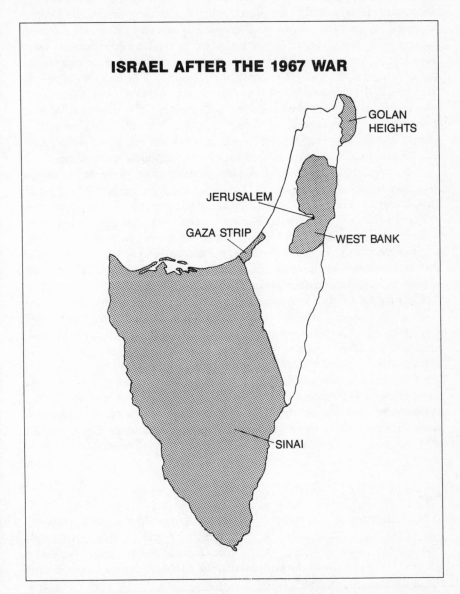

MAP 3.1 The white areas on the map represent Israel before the Six-Day War. The stippled areas represent territories occupied as a result of the Six-Day War.

exchange for peace with its Arab neighbors. However, the two chief combatants, Israel and Egypt, rejected this formula. The victors, the Israelis, preferred to keep the fruits of their victory and use them to negotiate directly with the defeated Arab states for a territorial settlement more favorable to themselves. The Israelis were also determined to redraw the borders in ways that would enhance their security. The Palestinian people who lived in the occupied territories were the most obvious losers. Nationalists who hoped to establish their own state rejected the UN resolution because it referred only to "refugees" and did not mention "Palestine." The occupation of the Sinai ensured Egypt's continued hostility and made the Arab-Israeli dispute technically an African issue as well as a Middle Eastern one.

Cyprus and India and Pakistan. United Nations efforts to mediate solutions for communal violence in Cyprus (1964) and the renewed battle for control of Kashmir between India and Pakistan (1965) also failed. These disputes were essentially settled by force of arms, with efforts at new regimes brokered by interested outside patrons (the United States, in the case of Cyprus; and the USSR, in the case of India and Pakistan). These two cases showed that even where a fairly extensive consensus about the nature of a conflict is present, coordinated international action can be difficult.

UN Financial Crisis. Moreover, UN operations in Cyprus were hampered by a serious financial crisis within the organization. Several states had refused to pay for peacekeeping actions in the Congo that they considered controversial. By 1964 both the USSR and France were technically ineligible to vote at the UN because of these arrearages, producing an ironic situation in which for one year (1964–1965) the United Nations conducted business without taking votes rather than force the issue. This meant that the Cyprus operations proceeded on the basis of temporary authority and voluntary contributions. (This episode was known as the Article 19 Crisis, named after the relevant section of the UN Charter.)

Supranational Issues

Movement toward supranational values and institutions was a relatively minor, but interesting, subtheme on the global agenda during this period. The United Nations served as a forum for discussions about codifying adjustments in the law of the sea, and in 1967 a UNGA declaration described the seabed as part of the "common heritage of mankind." This was a first step toward assertion of global economic rights and prerogatives, but it still was not clear what these "planetary property rights" might mean in practice. The need for international cooperation to solve problems of truly mutual concern was manifested also in ecological issues, but the conservation of natural resources was a very minor theme at this point, however.

The central global issue during this period was a larger security dilemma: management of conflict resolution in a politically fractious and still dangerous nuclear world. For the most part, ad hoc coercive solutions to conflict continued to be the norm.

THE EAST-WEST AGENDA

Weapons, War, and European Security

In Chapter 2 we noted that after the Cuban Missile Crisis both superpowers were prepared to make agreements to reduce the risks of war. The test ban treaty and the hot-line agreement also symbolized superpower consensus on the importance of reducing tensions. Normalization of East-West relations was an alternate conception of this issue. In the period from 1964 to 1968, both of these themes were prominent in East-West relations.

Active rivalries between the bloc leaders, the United States and the USSR, inhibited progress on improvements of relations in many specific areas. However, European states were particularly interested in cooperation on practical matters of commerce and travel. Acceptance of the territorial status quo in Europe and revision of European security arrangements were back-burner issues.

European security issues were being redefined. Within NATO, fears that a superpower standoff might leave Europe on its own made the reliability, form, and value of the U.S. commitment to European defense a central issue. Many in Europe doubted the reliability of the U.S. nuclear umbrella, despite President Kennedy's emotional rhetoric in 1963 about the willingness of Americans to "risk our cities for yours." Yet it could be and was argued that such worries were academic: The improvement in East-West relations after the Cuban Missile Crisis suggested that the risk of war had dropped and that the relative urgency of security issues should too. A controversial U.S. proposal to share operational control of some of NATO's nuclear weapons (the Multilateral Force) was designed to allay European anxieties but was abandoned when it created new ones about German participation in such a scheme. Assigning additional U.S. tactical nuclear weapons to NATO did not solve these problems. NATO strategy and the role of its military forces in Europe thus were important issues in East-West discussions.

French Independent Behavior

The controversy over alliance security was a stimulus to foreign policy independence among the NATO allies and to articulation of distinctive European positions on East-West issues. France was a leader in both respects. In 1966, President DeGaulle removed France from the military structure of NATO and advanced France's program to produce its own independent nuclear missile force. At the same time, DeGaulle undertook a series of direct approaches to the Eastern bloc states, in initiatives that incorporated "realism"—a willingness to accept the status quo and establish bilateral cooperative links between East and West. In practice French realism included diplomatic dialogue, high-level visits, and efforts to increase commercial and cultural exchanges. During a 1966 visit to the USSR, French President DeGaulle referred to a need for "détente, entente, and cooperation"; he also called the Cold War "silly."[1] Détente (reduced tensions) is the French word DeGaulle used to typify the new East-West relationship he sought. The German government elected in 1966 showed the same kind of relaxation when it proposed friendly relations with East Germany and eased its opposition to recognition of the GDR by other states. In October 1966, U.S. President Lyndon Johnson spoke in a similar way about the need to build "bridges" across political fissures in Europe.

Soviet and Eastern Bloc Responses

The Soviet bloc responded to these developments with proposals in 1966 and 1967 for the simultaneous abolition of military blocs, for détente, and for recognition of the status quo as one solution to European security. Interest in independent foreign policy initiatives in the service of new ties across the iron curtain was also evident within the socialist camp, particularly in Romania, Poland, East Germany, and Czechoslovakia. Leaders in these Communist countries who were willing to engage in direct diplomacy with Western states were generally also those who sought ways to assert their independence from Moscow—Romania and Czechoslovakia in particular.

Arms Control

The interest in "normalizing" East-West relations did not mean an end either to East-West military competition or to military efforts to control the evolving international balance of power during this period. The superpowers had come to recognize their mutual interest in reducing the risks of nuclear war (as indicated by both the test ban treaty and the hot-line agreement of 1963). East-West arms control negotiations were a natural complement to this support for reducing tensions, wherever mutual interests could be identified as clear and compelling.

Arms control as it appeared on the East-West agenda was different in some respects from arms control on the global agenda. On the East-West agenda arms control came to symbolize tension-reduction efforts between the superpowers, and the arms control negotiations served as a sort of thermometer of East-West hostility. The agreements to which we have referred as part of the global agenda presented an impressive list of achievements: the treaties banning nuclear weapons on the seabed and in outer space and the treaty to prevent nuclear proliferation. Yet we must note that these agreements really did not limit superpower arms nor did they reflect complete consensus on all issues.

For example, there were significant differences between the superpowers in interpretations of the purpose and meaning of the Nonproliferation Treaty (NPT). The United States saw the treaty as preventing the international destabilization that would be caused by the spread of nuclear weapons beyond Europe: Nuclear weapons in small states with radical or unpredictable leaders might be used to resolve a local war or to draw in the superpowers. However, for the Soviets, nonproliferation was a European issue: A nonproliferation treaty offered a means of controlling the spread of U.S. technology and arms to NATO, and to West Germany in particular. These Soviet concerns about the spread of nuclear capability to Western Europe led inevitably to tension between the superpowers concerning the U.S. proposal for a Multilateral Force (MLF) within NATO. Soviet insistence that it would not support a nonproliferation treaty so long as the United States pursued the MLF was one reason why the latter eventually abandoned this plan.

The NPT certainly reflected the clear mutual interest both superpowers had in controlling the spread of nuclear weapons and in achieving agreements between themselves. At the same time, the NPT discussions caused concern among the U.S. European allies who were reluctant to give up their own access to and control of nuclear weapons. The People's Republic of China had similar objections. The PRC, France, Brazil, India, Pakistan, Israel, and South Africa were nuclear or near-nuclear countries that refused to sign the treaty.

Antiballistic Missile Systems

There was one significant area where arms control did not succeed in the 1964–1968 period: antiballistic missile (ABM) systems. Each side had been working on a type of missile that could be used to attack and destroy incoming ICBMs. Many worried that the deployment of such antiballistic missile systems by either or both sides would change all existing calculations about the defensive protection provided by ICBMs and other strategic weapons. Insecurity would fuel the arms race because each side would feel compelled to develop countermeasures. All of this could raise the risks of accidental or preemptive war. Some discussions on the military implications of ABM systems took place between the superpowers from 1966 through 1967, but had no result.

The United States became increasingly concerned about evidence that the Soviets were both increasing their nuclear capabilities and building an

ABM system (see Figs. A.1 through A.4 in the Illustrations section). In response, the United States began to plan for deployment of a "thin" ABM system that could form the basis of a more extensive system should it not be possible to cap this aspect of the arms race.

Arms Limitation

This situation increased the incentives for a larger series of arms control talks, one in which the distinction between and control of "offensive" and "defensive" nuclear weapons would be discussed. A Lyndon Johnson–Aleksey Kosygin summit in Glassboro, New Jersey, in 1967 produced an agreement to begin such a series of Strategic Arms Limitation Talks (usually known by their acronym, SALT). However, this plan was dropped after the Soviet Union invaded Czechoslovakia in October 1968.

Ironically (or perhaps logically), as the two superpowers seemed driven by necessity to moderate the most dangerous aspects of their rivalry, they seemed increasingly less able to control the international agenda or their allies. East-West rivalry still diverted attention from the global agenda. This rivalry also persisted as a source of danger in unstable areas where superpowers were patrons for states involved in local conflicts.

On the Front Burner: The Limits of
Superpower Strength and Influence

Political conflicts in many regions continued to present opportunities and challenges to both superpowers. Yet most of these also demonstrated the increasing importance of issues that were independent of the East-West struggle. The superpowers were confronted with political change and instabilities and undesired political trends both within their alliances and major areas of influence, as well as in parts of the world where they previously had little interest. The problem and costs were worse for the United States in peripheral areas (represented by a politically and economically costly war in Vietnam). The Soviet Union, in contrast, faced its greatest challenges within its own alliance during these years. Despite the great potential of their dangerous nuclear arsenals, neither superpower was able to control these challenges.

The Third World Challenge

The prestige of both superpowers suffered because of their activities in the Third World. There were many opportunities to cultivate clients in the conflicts and political turmoil in the Third World or to capitalize on instabilities to win influence. But in the period from 1964 to 1968 the hazards of Third World involvements became more visible. Military aid did not guarantee control; instead, it often fueled costly local conflicts with real risks for the patron. Superpower patronage and East-West alignments in both directions did not survive political coups. Wars in the Middle East, between India and Pakistan, on Cyprus, within Nigeria, and in Vietnam challenged the stability of the system. Yet it appeared that the superpowers had neither the desire nor the power to eliminate such conflicts or to bend them easily to their own purposes. Conflict resolution should have been a global issue, but efforts to involve the United Nations proved irrelevant in most conflicts, since major protagonists preferred to trust in force.

Both superpowers, however, did use force in attempts to correct political and military situations they thought unfavorable. The United States used force to forestall political change in the Dominican Republic in 1965 and committed nearly one-half million troops to the war in Vietnam. The Soviets and PRC, in turn, committed vast resources to the support of North Vietnam. The Soviet Union's problems within its sphere of influence produced a use of force closer to home, when the USSR (in company with a Warsaw Pact force) invaded Czechoslovakia in 1968 to discipline a reformist regime.

The Arab-Israeli Conflict

The Arab-Israeli conflict created dangerous East-West tensions in the Middle East, since the United States and the Soviet Union served as rival patrons for the belligerents. The stunning Israeli military victory in the Six-Day War of 1967 discredited the value of de facto alignments with the Soviet Union, which had been chosen by Egypt and Syria. At the same time, the losses of additional Arab territory created growing pressure on the Soviets to help reverse the situation. Soviet support for Security Council Resolution 242 and for Israel's right to exist fell short of the most radical Arab positions and created suspicions about the USSR's real interest in advancing the Arab cause. Yet the firm ties between the United States and Israel left the Soviet Union as an important alternative source of arms, and Soviet shipments to replace weapons lost in the war soon began flowing to the Middle East.

For the United States, the Israeli conquests created new problems. Because of its role as arms supplier to Israel, the United States is criticized by many Moslem and Third World states for supporting "Zionist expansionism." Although the United States opposed the seizure of Jerusalem and proposed the city be internationalized, the Israelis were not dislodged, and diplomatic negotiations offered little hope of reversing the military victory.

Vietnam: A Test of U.S. Power

East-West tensions were also at a high level in Southeast Asia, where the conflict in Vietnam became an international issue again as the parties involved increased their levels of commitment to the war for control of South Vietnam. Controversy over proper classification of this conflict was an important aspect of this issue: U.S. policy treated the conflict as an East-West issue and charged North Vietnam with aggression. Much as Korea and Germany had been divided between East and West after World War II, Vietnam was split after the French defeat and withdrawal in 1954. U.S. policy was affected by the perception that the "loss" of South Vietnam to communism would be an unacceptable failure of the policy of containment, a failure that would weaken the general credibility of Western resolve and encourage additional communist challenges to exposed Western positions elsewhere. (This fear that a single communist victory would precipitate a chain of additional Western losses was called the "domino theory.")

The definition of the conflict as an Eastern challenge to Western positions was questioned on several grounds. The nature and course of the conflict lent credence to a variety of interpretations and also to a variety of practical criticisms. Many defined the conflict in Vietnam as a civil war or a social revolution and argued that South Vietnam was best left alone to resolve its own problems without interference either from North Vietnam or from the United States. Others believed that the United States was on the wrong side. Some opponents of U.S. involvement argued that efforts to replace the French in South Vietnam repeated the mistakes of neocolonialism and would fail. Others debated the appropriate tactics for defeating a local guerrilla movement with foreign military assistance.

U.S. Involvement in South Vietnam. The United States had been gradually increasing its financial and military aid to the South Vietnamese regime, which faced popular resentment and a growing communist insurgency aided by North Vietnam. In November 1963, Catholic leader Ngo Dinh Diem was removed by a military coup, and a succession of military governments followed. The domestic unrest caused by these regimes compromised U.S. efforts to bolster South Vietnam against internal and external opposition. (The North Vietnamese aided and helped to direct the South Vietnamese insurgency led by the Vietcong.) The Korean War had involved a clear, easily visible conventional offensive by regular armed forces across a border. The guerrilla warfare in South Vietnam provided no conventional military targets and demanded a different form of fighting. Furthermore, there was the constant possibility that expansion of the war to include attacks on North Vietnam could provoke Soviet or Chinese intervention, as had happened in the Korean War.

Tonkin Gulf Resolution. Nonetheless in August 1964, U.S. President Lyndon Johnson took advantage of a naval skirmish with North Vietnamese boats to secure congressional approval for reprisals against the North (the Tonkin Gulf Resolution). The U.S. president declared his desire to avoid a wider war but expected the threat of extensive bombing to persuade

North Vietnam to reduce its support for the Vietcong in the South. When initial bombing raids on North Vietnam and on nearby border regions in Laos failed to have the desired dissuading effect, the United States began large-scale bombing raids against North Vietnam in March 1965.

Soviet Warnings and Restraint. This air war started while Soviet Premier Kosygin was visiting Hanoi to discuss Soviet aid to a regime that was in many ways sympathetic to China's anti-Soviet position. The U.S. attacks on "our valiant fraternal Vietnamese allies" immediately became another point of Sino-Soviet contention. The Soviets denounced the U.S. attacks and issued ominous warnings that the USSR might send volunteers to Vietnam. Nonetheless, the Chinese accused the Soviets of preferring to negotiate rather than fight and charged that the USSR sought to gain control of the situation and make a deal with the United States. Despite some heavy criticism within the communist movement for its caution, the USSR preferred the indirect role of patron and arms supplier to the North Vietnamese. In fact, the Soviets sought to embarrass China by making an issue of China's refusal to cooperate in joint assistance to Vietnam. As long as the Vietnamese and Vietcong were holding their own, the Soviets could claim to be doing their part as a restraining force and arms supplier. U.S. efforts to observe some limits in its bombing attacks may also have persuaded the Soviets to hold back from actions that could have risked a direct Soviet-U.S. confrontation in Indochina.

U.S. Ground Combat Force Commitment. In fact, U.S. air attacks did not severely damage North Vietnam, nor did they prevent Vietcong victories in South Vietnam. The next step in U.S. involvement was a massive infusion of ground combat forces in 1965, which thoroughly Americanized the war. Although heavy U.S. involvement in the fighting brought some successes, it changed the political climate. North Vietnam and the Vietcong sought to capitalize on nationalist resentment of South Vietnam's reliance on foreigners. The fact that the South Vietnamese government demonstrated little staying power buttressed arguments that it was a puppet of the U.S. invaders.

After the U.S. escalation, the North Vietnamese repeatedly rebuffed intermittent U.S. efforts to offer them a negotiated end to the fighting. The North Vietnamese apparently gambled that they could outlast the Americans on the battlefield, endure, with the help of Soviet antiaircraft defenses, air attacks, and rely upon U.S. caution about Soviet and Chinese reactions to deter all-out attacks on North Vietnam itself.

Antiwar Sentiment in the United States. With the South Vietnamese government shaky and faction ridden, U.S. efforts to win this "war without fronts" were handicapped by the lack of a strong indigenous political base. As the fighting continued without evident result despite ever greater applications of U.S. technology, weaponry, and personnel, domestic criticism of the war increased. Frustration with the growing casualty rate and the apparent inability to prevail was an incentive for reappraisal: Proper definition of the issue involved in Vietnam became a point of contention in U.S. domestic political debate. Ultimately, President Johnson's motive for continuing the war was a negative one: to prevent a U.S. loss. But in 1968, he decided to halt the escalation, restrict the air war, and seriously seek a negotiated solution. In the end, the efforts to negotiate away the North Vietnamese interest in controlling South Vietnam would prove as fruitless for the Americans as it had for the French. The humiliation of withdrawal lay ahead for the Americans as well.

The Communist World: A Test of Soviet Power

Sino-Soviet Tension. Whereas the conflict in Vietnam appeared to reveal the limits of U.S. military power, the limits to Soviet power were demonstrated in the worsening crisis of authority within the communist camp. The split with China grew wider, to include open rivalry for control of the international communist movement. A more fundamental problem was the continued growth of nationalism among communist-ruled states, manifested in regular open defiance of Moscow in many areas of party and state relations. Soviet prestige, which had always been closely linked with its role as leader of the communist movement as well as of the socialist group of states, plummeted in this period as both positions were under attack. The decision of the USSR to sign the test ban treaty with the United States after the Cuban Missile Crisis had provoked new attacks from the Chinese, who denounced the treaty as an act of cowardice and appeasement. The Chinese were proceeding with their own nuclear weapons program and would test their first atomic device in 1964. They accused the Soviets of making plans for a deal with the United States to exclude the Chinese from the nuclear club. Accordingly, their official statement on the treaty warned that China would not be bound by any arms control agreements to which it was not a party. In public polemics, insults proliferated: The Soviets denounced Mao's personality cult and his ideological pronouncements. The Chinese pronounced the USSR an imperialist state that had abandoned Marxism. They called upon true Marxist-Leninists everywhere to abandon pro-Soviet communist parties and form their own parties with better ideological credentials.

Satellite Rumblings. Soviet efforts to rally the communist movement to denounce the Chinese and reaffirm Soviet leadership of the movement ran into opposition of several kinds. Key West European communist parties opposed any Soviet effort to "excommunicate" China because of the implications of such a move for their own autonomy within the movement. Some of the communist governments in the Eastern bloc states were also opposed to any reassertion of Soviet authority. Romania announced its belief in the principle of national autonomy in 1964 and declared that it would no longer participate in the Warsaw Pact's joint military maneuvers or permit such maneuvers on its territory. Various East European regimes also began to develop independent bilateral ties with Western European countries. Since the USSR was improving its own relations with West Germany and France at the time, it could do little. Nonetheless, loss of Soviet control of its satellites must have been a worrisome threat for Moscow.

Czechoslovakia. In light of these developments, prospects of political change in Czechoslovakia in 1968 were quite disturbing to the Soviets. A reformist independent-minded group within the Czech communist party forced President Anton Novotny to resign and held elections to bring new people into the party's ruling bodies. During a period known as the Prague Spring, the new group proceeded to relax censorship, introduce economic reforms, encourage political debate (even within the party), and rewrite the party statutes to permit the secret ballot in party elections. In August 1968, the USSR decided these developments had gone too far. Soviet military forces (in company with East German and Polish forces) invaded Czechoslovakia.

The Czech situation was not a repeat of Hungary. There was no revolt underway against the government; rather, a popular nationalist regime was quietly in revolt against Soviet-imposed political styles. Moreover, the Czechs did not challenge the invaders militarily; instead, the Soviets had to negotiate with the host government. It was several months before the Czechs agreed to sign a treaty legitimizing the invasion; nonetheless, the Soviets claimed afterward that their actions had been necessary to rescue Czech socialism, stating that

> every communist party is responsible not only to its own people, but also to
> all the socialist countries and the entire communist movement. . . . Any
> decision of theirs must damage neither socialism in their own country nor
> the fundamental interest of the other socialist countries nor the worldwide
> workers movement, which is waging a struggle for socialism.[2]

This statement came to be known as the principle of limited sovereignty, or the Brezhnev Doctrine.

Other Soviet Worries. The armed intervention in Czechoslovakia restored Soviet control in that country but created new problems for Soviet authority. China, Romania, Yugoslavia, and Albania denounced the invasion, as did several important European communist parties—most notably the French and Italian ones. The Chinese government quickly realized that the Brezhnev Doctrine could easily apply to them, and the war of words between Peking and Moscow heated up. Chinese Premier Zhou En-lai said that the Soviet leadership had "long since completely destroyed the socialist camp." He claimed that Soviet troops along the Sino-Soviet border had been increased and warned that China was ready to "smash any invasion launched by U.S. imperialism, Soviet revisionism, and their lackeys, whether individually or collectively."[3] Zhou also accused the Soviets of playing the standard imperialist "spheres of influence" policy. In November 1968, the Chinese proposed a renewal of diplomatic conversations with the United States. The possibility of a Sino-American rapprochement, clearly intended to stave off any Soviet designs on China, would figure importantly in the future development of East-West relationships.

Superpower Rivalry and Local Conflicts. Political instability and local conflicts looked like opportunities for superpowers to step in. However, these could also be traps, reducing freedom of action and producing long-lasting commitments to particular regimes. Winning clients by taking sides or offering support to a regime under challenge could also be risky business. Interference in conflict on the island of Cyprus in 1964 provides a good example. On the one hand, the USSR supported the Cypriots but also sought to capitalize on tensions between the United States and Turkey over the issue; on the other, the United States tried to mediate a solution that would prevent major conflict, thereby antagonizing both sides.

This situation was reversed in the renewed battle for disputed territory between India and Pakistan in 1965. A Soviet-Indian alignment took shape when the USSR not only sided with India in its 1961 border dispute with China but also sent large quantities of military aid. Subsequent Soviet economic assistance to India included support to several showcase state development projects that had been unattractive to Western investors. When India and Pakistan went to war over Kashmir in 1965, the USSR took care not to risk conflict with the United States, Pakistan's treaty partner in SEATO. Eventually the war was settled with Soviet mediation. Yet what had made the Soviet Union an attractive arms supplier was precisely its position as rival to the United States and potential threat to India's enemy; Soviet efforts to move beyond its partisan stance in search of a broader acceptance in the region were restricted by Indo-Pakistani rivalry. The limits of India's tolerance were demonstrated in 1968, when rumors that the USSR had offered to sell military equipment to Pakistan produced anti-Soviet demonstrations in New Delhi. The rumored deal never went through.

Setbacks to the USSR. Political change in the Third World could operate to frustrate assumptions about alignments. Ghana, Guinea, and Mali all had radical regimes that had been quick to affiliate with the USSR as an alternate source of aid and ideas for their political future, but between 1966 and 1968, all three of these African governments were overthrown. The new governments were not nearly so interested in the Soviet connection—in fact ties with the USSR were among the reasons for the coups. These setbacks prompted the Soviet Union to reassess Third World developments and raised questions about the value of alliances with fragile Third World radical regimes. The setbacks also threatened the assumption that time was on the communist side, or that anti-Westernism in the Third World assured easy political gains for the socialist camp.

THE NORTH-SOUTH AGENDA

Economic Reform

The North-South agenda during the period from 1964 to 1968 was dominated by the economic issue. Nonalignment suffered temporary political setbacks; Afro-Asianism died.

Post–World War II Restructuring of the World Economy

We mentioned at the end of Chapter 2 that the South launched intense efforts from 1961 through 1963 to promote a UN-based conference on economic issues. Our discussion of economic reform will begin with the developments leading the convening of that meeting, the first United Nations Conference on Trade and Development (UNCTAD I). The proposal to call such a conference articulated the Southern position on international economic issues, a position that called for a reexamination of a global matter in a global forum. As we have seen, however, the international economic restructuring that had been on the global agenda after World War II had produced trade and monetary institutions and practices generally reflecting the interests of the Northern, advanced economies that had designed them. By 1964, the South was experiencing a number of difficulties that focused its attention on economic confrontation with the North and raised the South's interest in attacking existing international economic institutions.

Barriers to the Economic Success of Southern States. Political independence had not automatically brought economic improvement to new states but instead often exposed serious weakness in their economies. Many states in the South had tried to isolate themselves from the international trading system through a policy of import substitution, which meant constructing their own industrial plants to produce items they had normally imported in the past. The new industries were often not competitive, however, and the limited industrialization that did result was very costly. Southern states generally were exporters of primary products (commodities)—minerals, lumber, and agricultural crops such as sugar, jute, rice, coffee, and cocoa. Commodity prices by nature are chronically unstable and subject to natural phenomena, overproduction or underproduction, and fluctuating world demand. Fluctuations in national revenue make economic planning difficult and expose all long-term projects to the possibility of financial disaster.

International economic strategies and organizations of Northern countries such as regional trade associations were logical targets for these Southern economic frustrations. Both the European Common Market (which included the major continental countries) and the Soviet bloc's Council for Mutual Economic Assistance (CMEA, or COMECON)[4] were closed markets.

GATT. The General Agreement on Tariffs and Trade (GATT) was another target of Southern resentments. As we saw in Chapter 1, this institution had been established after World War II to govern world trade. GATT's specific purpose was to promote free trade—a purpose appropriate to the advanced industrial market economies that sponsored it. But GATT held few benefits for the South and was regarded as a "rich man's club." The mutual concessions it required among signatory countries worked to the disadvantage of the South because of the weak competitive capacities of Southern economies; GATT's commitment to free-trade principles meant that Southern states belonging to GATT could not protect infant industries. At the same time, GATT rules did not cover many Southern exports. This permitted the North to maintain high trade barriers to these items. Although Third World states were not equally critical of GATT, the South had many complaints about its structure and orientation. Many Southern leaders came to believe that their countries' economic difficulties derived from circumstances of economic dependence and that the relative helplessness of Southern states in international economic matters reduced the value of the political independence they had recently acquired. Northern control of the international economic system was a logical target for these resentments.

Southern States Call for a New Conference

For all of these reasons, economic issues had moved up on the North-South agenda in the years before 1964; therefore, the Southern states sought to reopen the question of appropriate international institutions and procedures for the regulation of trade. The South's first step was to promote a UN trade conference. A joint resolution by Southern states from the Economic Commission on Latin America and the Organization of African Unity as well as some Asian states called for a UN Conference on Trade and Development (UNCTAD) in late 1963. Seventy-five of the states that supported this resolution plus two others formed a new Southern organization called the Group of 77 as a mechanism for lobbying in the UN for the economic interests of Third World states.

The Northern states were initially wary of any United Nations trade initiative. Once the conference had been called for, the North resisted the South's demands that the conference establish a new UN institution as a forum for discussions of trade and development issues because if it were to reflect the one-state-one-vote rule, the more numerous Southern states could outvote the North. Simple self-interest led the North to reject an institution in which its trade practices would be criticized. Northern states objected in principle to statements in the resolution that blamed the structure of the international trade system for contributing to the poverty and underdevelopment of states in the South. Moreover, there was the ever-present suspicion among the Western states (which were simultaneously part of the North) that the South was attempting to establish an anti-Western bloc. This suspicion was compounded by the fact that the USSR, in its own interest, had been lobbying for a UN trade conference since the 1950s.

UNCTAD I

Southern Consensus. Once UNCTAD I was convened in 1964, the South used its Group of 77 in order to confront the North with a unified voice, beginning the practice of working out within the group a consensus position on all issues ahead of time, which proved to be an effective tactic. The South sought unity in the UNCTAD forum to enhance its bargaining leverage, but this unity also served another purpose. The South was not politically or economically uniform; instead, there were distinct political and ideological differences as well as different economic strengths and weaknesses among the Group of 77 members. In the interests of group solidarity on economic matters, political differences were avoided, and the South's demands were set at the level of common agreement. This produced demands of a general kind, such as the call for restructuring of the international trade system, which were difficult for the North to discuss. The North preferred to negotiate smaller issues requiring less dramatic change, but that, in turn, would evoke the underlying differences within the South. The Group of 77 forum did permit the South to present a united front to the North, but it also produced contentious resistance by the North to Southern demands.

An International Trade Organization. At the first UNCTAD meeting, a number of issues were discussed, beginning with the question of whether a new institution was needed to govern international trade and to negotiate trade issues. The Third World states wanted an international trade organization with universal membership, but the North was satisfied with GATT and rejected this initiative. Instead, the North argued that any new institution such as that proposed by the South should be incorporated into the UN's existing coordinating body for economic issues, the Economic and Social Council (ECOSOC), and should be limited to examining only "the legal basis for trade relations."[5] Arguments also raged over voting arrangements: The North was well aware that the numerical strength of the South would give it exceptional power in an international trade organization if votes were equally distributed.

A compromise was eventually reached on these matters when UNCTAD acquired semiautonomous status as a permanent subsidiary organ of the UNGA on December 30, 1964. Although the North did not receive the power to veto UNCTAD resolutions, the South did not get an institution with the power to enforce its decisions. (UNCTAD can consider issues and make recommendations, but it cannot enforce those recommendations.)

A General System of Preferences. UNCTAD I's substantive agenda included discussion of manufactures (the South was encouraged to diversify and move away from primary products) and aid (terms for loans and repayments). Commodity price reform was another key issue. Although the final act specifically recommended the removal of barriers to commodity trade, the North and South were deeply split on how best to do this. The South presented a demand for a general system of preferences (GSP), a trading arrangement in which lower tariffs would be given to Third World exports (compared to developed-country exports), thus giving them improved access to Northern markets, therefore helping Southern states get started in manufacturing areas that are difficult to enter. The United States opposed this idea and argued that such preferences would in fact hinder free-market trade. Other Northern states, such as Great Britain, West Germany, and the Netherlands, were not so opposed to the idea of a special system of preferences. Nevertheless, agreement could not be reached on the issue, and the matter was referred to the Trade and Development Board for study. (The Trade and Development Board is UNCTAD's core decision-making body in between full UNCTAD meetings.)

UNCTAD I's Accomplishments. UNCTAD I did not result in a radical change in trade relations since the institution that it created could not compel states to adhere to its decisions. Nevertheless, the South had a new body in which to discuss trade problems; the Group of 77 proved to be a successful bargaining forum and would be useful in future negotiations with the North. In addition, there were a number of indirect effects of UNCTAD I, for example, the North agreed to some moderate reforms of GATT, including a new, but nonbinding, agreement on trade and development.[6]

UNCTAD II

UNCTAD II took place in 1968. In the interim, a series of discussions within GATT (called the Kennedy Round) had failed to act to ease Southern trading problems. But the South was not sitting idle during this time: The Group of 77 took steps toward a formal institutional structure at a group ministerial meeting in Algeria in October 1967. (By this time the Group of 77 had 88 members.) This meeting issued the Algiers Charter, which presented the group's position on important issues for the upcoming

UNCTAD II, including criticisms of the structure and the practices of the international institutions that distributed loans and aid. For example, the World Bank was taken to task for discriminating against states that engaged in extensive state planning for economic programs and in favor of states that let the private sector have more control.[7]

Despite the South's ability to present the North with a unified bargaining stance, it did not fare well at UNCTAD II, the major accomplishment of which was an agreement in principle to establish a general system of preferences. Accord, however, was not reached on increases in development assistance, on methods for increasing Third World access to markets, or on a global strategy for development. It should be noted that the Eastern part of the North, the socialist states, supported the South in principle but refused to take any responsibility for Southern development needs. The socialist states believed that the cause of Southern underdevelopment was colonialism and that the responsibility to help the South therefore lay with the West.

The South was discouraged by the results of UNCTAD II, particularly when it became clear that the Northern states were determined to resist practical steps to implement a generalized system of preferences. The Southern states disagreed about which items should receive preferential access to Northern markets, what kinds and amounts of preferences should be granted, and whether or not the system should be general or one based on a list of selected items.[8] UNCTAD II was considered a failure, and the North-South conflict intensified.

Nonalignment

Economic issues were of great concern to the nonaligned movement and dominated the nonaligned conference in 1964 at Cairo. But in other ways, the years from 1964 to 1968 were not good ones for the nonaligned movement as it entered into a period of crises and internal disarray.

Cairo Nonaligned Conference

When the Cairo nonaligned conference took place in 1964 it appeared that the relaxation of tensions between the East and West would make it possible for the North-South conflict to get international attention. Once again Tito, Nasser, and Nehru took the leading organizing role. This conference was attended by forty-seven states, nearly twice the number that had attended the previous nonaligned conference at Belgrade. Most of the additions were newly independent African states. Because of the expanded number, this group was quite a bit more diverse politically and ideologically than that at the previous meeting.

Two general issues dominated this conference: the need for economic development and the condemnation of intervention by the North in the affairs of the South. But despite apparent unanimity on the second issue, the participants had very different perceptions of the nature of the problem and thus preferred different responses to it. Some saw intervention as colonialism, some saw it as economic domination, some saw it as communist subversion, and others saw it as Western subversion.[9]

On related matters of principles and tactics for North-South relations, there was increased disagreement. The more militant leaders, such as President Sukarno of Indonesia, favored confrontation with the North. On Cold War issues, some, like Tito, continued to believe that the nonaligned should be mediators; Nasser favored a strong stance against Cold War–inspired superpower interference in the South.

No Unanimity Among the Nonaligned

It is indicative of these divisions that the nonaligned states were not able to take a unified position on the Vietnam War. In March 1965, when Yugoslavia sponsored a declaration requesting an end to the fighting and unconditional negotiations, only seventeen states supported the declaration. Some, such as Cuba and Mali, refused to support it because it was too mild; others because they did not want to invoke U.S. hostility by opposition on this issue. Criticism by nonaligned countries of the Soviet invasion of Czechoslovakia in 1968 was restrained, reflecting similar divisions of opinion. The nonaligned movement also suffered from political changes: A series of coups between 1964 and 1968 deposed several important nonaligned advocates including Presidents Kwame Nkrumah in Ghana, Ahmed Ben Bella in Algeria, and Sukarno of Indonesia. Indian enthusiasm for the movement faded when the nonaligned did not support India's position in its border conflict with China. Finally, regional conflicts like the Six-Day War in the Middle East in 1967 diverted attention from the issue of nonalignment. A 1968 Yugoslavian effort to promote another nonaligned conference generated little interest, but the movement was to experience a revitalization in the 1970s.

The events of this period demonstrated the strength of the East-West conflict when it imposed itself on the North-South agenda. Although the South looked at Northern intervention with dismay, it was unable to form a united opposition to it, and the South's own cohesion weakened as Southern states disagreed about the motives and intentions of East and West.

An Issue Leaves the Agenda: Afro-Asianism Fades

In the mid-1960s there was a significant amount of competition between the issue of nonalignment and that of Afro-Asianism. The major proponents of Afro-Asianism (as opposed to nonalignment) were China, Indonesia, and Pakistan. Many states sent delegates to both the nonaligned conference in Cairo in 1964 and an abortive second Afro-Asian conference in 1965. They were interested in both forums and the advantages each could offer.

But the Afro-Asian movement was torn by problems. Since the movement had included both the USSR and the People's Republic of China, the Sino-Soviet split had devastating effects. But there were other conflicts too that caused disagreements about who should be invited to the 1965 meeting: India wanted to exclude China, with which it had border disputes; Indonesia, which was friendly toward China, tried to have both its neighboring enemy Malaysia and the Soviet Union excluded; and Algeria wanted to exclude the premier of the Congo. These quarrels came out in the open after the unexpected overthrow of Algerian President Ben Bella delayed the scheduled June 1965 opening of the conference in Algiers. Some governments disliked the new Algerian government and decided on that basis not to attend. Further complications developed as it became clear that the USSR would be invited. China sensed that its own position would be weak and urged postponement, which, in turn, caused the Indians to insist that the conference take place as scheduled. Ultimately, the conference plans collapsed and so did Afro-Asianism.[10] By this time the emergence of the Southern unity movement in the context of the economic issues raised by UNCTAD offered an attractive alternative focus for the South.

*   *   *

Conclusions

The period of 1964-1968 was one in which the global agenda waned. Although a global agenda would appear again, it was never to regain the prominence it had in earlier years. During the 1964-1968 period similar issues appeared on several agendas, blurring the distinctions among them. Competition for definition of world political issues to some extent reflected a loss of control by the superpowers and a diffusion of effective political power to autonomous middle-sized and small states.

Notes

1. See Josef Korbel, *Détente in Europe: Real or Imaginary?* (Princeton: Princeton University Press, 1972), pp. 51-53.

2. *Pravda*, September 26, 1968. Cited in Joseph Nogee and Robert Donaldson, *Soviet Foreign Policy Since World War II*, 2d ed. (New York: Pergamon Press, 1984).

3. Cited in Richard Wich, *Sino-Soviet Crisis Politics: A Study of Political Change and Communication* (Cambridge: Harvard University Press, 1980), pp. 59, 71.

4. L. K. Jha, *The North-South Debate* (Atlantic Heights, N.J.: Humanities Press, 1982), p. 25. The Western part of the North already had a strictly Northern forum called the Organization for Economic Cooperation and Development (OECD). The Eastern part of the North had the Council for Mutual Economic Assistance (CMEA or COMECON), which also began to act collectively in UNCTAD. The CMEA includes the USSR, Bulgaria, Czechoslovakia, German Democratic Republic, Hungary, Poland, and Romania. Mongolia joined in 1962, Cuba in 1972, and Vietnam in 1978; Albania left the organization in 1961. Afghanistan, Angola, Ethiopia, Laos, Mozambique, Nicaragua, and PDRY attend as observers.

5. Gwyneth Williams, *Third World Political Organizations* (Montclair, N.J.: Allanheld, Osmun, and Co., 1981), p. 23.

6. These accomplishments are discussed in greater detail in Robert Mortimer, *The Third World Coalition in International Politics*, 2d updated ed. (Boulder, Colo.: Westview Press, 1984), pp. 17–18, and Joan Spero, *The Politics of International Economic Relations*, 3d ed. (New York: St. Martin's Press, 1985), pp. 235–236.

7. Mortimer, *The Third World Coalition*, p. 26.

8. For detailed discussion of the UNCTAD issues, debates, successes, and failures, see Branislav Gosovic, *UNCTAD: Conflict and Compromise* (Leiden: A. W. Sijthoff, 1972); and for a briefer examination see Spero, *The Politics of International Economic Relations*.

9. Mortimer, *The Third World Coalition*, pp. 19–20.

10. For a full history see David Kimche, *The Afro-Asian Movement* (New York: Halstead Press, 1973), p. 119.

Four / THE AGENDA SHIFTS: THE ERA OF DETENTE

The period from 1969 to mid-1975 is a distinctive and interesting one in world politics in which the two dominant agendas were redrawn. This was also a time when these two agendas seemed most distinct. Solutions for old problems changed the character of East-West issues, whereas the articulation of new problems brought greater conflict to the North-South agenda. Few exclusively global issues remained.

• **EAST-WEST AGENDA** Détente became a formal restatement of new relationships, expressed through a series of bilateral and multilateral agreements in many areas. The net effect was a substantial—albeit temporary—reduction of tension.

• **NORTH-SOUTH AGENDA** The North-South agenda acquired a new visibility as Southern states adopted more confrontational tactics. The South politicized issues relating to energy and economic equity in an increasingly open struggle to use international institutions to promote Southern interests. The net effect for this agenda was an increase in tension.

• **GLOBAL AGENDA** The global agenda included latent international economic issues and some conflict resolution problems. To some extent these were overshadowed by efforts to "globalize" issues from both the East-West and the North-South agendas.

THE EAST-WEST AGENDA

It is sometimes argued that the Cold War ended in this period. Although that conclusion is debatable, détente did involve some changes in strategy as well as a number of concrete agreements on several specific outstanding issues. Détente also raised new problems and expectations for East-West relations. In some issue areas détente between the superpowers offered new rules and perspectives for the management of conflict.

In sorting out the many developments that became part of détente, we will begin with a closer look at the ways in which East-West relations were redefined and the specific agreements that affirmed this redefinition. It is testimony to the centrality of the East-West agenda that almost all issues of world politics were viewed in this period as examples either of the advantages of East-West dialogue or of the disadvantages of East-West competition.

Détente: New Ideas About the East-West Relationship

Détente, a state of reduced tensions first discussed in the mid-1960s, became accepted as the preferred superpower relationship during the 1969–1975 period.[1] It involved some fundamental new perceptions, one of the most basic of which was an acknowledgment that since East-West conflicts simply could not be allowed to escalate to global war, East-West dialogue was essential. In part, this meant a recognition that the nuclear standoff severely inhibited both the United States and the USSR. For these two powerful states, the danger of escalation limited the utility of force (or threats of force) as a means of advancing or protecting their interests.

Another important perception was the acceptance of the international status quo in which East-West competition was less urgent and perhaps also less important. A more positive aspect of this acceptance was recognition of the possibility of mutually beneficial relations between members of the two camps. For some, this attitudinal change would be associated with a reduced sense of threat and diminished concern about ideological differences.

Neither of these themes was entirely novel. "Peaceful coexistence" and "normalization" were previous expressions of many of these ideas. In this period, however, the major powers explicitly embraced these elements and outlined a new code of conduct for their relationship.

As a redefinition of a hostile relationship, détente shifted the issues slightly away from the facts of competition to the manner and mechanisms of competition. In fact, specific pledges to normalize and improve East-West relations and abide by a code of reasonable conduct created new issues of compliance with the code. East and West also outlined a new, positive agenda appropriate to the more cooperative attitudes; however, these issues were of lower priority.

These developments did not mean that either side had become indifferent to the outcome of East-West competition. Détente was a policy choice, a strategy selected by East and West because of perceptions on both sides that a change to a nonconfrontational relationship could serve important foreign policy goals. Détente thus was dependent on evidence that this new policy offered tangible benefits.

U.S. Motivations for Détente

The motivations for a change in U.S. strategy stemmed from a general impression that the United States had overextended itself and that it should manage its power and international obligations more carefully. As one facet of this approach, President Richard Nixon urged U.S. alliance partners to share responsibilities for world order (an approach known as the Nixon Doctrine). Both U.S. withdrawal from Vietnam and détente with the Soviet Union were thus presented as prudent moves to trim global commitments.

Nixon's Rationale. From the perspective of U.S. leaders, détente did not mean a shift to amicable relations with the USSR. As President Nixon defined it in 1971, détente was a realistic approach in which the USSR was recognized as a global power, with legitimate interests of its own. On the one hand, Nixon cited specific figures about the size of the Soviet nuclear arsenal to acknowledge that the United States was no longer militarily "predominant"; on the other hand, he warned that the nation would resist Soviet expansion that affected U.S. interests:

> By virtue of its size and geography, the U.S.S.R. has traditionally had important security interests in Europe and East Asia. Her undoubted status as a global Power obviously creates interests in other areas where Russia has not traditionally been a factor. But the natural expansion of Soviet influence in the world must not distort itself into ambitions for exclusive or predominant positions. For such a course ignores the interests of others, including ourselves. It must and will be resisted. It can, therefore, lead only to confrontation.[2]

Kissinger's Definition. Secretary of State Henry Kissinger, the chief architect of détente, described it as a strategy that would combine specific rewards and punishments to induce the USSR to behave responsibly. Once the Soviets realized they had a stake in the status quo, he argued, they would have incentives to contain themselves by practicing self-restraint. Along with settlement of European Cold War issues, the United States was prepared to offer continued cooperation in arms control, a pledge of bilateral consultations in any significant crisis, and prospects of greater East-West trade. In return, the United States expected Soviet assistance in securing a negotiated settlement with North Vietnam and restraint in Soviet activities in the Third World. As a negative incentive, the U.S. leaders expected that the prospect of improved American-Chinese relations would prod the Soviets to agree.

Détente and Vietnam. The U.S. conviction that negotiations with the Soviets could help end the Vietnamese conflict on favorable terms was a key factor in the decision to pursue détente. President Nixon had vowed to seek an honorable peace but faced a compromised military situation in Vietnam and demands for withdrawal at home. No negotiated withdrawal was likely to avoid defeat of the U.S. client regime in South Vietnam. Meanwhile, the North Vietnamese proved stubborn and uncompromising in the U.S.-Vietnamese negotiations, which had begun in 1969. Although U.S. ground forces were being withdrawn to "de-Americanize" the war, U.S. involvement did not end: In an attempt to cut off North Vietnamese supply routes and sanctuaries, the Nixon administration escalated the air war and provided air and logistics support for South Vietnamese attacks into Vietnam's neighboring states, Cambodia (1970) and Laos (1971). These efforts intensified U.S. domestic criticism of the war effort without producing significant military gains or progress in the negotiations.

The United States pressed the Soviets vigorously to restrain the Vietnamese and urge them to accept a negotiated settlement that would permit an honorable U.S. withdrawal. Although the Soviets did not succeed in persuading the Vietnamese to be more accommodating, neither did they use Vietnam as a reason to back off from their pursuit of détente with the United States. Just after a U.S. presidential visit to China (in February 1972) and just before a Soviet-American summit (scheduled for May 1972), the North Vietnamese launched a major offensive across the Demilitarized Zone. The United States responded by bombing close to the capital, Hanoi, and by mining the Vietnamese port of Haiphong. Although some Soviet ships were damaged by mines and all seaborne commerce stopped, the summit in Moscow went forward as planned.

Negotiations between the United States and North Vietnam did proceed to a peace treaty in 1973 but not before the United States staged renewed air attacks on North Vietnam to force the pace of the talks. As it happened, the North Vietnamese did not respect the peace treaty, and the military situation continued to deteriorate in South Vietnam. In April 1975, the South Vietnamese regime fell to a large-scale Northern offensive.

Soviet Motivations for Détente

Détente offered several advantages for the Soviets. They had often proclaimed a willingness to conclude agreements that would formalize peaceful coexistence and reduce international tensions but were not always taken seriously. The new attitudes emerging in Western Europe offered the USSR a chance to achieve diplomatic recognition for East Germany by playing out this role of "reasonable peacemaker."

Soviet statements about the need for East-West dialogue were a mix of boasts and pleas. Leaders hailed a basic change in the "world balance of forces" in favor of socialism and pointed with pride to the military technology that had produced a strategic arsenal easily the equivalent of the U.S. one. However, they also warned of the mutual dangers of nuclear war, which made confrontational East-West relations dangerous for both sides.

The China Factor

The USSR and China. The so-called China factor was an important element of the calculations of both the USSR and the United States. Improved Soviet-American relations were certainly attractive for the USSR at this time of violent conflict with neighboring China, 1969. The situation became serious enough to generate fears of a full-scale war between China and the USSR over the long-contested Sino-Soviet border, which had been a site of skirmishes in the past. In the spring and summer of 1969, several major armed clashes occurred. To some extent these events were products of provocative demonstrations by the Chinese, who, domestically, were at the height of the radical and extremely xenophobic phase known as the Great Proletarian Cultural Revolution. However, a Soviet military buildup in the border regions gave credence to publicly expressed Chinese fears that the Soviets might be planning to use the Brezhnev Doctrine to justify armed interference in their affairs. At one point, high-ranking Soviet military officers made public statements about the feasibility of air strikes against Chinese nuclear facilities. The Chinese responded that their people would "rise up in revolutionary war" against any such aggression.[3] Eventually the tension eased when Sino-Soviet cease-fire talks were held in September and November, and the two sides agreed to upgrade their diplomatic relations by exchanging ambassadors once again.

American-Chinese Relations. These developments helped to explain why the prospect of better American-Chinese relations was alarming to the Soviets and why U.S. leaders believed that deliberate efforts to cultivate the Chinese could offer them useful leverage in East-West negotiations. (In the United States, this was referred to as "triangular diplomacy.") American-Chinese relations for a long time had represented a frozen front of the Cold War, but now, the United States took steps to thaw this front. The Chinese also welcomed the idea, apparently thinking that improved relations with the United States would offer a counterweight to the Soviet Union. Initial Chinese-American contacts took place in Warsaw in December 1969, just as the Sino-Soviet border crisis was subsiding, and at first relations improved rapidly, with beneficial effects on Soviet-American negotiations.

In June 1971, the U.S. government ended its embargo on nonstrategic trade to China. In July, it was revealed that Secretary of State Henry Kissinger had secretly visited Beijing in April 1971 and that President Nixon had accepted an invitation to visit the Chinese capital. In August the United States announced it would abandon its long-standing policy opposing the admission of the People's Republic of China to the United Nations. In October, the PRC replaced the Republic of China (Taiwan) in the Security Council and General Assembly. (A U.S. effort to retain representation for the Republic of China [ROC] in the General Assembly failed, and the

Taiwanese representatives were expelled.) Top-level talks improved Chinese-American relations by further reducing tension over Taiwan and by rejecting any "collusion" by two great powers against a third.

The Shanghai Communiqué. The Nixon visit to China took place in February 1972 (just three months before a scheduled Soviet-American summit). A joint declaration, the Shanghai Communiqué, sought to dispense with a prime Cold War issue in Asia: the status of Taiwan. The United States conceded that Taiwan was "part of China" but stated its interest in a peaceful settlement of this question: Thus although clearly opposed to any PRC effort to retake the island by force, the United States affirmed that all its military forces would ultimately be withdrawn from Taiwan. This withdrawal would proceed "as the tension in the area diminishes." The communiqué also included a declaration against "hegemony" in Asia. Since the Chinese had often used this word to refer to Soviet expansionism, this phrase sounded like a hint that the United States might be prepared to protect China against Soviet attack. After an initial flurry of activity and enthusiasm, however, relations between the United States and China advanced very slowly at this time.

Détente: Reconstructing East-West Political Relationships

Germany's Ostpolitik

The first important example of détente in action involved the oldest issue of the Cold War: the status of Berlin and of Germany. In this case a shift of attitudes that had occurred within Germany was decisive.[4] Willy Brandt, who was elected West German chancellor in 1969, undertook some bold steps to normalize West Germany's relationships with the East European states, extending the strategy called *Ostpolitik* (the Eastern Policy). Brandt's government offered to sign nonaggression pacts with the Eastern European regimes and with the USSR, provided negotiations on Berlin would begin among the four occupying powers. The West had contested the legitimacy of the Eastern European regimes and of their territorial boundaries ever since the end of the war, and the Eastern bloc states were no less vigorous in seeking recognition of their political and territorial status quo. In the case of Berlin, the Western states did not want to end their four-way occupation, whereas the USSR had pressed for change in the status of the city. The West German initiatives offered a trade: recognition of the status quo in Eastern Europe in exchange for an agreement that would keep the Western presence in Berlin, improve contacts among all Germans, and increase East-West trade.

The response was favorable on all sides. The USSR readily acceded, seeing an opportunity not only to achieve some important goals but also to erode the West's rationale for NATO. The United States cautiously followed the German lead. In December 1969, the four occupying powers agreed to begin negotiations on an agreement to stabilize the situation in Berlin. Meanwhile, West Germany concluded a nonaggression treaty with the USSR (August 1970) and one with Poland (December 1970). Chancellor Brandt's initiatives reduced the scope of the problem facing the bloc leaders. Moreover, the nonaggression agreements he negotiated were also an important prod, since none of them would be ratified without the agreement on Berlin.

Agreement on Berlin and Two Germanys

In 1971, diplomacy confirmed a status quo that confrontation and threat had failed to alter: The Quadripartite Agreement on Berlin, signed in September, reaffirmed the city's special status as not wholly part of either Germany. Although the city would of course remain physically vulnerable to a Warsaw Pact attack, the rights of the four allied powers to administer the city were confirmed, and access rights for all occupying parties were assured. Ratification of the nonaggression pacts followed swiftly. The two Germanys then signed a nonaggression treaty (December 1972) and exchanged diplomatic representatives. Both states finally became members of the United Nations in 1973.

Arms Control: The Top Issue for Détente

The superpowers had become increasingly concerned about the potential of small "hot" wars and crises to escalate into major superpower confrontations, and they were well aware of the concurrent need to make some progress in controlling the nuclear arms race as well. Arms control issues were in an important sense the leading issues of East-West détente. In fact, acceptance of the implications of a roughly equal strategic military balance was at the heart of détente. Arguments in favor of restraint, agreements, and East-West dialogue were most persuasive in this realm.

Considerable momentum had developed in East-West arms control negotiations in the 1960s. This picked up again in 1969 with the beginning of the Strategic Arms Limitation Talks (SALT talks) in December 1969. U.S.-Soviet conversations on strategic arms focused on stability of the overall strategic balance and qualitative and quantitative controls on both offensive and defensive weaponry.

Superpower Arsenals

The USSR had made a successful effort to catch up with the United States, and by 1969 the Soviets' strategic weapons outnumbered those of the United States in some categories (see Figs. A.1 through A.4). The rough equality of strategic arsenals was unsettling to the West, but it was widely believed in the West that such a standoff could be stable. Drawing conclusions about parity was a problem, however, because each side had a different mix of weapons and the weapons technology was changing all the time. Land-based ICBMs were the predominant Soviet strategic weapon, although the USSR was in the process of expanding its fleet of nuclear-powered missile-carrying submarines. At the same time, the United States was upgrading a number of weapons systems in its strategic "triad" of land, sea, and air-based forces. The major new U.S. development was a program to introduce ICBMs equipped with multiple, independently targeted reentry vehicles (MIRVs). The USSR was experimenting with MIRVs but was behind the United States at this time. MIRV technology could multiply the overall destructive capacity of existing arsenals very quickly.

A strategy to increase offensive capacity can be dangerous. On the one hand, additional offensive capacity can be regarded as improving one's ability to survive an attack—and therefore improving the chances an attacker would be deterred. Yet a state with large numbers of missiles could also be tempted to attempt a saturation attack on passive defenses such as reinforced "hardened" missile silos.

Defensive technologies presented similar problems. By this time both sides had taken the first steps toward protecting against the arrival of intercontinental missiles. Antiballistic missiles (ABMs) installed or under development raised the level of insecurity on both sides, since a state that could protect itself against incoming missiles might be tempted to strike first. Fortunately, the fact that defensive missile technology was expensive and unreliable made an arms race in these weapons unwelcome to both superpowers.

Quantitative increases in strategic arms, along with the qualitative improvements in weapons technology, underlined the sensitivity of the nuclear balance. Either offensive or defensive weapons could be dangerous, if they meant one of the superpowers would lose its fear of a nuclear exchange or become convinced that the other side was planning to strike first.

Between December 1969 and April 1972, the United States and USSR exchanged and debated a number of proposals on these matters. Although the negotiations were complex and difficult, both sides had a strong interest in agreement.[5]

The ABM Treaty and SALT I

In April 1972, the SALT talks produced two major arms control agreements. These were the Treaty on the Limitation of Anti-Ballistic Missile Systems (commonly known as the ABM Treaty) and the Interim Agreement on the Limitation of Strategic Arms (known as SALT I). The ABM treaty did not ban antiballistic missiles but restricted each side to two defensive missile sites and restricted the character and location of early-warning radar sites. The treaty also included a pledge by each side not to test or deploy any mobile antimissile systems or any that would be based in the air or in outer space. The SALT I treaty, which lasted only five years, was a complicated agreement that set specific limits on the numbers and characteristics of land-based ICBMs, ICBM launchers, submarine-launched ICBMs (SLBMs), and missile-launching submarines. The treaty banned new construction of land-based ICBM silos, set ceilings for various classes of submarines, and the modernization of weapons systems that it permitted had to be within specified ceilings and limitations. Verification for both agreements was left to "national technical means" (that is, to satellite imagery and electronic surveillance). A coordinating committee that could discuss problems arising in the implementation of the agreements was to be established. Formal signature of the two treaties took place at a Soviet-American summit in Moscow in 1972.

The ABM treaty and the SALT agreement were important first steps in limiting strategic weapons. Perhaps more important were the provisions in these agreements that helped to institutionalize arms control discussions and provided an agenda for future negotiations. However, SALT I left many kinds of weaponry unregulated.

Toward SALT II and Other Agreements

In November 1972, U.S. and Soviet representatives began a series of meetings to discuss further proposals on control of weapons technologies—toward a "SALT II," meetings that took place against a backdrop of rapid progress by both superpowers on MIRV technology. Another new problem was presented by cruise missiles—small, low-flying missiles resembling pilotless drones but designed to carry nuclear warheads. The United States had a significant lead in the development of cruise missiles, which would be relatively inexpensive, easily concealed, and difficult to detect in flight.

In October 1974, President Gerald Ford (who had replaced Nixon after his resignation in August 1974) met with Soviet Party Chairman Leonid Brezhnev in Vladivostok and agreed upon a framework of principles for the second SALT agreement. The most important feature of these discussions was the agreement to set equal, high ceilings for total numbers of various weapons. This did not really represent arms control in the sense of limitation but did reaffirm the principle of parity.

There were several other arms control pacts of importance during this period. These included a bilateral agreement on the prevention of nuclear war (PNW agreement) signed in 1973, by which the superpowers pledged themselves to restraint and mutual consultations to avert the risk of nuclear conflict. In 1974, they accepted limitations on underground nuclear tests, and the ABM treaty was amended to restrict each side to a single installation. Soviet-American agreement was also crucial to the successful negotiation of an international convention banning biological and toxic weapons in 1972 within the Conference of the Committee on Disarmament (CCD), which was an enlarged version of the Eighteen-Nation Disarmament Committee.

Détente was accompanied by an important first step toward multilateral negotiations to reduce the level of conventional armed forces in Europe. NATO proposals in 1970 for discussions on "mutual, balanced force reductions" (MBFR) with the Warsaw Pact countries led to a positive Soviet response in 1971, although actual East-West discussions about reducing conventional forces in Europe did not begin until January 1973, after the dramatic achievements in strategic arms control. Many disagreements surfaced: where reductions would occur, which types of forces would be reduced, and whether equal reductions or reductions to equal levels would be sought. Although the MBFR talks continued regularly, little progress was achieved in this forum, and multilateral conventional force reductions remained a back-burner issue for the time being.

The Documents of Détente

The Basic Principles Agreement

Progress in arms control and on the German question prepared the way for a major East-West reconciliation. This came in the form of a Basic Principles Agreement (BPA), negotiated by the United States and the USSR to be signed at the Moscow summit of May 1972 as a companion document for the SALT and ABM treaties. The USSR has attached great importance to this agreement, whereas U.S. officials have stressed the value of the arms control treaties. Nonetheless, the BPA is a remarkable document that outlined very clearly the principles and aspirations of détente. In this document, the United States and the USSR, "mindful of their responsibility for maintaining world peace and for facilitating the relaxation of international tension," pledged to "remove the vestiges of the Cold War . . . in order to move into a new era" in U.S.-Soviet relations. The BPA provided a code of conduct for responsible, restrained superpower competition:

They will proceed from the common determination that in the nuclear age there is no alternative to conducting their mutual relations on the basis of peaceful coexistence.

They attach major importance to preventing the development of situations capable of causing a dangerous exacerbation of their relations. Therefore, they will do their utmost to avoid military confrontations and to prevent the outbreak of nuclear war. They will always exercise restraint in their mutual relations, and will be prepared to negotiate and settle differences by peaceful means. Discussions and negotiations on outstanding issues will be conducted in a spirit of reciprocity, mutual accommodation and mutual benefit.

Both sides recognize that efforts to obtain unilateral advantage at the expense of the other, directly or indirectly, are inconsistent with these objectives. The prerequisites for maintaining and strengthening peaceful relations between the U.S.A. and the U.S.S.R. are the recognition of the security interests of the parties based on the principle of equality and the renunciation of the use or threat of force. The development of U.S.-Soviet relations is not directed against third countries and their interests.[6]

The Helsinki Accord

The idea that the two superpowers might cooperate to limit or contain local conflicts (particularly in the Third World) to regulate them in the interest of avoiding escalation into global nuclear conflict may be seen as an East-West agenda cooptation of an item long on the global agenda. Commitment to refrain from seeking "unilateral advantage" was accompanied by pledges to pursue positive changes in Soviet-American relations: continued arms control efforts, expanded East-West trade, cooperation in space exploration, scientific, technical, and cultural exchanges. The reduction in tension between the superpowers naturally led to expectations that NATO and the Warsaw Treaty Organization could redefine their relations. Eventually the two sides agreed to an expanded European meeting. Thirty-five states, including the United States and Canada, attended the Conference on Security and Cooperation in Europe (CSCE), which met in Helsinki and Vienna between 1973 and 1975. This conference produced a multilateral agreement that expanded the definition of détente. In fact, this agreement specifically stated that its purpose was to "broaden, deepen and make continuing and lasting the process of détente."[7]

The final act of this conference (generally referred to as the Helsinki Accord) is the second major document of détente. This act included a package of several elements, including a set of principles, which may be taken as expressing what was understood by détente in East-West relations: nonintervention; peaceful settlement of disputes; and respect for sovereignty, existing borders, and territorial integrity of all states. Specific references to the borders in Europe implicitly conceded legitimacy to the territorial arrangements left officially unratified after World War II, particularly, the division of Germany and the altered postwar borders of Poland. For this reason, the Helsinki Accord has been considered the "missing peace treaty" of that war.

The signatories also pledged to respect human rights and fundamental freedoms and to cooperate to promote mutual understanding and good neighborly relations, a section of the treaty of special interest to the Western states, which also insisted that provision be made for subsequent meetings to monitor performance of all signatories on human rights issues. Also of special interest to the West was a set of commitments to increased and improved flow of information and improved treatment for journalists in Eastern bloc countries. With respect to security matters, the agreement included a commitment to confidence-building measures (such as prior notifications of military maneuvers in Europe). The states present also agreed to a set of principles for development of economic and commercial relations, scientific and technical exchange, environmental protection, trade and tourism.

The Helsinki final act provided for follow-up meetings that would "exchange views" on the implementation of the agreements and compliance with the pledges it contained. Thus the new East-West agenda included a pledge to establish and deepen détente but also meant that improved East-West relations would depend on Western assessments of Soviet behavior. In practice, this arrangement kept compliance with the ideals of détente near the top of the East-West agenda.

Détente and the Dangers of East-West Competition in Regional Conflicts: A Hot Issue

The hazards of East-West competition were amply demonstrated through a number of indirect superpower confrontations in the Third World. Each of these situations involved conflicts between clients of East and West.

The Middle East

The Middle East produced several serious crises. For the Arab states, Israel's retention of captured Arab lands was the major regional issue. For the Palestinians, self-determination was at stake. For Israel, the issue was security. Various outside powers sought to promote stability or to protect their own interests amidst the conflict. Attempts to resolve these issues by force inevitably drew in the superpowers.

The first indirect confrontation occurred at the Suez Canal. A cease-fire had been arranged between Israel and Egypt after the 1967 war, but no progress had been made toward returning the territories captured by

Israel. The canal remained closed to shipping, with Israeli and Egyptian forces arrayed on either side. In 1969, Egypt's President Nasser decided to change the military situation with help from his Soviet ally. In April Egypt abrogated the cease-fire of 1967 and launched a War of Attrition—essentially an artillery campaign against Israeli emplacements and defenses near the canal. By October, Israeli forces had achieved air superiority and began bombing raids deep into Egyptian territory. U.S. shipments of new aircraft to Israel were approved in the midst of these developments. Nasser, in turn, pressed the Soviets for more assistance with air defenses and for advanced fighter aircraft. In a pattern that became familiar, the Soviets warned the United States about the risks of Israeli military action, then escalated their own military involvement by sending surface-to-air missiles (SAMs). Soviet pilots began flying combat missions against Israeli planes in April 1970. The U.S. response warned the Soviets about "seeking predominance" in the area and pledged to maintain Israeli military strength.

A new cease-fire in June 1970 did not produce any progress toward a diplomatic settlement. Moreover, the Egyptians used the cease-fire respite to enlarge their antiaircraft defenses along the canal; this then provided a justification for large new U.S. shipments of arms to Israel. Intransigence of both Egypt and Israel left the superpower patrons in a continuing stalemate.[8] Although at several points in 1970 and 1971 the Soviets and Americans discussed proposals for a jointly devised Middle East solution, the pattern remained competitive arming of independent-minded local rivals.

A second indirect Soviet-U.S. confrontation arose over related events in Jordan. One consequence of the 1967 war had been a massive displacement of Palestinian Arabs, who had left the West Bank (now occupied by Israel) and moved into camps within Jordan and Lebanon. Lack of progress toward an Israeli withdrawal encouraged the growth of radicalism among the refugees. Many of them had joined together in the Palestine Liberation Organization (PLO), formed in 1964 as a loose association of groups determined to "liberate" Palestine and replace Israel with a Palestinian-controlled state that they promised would be secular. Although the weak government of Lebanon had accepted Palestinian guerrilla activity within certain limits, King Hussein of Jordan was not willing to do the same. In September 1970 when a PLO splinter group hijacked two airliners and blew them up on the Jordanian desert, the king sent his army against them.

Syria's profoundly anti-Israeli government had been heavily armed by the USSR and now moved, together with some Iraqi units, to protect the Palestinians. As these troops neared the Jordanian border, the United States and Israel warned them not to invade. The Syrian columns halted, leaving the Palestinians to be driven out of Jordan by Hussein's forces—a confrontation U.S. President Nixon referred to as a "sobering experience."[9] Although overt conflict subsided, diplomatic efforts to promote negotiations made little progress, and continued arms deliveries to the belligerents by the United States and the USSR kept the situation dangerous.

South Asia

Another indirect East-West confrontation occurred in 1971 in South Asia, where the superpowers served as rival patrons for India and Pakistan. Pakistan had joined both SEATO and CENTO and had been receiving military aid from the United States. Pakistan had also established friendly relations with China, India's enemy to the northeast. India, in contrast, had friendly ties with the USSR and had become a major purchaser of Soviet arms. In 1971, India and Pakistan went to war again, this time over the secession of East Pakistan.

Pakistan's two parts were a thousand miles apart, and the eastern region had many grievances against the dominant west. When a separatist party won elections in East Pakistan in 1971, Pakistan's military ruler ordered the arrest of its leader and sent in the army to restore order. Resulting violence created a flood of millions of refugees—most of whom fled into neighboring India. When India mobilized to intervene, both the United States and China warned against it. India promptly signed a Peace and Friendship treaty with the USSR (August 1971). After clashes between Pakistani and Indian forces began in December, a U.S. naval force was ordered to the region, but no U.S. military action was taken. Although India did not attack West Pakistan, it intervened in sufficient force to ensure defeat for the Pakistani military forces in East Pakistan. Formal secession of East Pakistan—renamed Bangladesh—followed swiftly.

East-West competition and interference in regional conflicts did not stop during this period. Despite détente, the superpowers did not achieve a new approach to managing those conflicts. Continuing crises and another war in the Middle East illustrate this point.

The October War

The advantages of superpower détente received a test during the Middle East war that began with Egyptian attacks on Israel in October 1973. The Soviets are not blamed for this war, although they adopted a position in favor of Arab grievances against Israel. In fact, Egypt had expelled its Soviet military advisers in 1972 after the Soviet-American summit, amidst complaints that the USSR was not adequately supporting the Arab cause. Nonetheless, once the war began, direct U.S. and Soviet discussions became an important part of the conflict-management process. A cease-fire agreement was actually worked out by American envoy Kissinger in Moscow, then delivered to the Egyptian and Israeli leaders. When the Israelis broke the cease-fire to cross the canal and encircle a large Egyptian force, the Soviets suggested a joint

U.S.-Soviet action in response. The United States had consistently rejected such proposals before, but this time the Soviets indicated that they would be willing to act unilaterally if the Israelis could not be restrained.

At this point superpower contention over proper resolution of the war between their clients became the important issue. On the one hand, the United States shared the view that the Israelis should relax their siege of the Egyptian force and convinced the Israelis to do so. On the other hand, the U.S. responded with great hostility to the prospect of Soviet involvement and demonstrated this hostility with a global military alert of U.S. forces. Eventually U.S. diplomacy proceeded independently to help secure a series of disengagement agreements between Egypt and Israel and between Syria and Israel.

East-West Trade

Increased East-West trade was another advantage offered by détente. The USSR and its socialist allies were clearly interested in expanding trade with the West. Confident declarations about socialism's ability to prevail through peaceful economic competition with capitalism masked a real need for increased access to Western technology, markets, and financial resources. Economic stagnation, rising energy needs, and the burdens of poor agricultural productivity were pressing problems within the Eastern bloc, and Soviet efforts to negotiate improved terms of trade with Western states had been intensifying for some time. As it happened, some in the West saw this Eastern need for trade as an instrument that could be used to the West's advantage, and others emphasized the direct benefits of expanded trade with the East.

The West had erected so many barriers to East-West trade during the Cold War that a political accommodation between the blocs appeared necessary for any economic changes. Most-favored nation (MFN) status (which ensured equally favorable terms of trade to all customers in that category) had been withdrawn from Eastern states in 1951. The United States had refused loans to the USSR on the grounds that the Soviets had failed to repay wartime debts. Sales of Western technology to the socialist states were restricted by NATO prohibitions on export of potentially strategic materials to the communist countries. A few of these restrictions were modified in the 1960s, but the most dramatic change in East-West commercial relations came as a result of détente. Although Soviet and Eastern European trade with Japan and with Western Europe grew very quickly, conditions of Soviet-American trade changed more slowly.

In 1972, the United States and the Soviet Union concluded a major grain sale. The two nations also signed a comprehensive trade treaty that extended most-favored nation status to the USSR and included a debt settlement that opened the prospect of access to Western loan funds. Implementing expanded trade proved to be politically difficult in the United States, where political pressures mounted for some evidence that the increased trade and access to Western markets would have tangible results in an improvement in the condition of Soviet Jews (whose emigration from the USSR had been severely restricted). When the key trade bill emerged from the U.S. Congress, most-favored nation status for the USSR was made contingent upon increased levels of Jewish emigration in an attachment known as the Jackson-Vanik Amendment. The Soviets denounced this as "gross interference" and a "slander" and eventually rejected the treaty altogether.[10]

THE NORTH-SOUTH AGENDA

International Economic Issues

The years from 1969 to 1975 were years of confrontation between the North and South on crucial economic and developmental issues with potentially far-reaching implications for the shape of the entire international economic system. A new strategy designed to augment Southern bargaining power enabled the South to define the North-South agenda in more explicit and more confrontational ways. By 1970 international economic issues were on the front burner and stayed there throughout this period. Efforts by Southern countries to coordinate promotion of their common interests took on new forms. They developed a detailed program of desired reforms in the international economic system that brought a new focus to the North-South agenda. The nonaligned movement revived and became the initial vehicle for the development of the new strategy.

The Southern Economic Agenda

At a nonaligned meeting in Lusaka, Zambia, in September 1970, a Southern economic agenda was put forward. President Julius Nyrere of Tanzania set the tone by arguing in a speech that dependence upon the existing international economic system was as threatening to the Southern countries as military pressure from the superpowers. He urged self-reliance and mutual aid among Southern states in order to promote economic independence. Specific proposals to enhance South-South cooperation included improved South-South trade, creation of Southern-owned transnational corporations, Southern free-trade zones, support for Southern producer associations, and joint research institutions to help reduce Southern dependence on Northern technology.

The new focus was organizational as well. After Lusaka the nonaligned movement expanded its institutional structure, moved toward more formal, regularized meetings, and linked its work more directly to that of the Group of 77. The Group of 77 supported the nonaligned's Algiers Charter and built on it to produce its own program of action in 1971. This program demanded that the United States remove its 10 percent surcharge on imports from the South, that the general system of preferences be established, and that the South attain more voting power in the International Monetary Fund.[11]

UNCTAD III

At UNCTAD III (Santiago, Chile, April and May 1972), the North-South confrontation began to crystallize. The South continued to press for stabilization of commodity prices and improved access to Northern markets along the lines of the positions prepared by the Group of 77. Another contentious issue concerned the failure of Northern states to increase their commitments to world development needs, as promised in previous meetings. It was also proposed that Third World countries be given more influence in global trade and monetary issues through a new relationship between UNCTAD, the IMF and GATT.[12]

The Southern proposals got nowhere. At this point, the Western portion of the North was suffering from a number of severe economic problems and instabilities. Western European states expressed some sympathy for Southern demands, but the United States strongly resisted them. The Eastern portion of the North was in a difficult position during this UNCTAD meeting. Some in the South had proclaimed the East as part of the rich North, an idea naturally rejected by the Soviets who insisted that they were increasing their own trade and aid for the South.[13] In the end the North made very few concessions and turned down the South's major demands. Thus the South did not accomplish much at UNCTAD III aside from an agreement on aid to the poorest of the Southern countries.

A Framework for Reform

Northern resistance radicalized the South. At a nonaligned summit in Algiers in September 1973, the Southern countries put forward a framework for major structural reform in the international economy, which they called the New International Economic Order (NIEO). This was a comprehensive platform that attacked the existing economic system as fundamentally and structurally inequitable. Southern leaders were well aware of the asymmetry of international power, the many weaknesses of the South. By acting together the Southern states were able to advance a common set of proposals. But the South seemed to lack ways to force the North to make concessions or to convince the Northern states of the merits of Southern positions, and solidarity alone was apparently not enough to gain major concessions. In

1973, however, important events took place that indicated that some of the Southern states had other power-enhancing options available.

Petroleum

On October 16, 1973, shortly after the beginning of the war in the Middle East, the Arab oil ministers of the Organization of Arab Petroleum Exporting Countries (OAPEC, most of whose members were also in the Organization of Petroleum-Exporting Countries—OPEC) cut oil production and announced an embargo on sales of oil to states that supported Israel, which was applied to the United States and the Netherlands. OAPEC increased the price of oil in October. In December, OPEC as a whole doubled that price. Within a year, the price had quadrupled compared with that of early 1973. The embargo and the price hike severely damaged the international economy at the same time that it demonstrated the vulnerability inherent in the West's energy dependence.

The West was relatively impotent in the face of solidarity among the oil producers. Most small developing states of the Third World were energy importers and stood to suffer severely as oil became more expensive. Nonetheless these states supported the OPEC effort and the Palestinian cause. Promises from the oil-rich states to make special arrangements to assist the poorest states and thus help them escape the damaging effects of the price hikes were one incentive; however, the major reason the Southern states rallied behind OPEC and the Arab states was clearly political: OPEC's actions offered an opportunity to use Southern power, limited though it was, to influence the North in a forceful way.

The United States and the Netherlands defied Arab pressure and urged others to do so as well. However, they were not supported by Japan and the Western European states, who were heavily dependent on imported oil from the Arab states and less closely linked to Israel. Most of these states escaped the embargo by their willingness to support Arab positions on Palestinian rights. Despite U.S. warnings about possible uses of force in the event of "resource denial," there is little doubt that the oil embargo was an important factor in Middle East negotiations in the winter of 1973–1974. Discussions about the circumstances under which the embargo could be lifted paralleled U.S.-sponsored negotiations between the belligerents. At a low point in the sequence of diplomatic discussions, oil prices were doubled. At various points Egypt and other Arab states made it clear they would support an end to the embargo once a diplomatic settlement to their liking had been arranged.[14]

By the time the embargo was lifted by most Arab oil producers in March 1974, several steps had been taken to promote negotiations. Most notably, an international peace conference cochaired by the United States and the

USSR had been convened in Geneva to discuss the situation in the Middle East. Although this initiative was a failure, unilateral U.S. efforts had borne fruit: U.S. Secretary of State Kissinger traveled back and forth among the relevant capitals (this was called shuttle diplomacy) to mediate an Egyptian-Israeli disengagement agreement in January 1974. This agreement included pledges by the United States to monitor compliance and to continue to press for Israel's return of the occupied territories. U.S. pressure was also of central importance in securing an Israeli-Syrian disengagement agreement in May 1974—again with U.S. pledges to continue working for implementation of relevant UN resolutions on return of Arab lands. Diplomatic relations first between the United States and Egypt and then between the United States and Syria were restored shortly afterwards. Although it is hard to be certain of the exact impact of the "Arab oil weapon," the potential value of a source of Arab pressure on the United States was clearly demonstrated. Although Arab states did not recover the territory lost in 1967, Israel's strong military position made the deals seem realistic to all but the most radical Arabs.

Although OPEC's power had been building for years, OPEC's strong response to the Middle East war and the subsequent price rises caught the North by surprise. This was the first time a major international crisis had occurred in which the South as a unit was a major actor. The situation had many important symbolic aspects. The fact that so many states of the South supported OPEC's actions caused the North to recognize Southern solidarity as a force to be reckoned with. Northern states, by contrast, had been split in their reactions to the crisis. The USSR is a major oil exporter and benefited indirectly from the embargo, which it encouraged. Nonetheless the economic side effects were serious for Soviet allies and clients that relied on the USSR for petroleum products. The United States took OPEC's moves as a challenge and sought to organize a consumer cartel to fight back. The other industrialized states, which were heavily dependent on imported oil, were not interested in confrontation. While the North was in disarray over OPEC's political and economic challenges, the South pressed forward its major issue of this era: the New International Economic Order.[15]

The New International Economic Order

Frustration with the slow pace of change in international economic relations together with the excitement generated by OPEC's economic coercion of the industrial North galvanized searches for development strategies that would not involve dependence on the North. It had become increasingly clear that the economic programs the South had been following had not and would not work. For a long time development economists had assumed that integration with the world market would produce an international trickle-down effect wherein industrial growth in the North would generate a demand for more Southern exports. This Northern industrial growth, in turn, would produce revenues that could be used to increase industrialization in the South. The entire scheme hinged on Southern access to Northern markets and continued economic expansion in the North. In short, Southern economic progress was viewed as dependent on continued Northern growth.

But economic developments in the 1960s had not resulted in growth and industrialization on a large scale in the Third World. The Northern economies had expanded for most of the 1960s, and they had required more raw material imports from the South. But the South had not acquired a bigger share of the international market and economic prosperity. In fact, Southern states had suffered from a declining share of world trade, their exports had remained overwhelmingly primary products, and they had continued to import manufactured items. At the same time the prices they received for the primary products they sold had declined, while domestic agriculture suffered from excessive emphasis on the more industrialized sectors of Southern economies.[16] All this actually had increased Southern dependence on the international marketplace, since a majority of Southern countries could not produce items essential for their own survival.

The New International Economic Order (NIEO), first proposed at a 1973 meeting of the nonaligned movement, incorporated a number of measures to improve the South's domestic and international economic prospects. These included better access to Northern markets, increased flows of finances for development, and reform of the international monetary system, as well as the right of states to control their own natural resources through nationalization and efforts to control multinational corporations. The Group of 77 took this Southern proposal, with a few additions and refinements, and prepared to press for its adoption at a Sixth Special Session of the United Nations General Assembly on raw materials and development issues, scheduled for April 1974.

UN Action on the NIEO

The session ended on May 2, 1974, with the adoption by the General Assembly of the "Declaration on the Establishment of a New International Economic Order" and the "Program of Action on the Establishment of the New International Economic Order." Although these documents were adopted by consensus, the North was fundamentally opposed to them. Several states, including the United States, announced major reservations emphasizing their disagreement with key provisions. Amendments submitted by the United States, the European Economic Community, and the Soviet Union were all rejected.[17]

The numerical dominance of the Southern states ensured that the final details of the proposed NIEO were quite similar to their original proposals:

The UN resolution explicitly aimed for equality for all states, rich or poor. The documents contained twenty principles that were supposed to guide the reconstruction of the international economy to accomplish this equality and identified four categories of economic problems: international resource transfers; the need to restructure markets for primary products and manufactured goods; the need to reorganize international financial and managerial institutions; and development aid and debt relief. Specific economic measures advocated the creation of additional producer's associations, including joint marketing arrangements; improvements in terms of trade for Third World exports; more orderly commodity trading; the promotion of commodity agreements; and improved arrangements for a general system of preferences. The Southern states sought debt relief in the form of debt cancellations and additional aid at lower interest. Proposals for monetary reforms urged stabilization of exchange rates, control of inflation worldwide, special IMF efforts to shelter the South from the effects of international inflation, and greater participation by the South in the IMF decision-making agencies. In addition, the NIEO declaration criticized the behavior of multinational corporations and affirmed the right of all states to nationalize property.[18]

A few months later the UN General Assembly in its regular session adopted the "Charter on the Economic Rights and Duties of States," which echoed some NIEO themes and specifically reinforced the South's insistence on the right to nationalize foreign-owned properties. Although these Southern victories at the United Nations were impressive, they lacked substance. In a pattern that would become familiar, the five or six states representing the most powerful international economic actors voted against Southern resolutions.

Northern Resistance to the NIEO

The Northern countries had many objections to specific aspects of this program, and they resented the language of the resolution. The objections of the North fell into East-West lines: Western countries were irritated by a section that asserted the right of all states or peoples "under foreign occupation, alien and colonial domination or apartheid" to "restitution and full compensation" for past exploitation of natural resources.[19] This seemed to imply that European imperial states owed huge debts to their former colonies. Western states also protested the program's failure to recognize the principle of fair compensation for assets seized by host countries. The East applauded many points of the declaration—particularly the condemnation of "neocolonialism" and assertions of sovereignty over natural resources—but complained that it should have been more consistently "anti-imperialist" (that is, exclusively anti-Western).

More Favorable Northern Responses

Diplomatic encounters between North and South were sometimes confrontational but gradually some willingness to negotiate did appear, as the
Group of 77 dropped some of its more far-reaching positions and as the
Western states took steps to respond to some specific Southern demands.
Several West European states and Japan moved to improve terms of trade
with Southern states, particularly in commodities. In February 1975, conclusion of the Lomé Convention (to be known as Lomé I) between the
European Economic Community (EEC) and forty-six African, Caribbean,
and Pacific (ACP) countries provided a system of financial assistance to
commodity trade and special terms for access to European markets.

The international political economic climate was growing very serious.
By 1975 the world economy was in a deep recession, and the OPEC states
had announced that future price increases would be influenced by the
outcome of the North-South deliberations. A Seventh Special Session of
the UN General Assembly devoted to development issues adopted a resolution
on the need to "study" a host of specific problems raised by the South,
including measures to use the IMF to alleviate the consequences of export
revenue fluctuations; to improve access to Northern markets and accelerate
and/or expand tariff reduction negotiations; to increase World Bank funds
for the International Finance Corporation; to establish producer-consumer
organizations for important primary products; and to improve food supplies
to prevent starvation.[20]

The North rejected other proposals, which in some cases were much
more significant in their implications for the nature of the international
economic system, for example, the indexation program. The Southern states
argued that this plan to link commodity pricing to worldwide price trends
would help shelter them from deteriorating terms of trade and worldwide
inflation, but key Northern states rejected it as too restrictive of trade.
Proposals to ease access to World Bank funding for development needs
were also rejected by the North.

Simmering Issues: Nationalizations
and Producer Associations

Nationalizations: Pro and Con

Two issues on the North-South agenda as articulated in the period from
1969 to 1975 deserve special comment. One was nationalizations, which
had increased in the late 1960s and early 1970s as Southern states sought
to gain control of their natural resources. Mineral and agricultural wealth
in many Southern states was controlled by foreigners and often by multinational corporations. Multinationals were often accused of a variety of

exploitative practices ranging from draining local capital, driving local producers out of business, employing skilled workers in countries that needed jobs for unskilled workers, evading taxes, taking excessive profits out of the country rather than reinvesting, and so on. The Southern states in many cases considered it politically and economically advantageous to take these companies over, particularly those that controlled industries or subsoil minerals that were crucial to the states' economies.

The North's position was that nationalization was permissible but only after the company had received "adequate" compensation—a figure often set by the expropriated company. Many in the West tended to identify nationalizations with radical leftist policies and regarded the act of nationalization as an indicator of such political predispositions. The USSR and the other socialist states, however, applauded the nationalizations. In these circumstances the East-West conflict blended with the North-South conflict, and for the United States the former took precedence. Thus governments that nationalized privately owned assets were frequently seen not only as irresponsible, but also as real or potential allies of the Soviet Union. This view was provocative to Southern political leaders, who knew that a number of coercive actions had been taken by Western countries in response to nationalizations or threatened nationalizations by reformist regimes (Iran, 1953; Guatemala, 1954; Egypt, 1956; Peru 1969-1970; Chile, 1971–1973).

Producer Associations

Another issue that deserves some special consideration is producer associations, that is, associations of producers of primary commodities established in order to control price and supply. The development of such groups became a popular Southern objective in the late 1960s and early 1970s, in part because of OPEC's success, and was seen as a good technique for increasing Southern bargaining power and control over all stages of resources exploitation: extraction, refinement, and marketing. After the 1973 oil embargo and price increases many new producer associations were formed, and many old ones gained new members.

Producer associations entail considerable risks to participants because they must trust each other to abide by their agreements and not attempt to undersell other members. The North has opposed producer associations in principle and in practice, arguing that producer associations fix prices at an artificially high level, disrupt the market, and distort the international economy. In fact, producer associations can backfire by reducing demand for a commodity by raising prices too high.

Additional Agenda Items

The efforts of the Southern countries to articulate their economic demands presented a very full agenda. The response of the North made nearly all its issues very contentious. The North-South agenda included political issues as well. Although the Southern countries differed considerably in their political viewpoints, the coalition tactics that were so important in the definition of the NIEO also produced cooperation in support of several symbolic decolonization and national liberation issues: Palestinian rights, the struggle for black majority rule in Rhodesia and South Africa, and independence for Namibia. These were not solely Southern issues: They resided on the global agenda as well.

THE GLOBAL AGENDA

The global agenda was very weak in the 1969–1975 period in comparison to the East-West and North-South agendas. Few issues received genuinely multilateral treatment as matters affecting the interests of all states, although global status was sought for key issues of both the East-West and North-South agendas. However, international economic issues were an exception to this situation.

Collapse of the Postwar Economic System

The international monetary system that had been established after the war collapsed during this period, creating a major global issue. The demise of the Bretton Woods system reflected global economic trends but was symbiotically related to severe problems in the United States. Thanks to the vigor and strength of the U.S. economy, the dollar had served as an international currency and was accepted all over the world in payment for goods and services. Technically, the dollar was on a "gold standard," meaning that it was a piece of paper that could be exchanged for gold. But confidence in the U.S. economy meant that Americans could spend dollars freely, without worrying about whether or not the country had enough gold to back up the dollars being used worldwide. The strength of the dollar also financed the very large U.S. official presence around the world, including military and economic aid programs, military bases, and military operations like the war in Vietnam. Businesses and governments in other parts of the world were happy to have dollars because they could use dollars to purchase other goods on the international market.

U.S. Financial Troubles

By the late 1960s the favorable circumstances of the U.S. economy and currency had begun to change. The costs of the war in Vietnam were one factor diminishing confidence in the dollar; another was a growing U.S. trade deficit: For decades, the United States had exported more than it imported, but by 1971 this situation had reversed. Foreign bankers feared that as the deficit grew, the United States would devalue the dollar. Currency devaluation, a technique frequently used to reverse an unfavorable trade balance, makes imported goods more expensive, which promotes purchases of domestically produced goods and helps correct a deficit, but it also reduces the value of dollars held overseas. If a devaluation is anticipated, creditors hesitate to accept the currency, and foreigners holding large amounts of it become concerned about potential losses. Thus, foreign bankers and friendly foreign governments together with domestic political exigencies put pressure on the United States to do something about its economic situation.

The U.S. government responded to these problems with a series of policy decisions that shocked the allies and changed the international economic system forever. In 1971, President Nixon announced that the dollar was no longer convertible into gold, an act that essentially ended the Bretton Woods system for currency regulation. Nixon also imposed a 10 percent surcharge on goods imported into the United States, making them immediately more expensive. The feared devaluation of the dollar occurred in December 1971 and a second devaluation followed in February 1973. Collectively, these actions were known as the Nixon shocks.

World Economic Problems

Dramatic oil price increases and the oil embargo of 1973-1974 were another blow to the world economy. Soaring energy costs contributed to a general economic recession, which had the effect of reducing interest in global cooperation to tackle trade and currency problems. These developments threatened the ideal of an open international trading system—a major goal of the postwar international economic order. The need for replacement of the Bretton Woods system became a serious global issue, although international discussions in 1973 failed to produce a consensus about the shape of a reformed system.

Other Items

Interdependence

While governments wrestled with the dilemmas of these new difficulties, nongovernmental actors took the lead in bringing a new issue to the global agenda: interdependence. According to this concept, economic, social, demographic, and ecological issues cannot be solved by individual states, but require cooperative, global solutions. A number of organizations were formed to wrestle with "ecopolitical" issues such as the depletion of the world's energy resources, the "population bomb," the impact of technological changes, problems of food and famine, and transnational environmental pollution.

One such group, the Club of Rome, was particularly influential during the early 1970s as a voice advocating that the international community attend to the "limits to growth." The club's studies indicated that the world simply could not sustain high levels of industrial growth and predicted that an increase in growth would bring catastrophe through pollution, starvation, and the depletion of resources. Although there have been many criticisms of the Club of Rome, its position reflected real concerns on the global agenda during this era.[21]

The Palestinian Issue

A number of political issues were framed in global terms during the period from 1969 to 1975, although few were purely global. Palestinian rights is an example of a Southern issue that shifted to the global agenda during this period. Palestine had disappeared in 1948, with some portions absorbed into Israel and others into Jordan. But Israel's repeated military victories and the 1967 seizure of extensive tracts of territories (including the Sinai, which had never been designated as Palestine) offended all those who reject the acquisition of territory by force of arms and gave sharper focus to the complaints of the displaced Palestinians. Palestinians became more visible and more controversial after their terrorist campaigns and stepped-up guerrilla attacks on Israel in the early 1970s.

For various reasons, a number of Southern states labored diligently in this period to make Palestinian rights a matter for global attention and solution. Many African states were won over to the Palestinian side in the early 1970s, after an OAU mediation mission was rebuffed by the Israelis. Those that did not break off relations with Israel at this point did so after the 1973 war and the oil embargo. Interest in the Palestinian demand for "self-determination" gained ground in 1974, after the League of Arab States formally recognized the Palestine Liberation Organization (PLO) as the spokesman for the Palestinian Arabs. Many of the European states became sympathetic to the PLO. Even U.S. government spokespersons began referring to "Palestinian rights," and Palestinian representatives were supposed to participate in the Geneva international peace conference of 1974.

Although the PLO has never declared itself a government-in-exile, it has functioned in many ways like one. The PLO's status as a "non-state actor" achieved recognition at the United Nations in 1975 when PLO Chairman Yasser Arafat was invited to address the assembly, and the PLO was awarded observer status. Partisan PLO positions proved less popular: A General Assembly resolution that condemned Zionism and equated it with racism produced an East-West voting split. Discord about the legal status of this group continues.

The UN and Southern Africa

Domestic policies of the white minority governments in Rhodesia and South Africa had been treated as global issues for some time. In the period from 1969 to 1975 differences in approach to these problems were reflected in a split between the UNGA and the UN Security Council. The Southern countries, with support from the Eastern bloc, pressed for more rapid solutions, while the major Western states resisted confrontational tactics. Both UN bodies criticized the South African system of legalized racism, or apartheid, and condemned South Africa's control over Namibia (formerly German Southwest Africa), which persisted in defiance of the United Nations and international law. The General Assembly endorsed armed struggle against South Africa, voted to expel South Africa's delegation from its meetings, and recognized opposition groups as "authentic representatives" of the South African people with observer status. The South-West African People's Organization (SWAPO) represented Namibia, and two groups represented the South Africans: the African National Congress (ANC) and the Pan-African Congress (PAC). By contrast, in the Security Council, Western opposition defeated efforts to strip South Africa of its UN membership. A proposed mandatory arms embargo on South Africa was also rejected.[22]

*   *   *

Conclusions

This is an interesting period in which special attention was drawn to the agendas of world politics. Almost every conflict or problem in international affairs was in one way or another redefined with careful attention to the ways in which larger relationships might be affected. Not all states were happy about this. Whether the redefinitions meant greater tension (as in the case of the North-South agenda) or much less tension (as in the case of the East-West agenda), the merits of specific positions or circumstances faded in favor of larger purposes.

As we shall see, the overall reorientations reviewed in this chapter were too extreme to last: The dramatic reduction in East-West tension presumed a level of collaboration that did not emerge. The high tensions in North-South relations produced by the NIEO proved counterproductive in the search for negotiated agreements to implement its goals. Meanwhile, severe global economic problems remained unresolved. North-South tensions intruded upon the global political agenda and defined some new issues.

Notes

1. *Détente*, the French word for relaxation of tensions, is used throughout the West. The Soviets use the equivalent Russian phrase *razriadka napriazhennosti* or, simply, *razriadka*.

2. President Richard Nixon's Report to Congress on U.S. Foreign Policy, February 25, 1971, as reprinted in *Keesing's Contemporary Archives*, 1971, pp. 24541–24545.

3. For details, see Raymond L. Garthoff, *Détente and Confrontation: American-Soviet Relations from Nixon to Reagan* (Washington, D.C.: The Brookings Institution, 1986), Chapter 6; and Richard Wich, *Sino-Soviet Crisis Politics: A Study of Political Change and Communication* (Cambridge: Harvard University Press, 1980).

4. In 1967, the West German government had given up its Hallstein Doctrine (nonrecognition of any state that recognized the GDR). Although Romania established diplomatic relations with West Germany in 1968, the rest of the Warsaw Pact states stuck to their policy of not recognizing the Federal Republic until it recognized the GDR. For background see Chapter 3.

5. The atmosphere was improved by progress in related areas. In February 1970, multilateral negotiations on a treaty to ban nuclear weapons from the seabed were completed at the United Nations. In September 1971, two Soviet-American agreements were reached on collateral issues: an agreement to upgrade the U.S.-USSR hot line and one on consultations to prevent accidental nuclear war.

6. Text of the Basic Principles Agreement may be found in *Keesing's Contemporary Archives*, 1972, pp. 21513–21514; and in *Facts on File*, 1972, p. 396.

7. For the text, see *Conference on Security and Cooperation in Europe* (Washington, D.C.: U.S. Department of State Publication 8826, 1975).

8. See William Quandt, *Decade of Decisions: American Policy Toward the Arab-Israeli Conflict 1967–1976* (Berkeley: University of California Press, 1977), Chapters 3–5; and George Breslauer, "Soviet Policy in the Middle East, 1967–1972: Unalterable Antagonism or Collaborative Competition?" in Alexander George, ed., *Managing U.S.-Soviet Rivalry: Problems of Crisis Prevention* (Boulder, Colo.: Westview Press, 1983), pp. 65–105.

9. Nixon's February 25, 1971, speech, cited above (note 2), p. 24545. A Palestinian terrorist group called itself Black September to mark what it considered a betrayal by King Hussein.

10. See Franklyn D. Holzman, "East-West Trade and Investment Policy Issues: Past and Future," in *Soviet Economic Prospects for the Seventies: A Compendium of Papers*, Joint Economic Committee, U.S. Congress (Washington, D.C.: Government Printing Office, June 1973), pp. 660–689.

11. For a full discussion of the combined efforts to institutionalize the nonaligned movement and to formulate a common position between the nonaligned and the Group of 77 for UNCTAD, see Odette Jankowitsch and Karl P. Sauvant, "The Initiating Role of the Non-Aligned Countries," in Karl P. Sauvant, ed., *Changing Priorities on the International Agenda: The New International Economic Order* (New York: Pergamon Press, 1981).

12. Robert Mortimer, *The Third World Coalition in International Politics*, 2d updated ed. (Boulder, Colo.: Westview Press, 1984), p. 35.

13. Gwyneth Williams, *Third World Political Organizations: A Review of Developments* (Montclair, N.J.: Allanheld, Osmun and Co., 1981), p. 34.

14. See Quant, *Decade of Decisions*, Chapter 7.

15. A full discussion of the political impact of OPEC on North-South relations and the South's political power can be found in Mortimer, *The Third World Coalition*, pp. 44–48.

16. Karl P. Sauvant, "The Origins of the NIEO Discussions," in Karl P. Sauvant, ed., *Changing Priorities on the International Agenda: The New International Economic Order* (New York: Pergamon Press, 1981), p. 17.

17. See United Nations, *Official Records of the General Assembly, Sixth Special Session, Plenary Meeting, Verbatim Records of Meeting 9 April–2 May, 1974*, for details of these reservations. This document can also be found in Sauvant, ed., *Changing Priorities*, pp. 183–206.

18. The declaration and program of action are United Nations Resolutions 3201 (S-VI) and 3202 (S-VI), available in *U.N. Documents* A/9559 and in Sauvant, ed., *Changing Priorities*, Appendix A.

19. The Declaration on the Establishment of a New International Economic Order, Resolution 3201 (S-VI), as reprinted in Sauvant, ed., *Changing Priorities*, Appendix A, p. 171.

20. Mortimer, *The Third World Coalition*, p. 68.

21. See Donella H. Meadows et al., *The Limits to Growth: A Report for the Club of Rome's Project on the Predicament of Mankind* (New York: Universe Books, 1972). Also relevant to these issues are Lester R. Brown, *World Without Borders* (New York: Vintage Books, 1973), and, more recent, Barry B. Hughes, *Alternative World Futures* (Lexington: Lexington Books, 1986).

22. See *Everyone's United Nations*, 9th ed. (New York: United Nations Publications, 1979), pp. 96–100.

1975–1980

Five / THE AGENDA DRIFTS BACK: COMPETITIVE GLOBALISM

From mid-1975 to 1980, the redefinitions of the East-West and North-South agendas established during the previous period proved fragile. In fact, the comprehensive new agendas themselves were at issue. Détente and the NIEO had supplied sets of issues bound up by particular perceptions about East-West and North-South relations. As these assumptions came under attack, the issues on both agendas changed.

• **EAST-WEST AGENDA** In the case of East-West relations, the consensus on the new agenda began to dissolve, and East-West tensions rose. Détente had suggested a simplification of world politics in which all outstanding issues could be cast in East-West terms and their solution facilitated by East-West concord (or condominium). This conception of a "globalized" East-West agenda began to break down as a proliferation of new conflicts and problems that did not fit onto the East-West agenda frustrated hopes that a "new era of negotiation" between the superpowers would make problems everywhere more tractable. Thus the superpowers proved unable to control the international political agenda, and as a result, the East-West agenda declined in relative importance and became constricted in scope.

• **NORTH-SOUTH AGENDA** The North-South agenda had been very clearly defined by the proposals for the New International Economic Order. However, difficulties in promoting action on the issues raised by the NIEO illustrated that defining a coherent agenda is not enough: The perceptions underlying it must be shared. The NIEO was a "globalized" Southern agenda that implied that a Southern numerical majority could work within both new and old multinational institutions to restructure the international economy. Reluctance of the Northern states to permit this restructuring stalled progress toward implementation of the NIEO and emphasized the realities of Northern economic power. Thus although the agenda of North-South issues remained clear, it also remained contentious.

• **GLOBAL AGENDA** Partly because of the atmosphere created by the détente idea and partly because of transformations in U.S. politics, a tentative

117

mixture of the East-West and North-South agenda occurred during these years on several issues of international economics, racism, and political change in the Third World. The overlapping of agendas gave new credence to the global agenda, and to the prospects for global solutions to some political problems. Yet it was also clear that such global solutions depended on the willingness of major actors to admit a broad range of states to participate in deliberations. Such willingness proved elusive, even in matters such as the need for new order in the global economy.

THE EAST-WEST AGENDA

The Narrowing of Détente

The East-West agenda during the period from mid-1975 to 1980 included arms control and European security. But a major issue was the status of détente—that is, whether East and West were acting in ways consonant with their pledges to restructure relations with each other on the basis of parity and cooperation and relations with other states on the basis of restraint. The superpower "code of conduct" was severely tested during this period. Developments in East-West trade and political relationships reflected many strains.

Arms Control on the Front Burner

The superpowers clearly recognized arms control as an area where mutual interests were still strong. The arms control agenda had been set by previous discussions and by the agreements already reached. In matters of the bilateral strategic nuclear balance, the need for parity and avoidance of confrontation was clear.[1] Although the issues were becoming more technically complex, there was general consensus on identifying outstanding tasks.

Quantitative and Qualitative Limits

The overall problem was still how to establish an acceptable balance and mix of weapons. Thus, both types and levels of strategic weapons were at issue. The ABM had severely limited defensive systems; SALT I had frozen the number of land-based missile launchers and specified upper limits on submarine missile launchers, but numerical limits were no longer enough. The innovations in weapons technology appearing in all weapons categories made qualitative arms control an urgent need.

Many weapons developments were viewed as destabilizing because they added uncertainty to calculations of the two sides about capabilities and intentions. Moreover, discovery and deployment of new weapons technologies were occurring unevenly during the late 1970s. Both sides were making improvements in missile accuracy and in MIRV technology, although the United States was apparently ahead in both these categories and in cruise missiles. The Soviets developed a new bomber (the Backfire) with potential for use against the United States, mobile launch platforms for improved intermediate-range missiles, and more powerful booster rockets permitting heavier missile payloads. Each of these new developments complicated the task of maintaining a stable strategic balance that would be perceived as roughly equal. The trick was to find acceptable and effective ways to agree to regulate the manner and measure of the impact of these innovations on the strategic balance.

Verification Issues. Verification of any qualitative limitations posed another vexing problem because many of the most important qualitative weapons improvements would be difficult to monitor simply by photo reconnaissance or electronic surveillance. MIRV technology, the development of mobile launching, and improvements in missile accuracy could be detected to some extent by observing tests. But it would be difficult to tell whether an older missile had been replaced by an update of significantly greater capabilities and accuracy. The impact of improvements in other capabilities that were not directly strategic also raised problems.

SALT II. Qualitative arms control is very tricky; nevertheless, the momentum of arms control negotiations and the strong commitment given to the overall goal by both sides carried the process along. In June 1979, after a long and complex set of negotiations, Soviet and U.S. negotiators agreed on a draft treaty for a second major phase in arms control. This draft, called the SALT II treaty, essentially provided for a limited menu of choices. To keep the strategic balance roughly equal, allowing for differences that had developed in the types of weapons deployed by each side, the draft proposed the following arrangement: an overall limit for each side of 2,400 (later 2,250) strategic launchers; of these, 1,320 could be either cruise missiles or MIRVed ICBMs. The maximum permitted number of MIRVed ICBMs was 1,200; of these, a maximum of 820 could be land based. Limits were also set on the number of warheads that could be carried by one vehicle and on improvements to existing missiles. The treaty was an ingenious package that provided options within ceilings. Sticky issues that remained were dealt with in protocols or left for later resolution.[2]

European Security and NATO

Arms control had its multilateral aspects too. European security issues received much attention in the 1975–1980 period. The Helsinki Final Act of the CSCE had mandated some confidence-building measures for Europe (such as prior notification of military maneuvers) intended to reduce tensions and the risk of war. Although the MBFR talks on cuts in conventional arms continued fitfully during this period, they were limited to exchanges of proposals. In fact, NATO's disadvantage in conventional forces faded as an issue in this period, to be replaced by concern about the stability and parity of the European strategic balance. Theater nuclear forces (TNF) became a major issue in Europe, primarily because the USSR was modernizing its intermediate-range ballistic missiles (IRBMs) by deploying a triple-warhead mobile missile, the SS-20, targeted on Europe.

In response to this Soviet buildup, NATO sought ways to achieve some kind of nuclear weapons parity within the European theater of operations. These efforts included proposals to introduce improved tactical nuclear weapons (including a warhead with enhanced radiation known as the neutron bomb), improved intermediate-range ballistic missiles, and cruise missiles. In early December 1979, the NATO ministers adopted a "two-track" policy: to move forward with East-West negotiations aimed at reducing Soviet intermediate missile forces in Europe, but also to proceed to modernize NATO's "Eurostrategic" arsenal through deployment of both ground-launched cruise missiles (GLCMs) and a U.S. IRBM, the Pershing II.[3]

Questions About Arms Control Agreements

The uncertainties of weapons development and deployment decisions left considerable room for doubt on both sides about the value of East-West cooperation on arms control issues. The history of weapons research suggested that a breakthrough of a technical nature could emerge at any time to nullify existing strategic plans and programs or suddenly confer an advantage. Apprehension about such possibilities made some hesitate to rely on arms control for security. The acceptance of arms limitations requires willful abandonment of potential advantages over an adversary not readily seen as trustworthy and substitutes trust in written instruments and promises.

Political forces and factions within both the East and the West had reservations about the SALT II agreements. Western doubts were directly related to the Soviet IRBM deployments in Europe, to Soviet activism in the Third World, and to perceptions about unfavorable developments around the world. In fact, U.S. President Carter withdrew the SALT II treaty from Senate consideration in January 1980, after the Soviets invaded Afghanistan. Although the agreement was thus never formally ratified, the U.S. government declared that it would abide by the terms of the treaty as long as the Soviets did so.

The Status and Value of Détente

Normalization of East-West relations was still on the agenda, but there were differences over the desirability of this goal. Within Europe, sentiment for and interest in normalization was strong, and levels of trade, tourism, and immigration increased markedly throughout this period. These ties were creating just the sort of vested interest in détente that had been sought by some of its sponsors. However, although East-West trade did increase dramatically during this period, it did so unevenly.

U.S.-Soviet relationships did not develop smoothly: The collapse in 1975 of the U.S.-Soviet trade treaty that was to have been a centerpiece of détente limited the improvement of Soviet-U.S. commercial relations. The treaty would have permitted extension of credit to the USSR for purchases of U.S. goods, and failure to obtain access to these credits was a serious loss for the Soviet Union. Nonetheless, easing of licensing arrangements meant that where interest was strong on both sides, agreements were easily reached—such as a long-term agreement for Soviet purchases of U.S. grain. The United States did extend most favored nation status without incident to Romania (1975), Poland (1978), and Hungary (1978).

Human Rights: Helsinki and Belgrade

Compliance with the human rights portions of the Helsinki Accord of 1975 became a new and prominent issue between East and West. The Western states had clearly expected improvements by the communist states on specific matters. However, the broad language of the agreements made it possible for the West to raise very general and basic complaints about the legal and political systems of all communist states, which did not share the Western view that individual citizens had rights to protection from their own government. The Final Act had included a pledge to publicize the agreement, including clauses that pledged to respect freedom of speech and religion, and to remove some restraints on emigration. Indeed, citizen "Helsinki monitoring groups" formed in the USSR and in Eastern Europe to review the degree of government compliance with the Final Act. Once it became known that the Soviets were persecuting these groups, treatment of dissidents and of political prisoners became a formal East-West issue. Soviet discomfiture with this aspect of détente was enhanced by the actions of European communist parties during this period, which were articulating— in the form of "Eurocommunism"—their ideological defiance of Soviet authority. These parties openly criticized the Soviet political system and often joined with European socialist parties to champion the cause of political prisoners and dissidents within the USSR.

A follow-up meeting to the Conference on Security and Cooperation in Europe was held in 1977 in Belgrade. This meeting proved very uncomfortable for the USSR and its allies because Western delegations used the sessions to prod the Eastern bloc about its failures to move quickly enough or far enough in improving East-West contacts, working conditions for journalists, and the treatment of their citizens. Testimony by former political prisoners from Eastern bloc countries provided highly public criticism of the Soviet system and called attention to fundamental differences in Eastern and Western political philosophies. The human rights issue increased pressure on the East, while it raised doubts about détente in the West. For both sides, questions were raised about the value of détente as a mechanism to serve real interests. In the United States (and in several other countries) Soviet human rights violations became an important domestic political issue.

Formal Chinese-U.S. Relations

Increasing U.S. discontent with the state of U.S.-Soviet relations was reflected in steps to improve relations with China: In 1978, while trade with the USSR was being restricted, restrictions on trade with China were eased; formal diplomatic relations between the United States and the PRC were established in January 1979. When the Chinese Vice Premier Deng Xiaoping visited the United States in February, his public criticisms of Soviet policy and appeal for anti-Soviet cooperation with the West elicited Soviet protests. Soviet worries about implications of improved Chinese-U.S. relations were raised by the coincidence that China's attack on Vietnam began just after Deng's visit to the United States.[4] Thus, although economic and commercial contacts between East and West did increase significantly, the old Cold War patterns of mistrust, suspicion, and competition were still visible.

Superpower Crisis Diplomacy: Condominium or Competition?

Détente had promised Soviet-U.S. consultation to avoid crises that could escalate into nuclear war. It was evident in the 1975–1980 period that although avoiding nuclear war was a genuine common interest, the superpowers would continue attempting to advance their own interests while containing or reducing each other's influence wherever possible. The best and most important example of this process occurred in the Middle East.

Arab-Israeli Dispute

A brief effort was made to solve the Arab-Israeli conflict through superpower cooperation in 1977. This came in the form of a proposal to reconvene the Geneva Conference on the Middle East under U.S.-Soviet joint chairmanship. When this failed (basically because the parties refused to meet with each other), efforts toward peace proceeded with U.S. sponsorship.

Egyptian Initiative. Egypt's President Anwar Sadat had continued to distance himself from the USSR by abrogating the Egyptian-Soviet friendship treaty in 1976. In November 1977 Sadat decided upon his own dramatic initiative to promote a settlement with Israel. In order to demonstrate the sincerity of his interest in a peace agreement that would secure the return of the Sinai, he traveled to Jerusalem and addressed the Israeli parliament. This was a powerful conciliatory gesture because the Arab states had taken a rigid stand of not recognizing Israel and specifically rejected the legitimacy of Israeli control of all of Jerusalem. The United States then took an active role in promoting an agreement: In September 1978, U.S. President Jimmy Carter personally mediated Israeli-Egyptian negotiations held in the United States at Camp David, Maryland. These discussions produced a framework both for a comprehensive agreement and for an Egyptian-Israeli peace treaty (signed in March 1979). The U.S. role included providing observers in the Sinai and assuring steady oil supplies to Israel (to replace sources that had been developed by the Israelis in the Sinai).

The Peace Treaty and Its Consequences. Despite some euphoria in the West about this diplomatic success (Sadat and Israeli Prime Minister Menachem Begin later received Nobel Peace prizes), the situation in the Middle East actually worsened in some respects. The accords reached at Camp David inflamed other Arab states, which for a brief period were united in their anger at Egypt. The 1979 treaty satisfied Egypt's desire to recover the Sinai, but Jerusalem, the Gaza Strip, the Golan Heights, and the entire West Bank were still in Israeli hands. The Arab states had failed to recover these lands by force in the 1973 war and without Egypt's help, it was unlikely they would now ever be able to do so. Moreover, Israel's continued control of the Palestinian lands meant an independent Palestinian state was impossible. The Camp David "framework for peace" included a pledge by the Israelis to move toward "autonomy" for a Palestine entity on the West Bank. Although this concept was a major concession for Israel and a product of heavy U.S. pressure, it was still far from what any Palestinian group would accept. Thus the Camp David agreements became a symbol of sellout for many Arabs. Egypt was expelled from the League of Arab States, and the most radical Arab states (led by Libya and Syria) tried to organize sanctions against Sadat's regime.

The Egypt-Israeli negotiations also confirmed the United States as the only outside power able to secure concessions from the Israelis. However, the Soviet Union, as chief arms supplier to the Arab supporters of the Palestinian cause and patron of the anti-Israeli forces, had fewer options. The Soviets could become an important actor in the event of another war or if the pro-Palestinian forces became much more powerful. But the strength of the Israeli military position, Arab disunity, and Soviet reluctance to be drawn into direct fighting were all factors that made negotiations the only apparent means to promote Arab interests. For all these reasons, the Camp David achievements drove the radical Arab states closer to the Soviets and froze the peace process around the issue of Palestine autonomy.

The Palestinian Issue. The status of the Palestinians was a serious and somewhat separate issue, and not strictly an East-West one. Although the USSR publicly supported Palestinian rights and established contacts with the PLO and Yasser Arafat, the Soviets also supported Israel's right to exist. Although the United States supported Israel, the United States was also pressing Israel to make peace with its neighbors, return territories seized in 1967, and surrender Jerusalem to international control. However, the Palestinians were determined to define the issue in their own way—as a question of national rights frustrated by "Zionist imperialism." Displaced Palestinians became a potentially disruptive political force wherever they located, pushing many Arab governments to espouse their cause vigorously.

Fighting in Lebanon

Violence in nearby Lebanon revealed the volatility of the Palestinian issue. In 1976, problems caused by the presence of Palestinian forces sparked a civil war that injected new instabilities into the region. The Christian-dominated government of Lebanon was at odds with many Muslim groups, and its unsuccessful attempts to control the Palestinian guerrillas multiplied its domestic political difficulties. When fighting broke out between the Lebanese army and the Palestinian irregulars, various armed factions in Lebanon took sides. The breakdown of order in 1976 provoked an intervention by the Syrians, who tried to mediate a political settlement that would create a more stable Lebanese government and regulate Palestinian activity at the same time. The Syrian intervention was ultimately legitimized by an Arab summit that accepted the Syrian forces as components of a multinational Arab peacekeeping force.

Lebanon was the scene of conflict again in 1978, when Israeli forces intervened to clear Palestinian base camps out of the border region and establish order in South Lebanon. The prospect of a Syrian-Israeli confrontation that this raised was alarming; so was the prospect of a partitioned Lebanon. Syria was a treaty partner and favored arms customer of the USSR; thus an escalation that could involve the United States and the USSR was always a possibility. The superpower patrons maneuvered cautiously to protect their clients' interests and to restrain their military action. Eventually a multilateral solution was sought: A United Nations interim peacekeeping force was dispatched to the Israel-Lebanon border area to police a demilitarized zone, but the situation remained unstable.

Third World Crises Leading to a Mixture of the East-West and North-South Agendas

Third World crises were another front-burner issue that increased in intensity from 1975 to 1980. These crises, wars, and revolutions divided the South, caused increased tensions between East and West, and irreparably damaged détente.

Détente had involved a pledge by the superpowers "not to seek unilateral advantage." Any hopes that this meant restraint in Third World conflicts were dashed by the end of this period. Many new sites of conflict and political change that presented tempting opportunities for the East and growing fears for the West emerged. These included Angola, the Horn of Africa (Ethiopia and Somalia), Iran, Lebanon, Vietnam and Cambodia, Afghanistan, South Yemen, and Nicaragua.

Political changes in these countries were also of great significance on the North-South agenda. Revolutions, instabilities, and wars for independence—as former colonies achieved freedom and sorted out their political futures—were seen by many states in the South as logical and inevitable outcomes of Northern domination. Other Southern states were less interested in blaming the North for the origins of these conflicts but keenly critical of intrusions by both East and West as each side's attempts to influence the political outcomes inflamed the crises and placed them on the East-West agenda.

By the end of the 1970s there was a growing split in the West about the priority to be given to the Third World. Some countries, such as the Netherlands, Sweden, France, and Spain, perceived Third World crises as local problems or North-South issues, whereas others (the United States and Great Britain in particular) blamed the USSR for abandoning détente and moving onto the offensive. To the Soviets, it seemed that the West was having trouble accepting the "forward movement of historical forces." Nonetheless, net gains for the socialist camp, taken in conjunction with obvious growth of Soviet military strength, made appropriate Western responses to Third World crises an important issue for some.

Changes in Sub-Saharan Africa

Rapid political change was occurring in sub-Saharan Africa, caused primarily by the collapse of the Portuguese empire. In 1974, a military coup in Portugal had produced a leftist government, which announced it would abandon efforts to suppress armed rebellion in the Portuguese colonies and would move swiftly to grant them independence. This meant not only an end to white rule in Angola, Mozambique, Guinea-Bissau, and São Tomé and Príncipe but also the accession to power of political and military movements that had a long history of struggle against the West and close associations with socialist states and communist parties. The political situation would change drastically for South Africa and for Rhodesia, since it could be expected that the black governments that would emerge in Portugal's ex-colonies would support the liberation movements in South Africa, Rhodesia, and Namibia. This could deprive the landlocked Rhodesians of their safe transit to the sea and bring safe bases for the African National Congress (ANC, the armed liberation movement of South Africa) and the South-West African People's Organization (SWAPO, the liberation movement attacking South Africa's occupation of Namibia).

Soviet-Cuban Military Interventions

The two Soviet-backed Cuban military interventions in Africa (in Angola and in the Horn of Africa) that occurred during the latter half of the 1970s were important episodes in the demise of détente. The Cuban influence on political change in Africa was an innovation. Western fears that this signaled a new more aggressive phase of Soviet pursuit of influence in the Third World helped to discredit détente and rekindle fears of communist expansionism.

Angola. In Angola, independence was offered in 1975 to a coalition of three separate liberation movements, but these groups set to fighting among themselves for control of the emergent government before the scheduled independence date of November 1975. The U.S. government decided to send covert aid to the FNLA (National Front for the Liberation of Angola); the USSR and Cuba were linked with the MPLA (Popular Movement for the Liberation of Angola); and the Chinese and South Africans had been aiding Jonas Savimbi's UNITA (Union for the Total Independence of Angola). As the civil war progressed, South African and UNITA forces made a dash for the capital city. At this point the Cubans, assisted by the Soviets, rushed in troops and supplies to beat back UNITA. In December 1975, after the U.S. Congress resolved not to become involved in this struggle, the South Africans decided to withdraw to bases in Namibia (their support to Savimbi's forces in southern Angola continued, however).

Cuban troops and Soviet weapons had saved the day and helped the MPLA emerge victorious. The new government, the People's Republic of Angola, was accepted into the Organization of African Unity in 1976. The United States was displeased with this outcome and the idea of détente grew less popular. In March 1976, President Gerald Ford announced he was dropping the word *détente* as no longer appropriate as a goal or description for East-West relations.

Ethiopia and Somalia. Another case of Soviet-supported Cuban military intervention in a Third World political crisis occurred in the Horn of

Africa a year later. The pro-Western Ethiopian Emperor Haile Selassie had been overthrown in 1974. He had soon been replaced by a group of radical army officers who declared their intention to lead Ethiopia in a socialist direction. This new regime faced internal strife and an active secessionist movement in the coastal province of Eritrea. Ethiopia also faced an external threat: Neighboring Somalia had long claimed a piece of Ethiopian territory, the Ogaden (a desert area inhabited by ethnic Somalis). When the Somalis sought to take advantage of Ethiopia's internal disarray to seize the Ogaden, the Ethiopians asked the USSR for help. Although the Soviets had close relations with Somalia and were its chief military supplier, this chance to gain a new ally was attractive to the Soviets. They agreed to help the Ethiopians and tried to persuade the Somalis to make peace with their ancient enemy. The Somalis were unwilling to make peace with Ethiopia just because the Soviets thought it might be a good idea and decided instead to oust the Soviets, abrogate their friendship treaty with them, and proceed with an invasion of Ethiopia.

The shift of alignments was dramatic. Over a few months in the winter of 1977–1978, the USSR switched its support to Ethiopia's new government, sending military aid, while Cuban troops helped the Ethiopians secure their own regime and fend off the Somalis. The United States responded positively to Somali requests for assistance at this juncture but would not endorse a Somali invasion across recognized boundaries. By February 1978, at the point when the Somalis had been driven back by Cuban troops, U.S. backing became more important for its defensive value: to deter the Ethiopians from attempting punitive movement into Somali territory. Although no direct superpower confrontation occurred in a military sense, U.S.-Soviet tensions rose significantly over this incident.

Western Initiatives in Africa

One effect of these Soviet activities and the leftward political changes in Africa was an increase in the salience of Africa for the West. Both independently and in conjunction with other Western states, the United States undertook several initiatives in Africa. Efforts by the Ford administration to treat African problems as East-West issues were not well received in Africa. The Carter administration's view that these conflicts were local in origin and required African solutions was closer to that of African leaders, although Carter still believed his policies would indirectly preempt a growth in Soviet influence. His administration focused on the decolonization process in Rhodesia and the long-stalled efforts to free Namibia from South African control.

In 1978, a U.S. initiative was important in forming the Western Contact Group, comprising the Western members of the United Nations Security

Council; the group undertook to negotiate with the South Africans to secure independence for Namibia. An important motive in these efforts was a desire to ensure that future governments in Africa would be favorable toward the West, whatever their political ideology.

Southeast Asia

Political changes occurring in Southeast Asia produced a new set of issues. Vietnam, which had already extended its influence over neighboring Laos with relative ease, in 1978 took advantage of its military superiority in the region to invade Cambodia (called Kampuchea since 1975). The Marxist, pro-Chinese Pol Pot government was overthrown and a pro-Vietnamese government installed under Heng Samrin in 1979. The Pol Pot regime in Cambodia had been a brutal one, and its forcible campaigns to eliminate cities and "capitalist elements" involved so much killing that charges of genocide were raised; nevertheless, the Vietnamese invasion and political takeover was alarming to many states. The credentials of this new Kampuchean government subsequently became an issue at the United Nations and at meetings of the nonaligned.

The invasion of Kampuchea also affected relations between Vietnam and China, which had been poor for some time. In February 1979, Chinese forces invaded Vietnam from the north in a "punitive exercise" probably intended to frighten the Vietnamese. The Chinese were not very successful militarily and withdrew after suffering high casualties. The possibility of additional Vietnamese expansionism in Southeast Asia accordingly became an issue in that region.

Revolutions and Regime Changes

From 1978 to 1979 several revolutions and regime changes that affected perceptions about the nature of East-West and North-South relations occurred in the Third World. Again, interpretations of their causes and consequences varied depending upon whether one looked at the North-South or the East-West agenda. In all of these cases, pro-Soviet regimes or less pro-Western ones emerged: Eastern gains were registered in Afghanistan and South Yemen; Western losses occurred in Iran and Nicaragua. These political changes contributed to Western perceptions of loss and served to encourage domestic criticisms of détente as a Western strategy for better relations with the East.

Afghanistan. Afghanistan had always maintained friendly relations with its neighbor, the USSR. However, Afghanistan had been neutral and receptive to aid and contact with Western states as well. In April 1978, communists in Afghanistan carried off a coup against the government of Mohammed Daoud. The new regime swiftly became embattled against internal opponents to its policies and moved to acquire help from the USSR in maintaining order. A friendship treaty was signed with the Soviet Union in December 1978, and increasing amounts of Soviet military assistance were forthcoming to assist in keeping order against internal opponents.

South Yemen. In June 1978, Cuban troops and Soviet military equipment were involved in a coup that put pro-Soviet Marxists firmly in charge of the People's Democratic Republic of Yemen (PDRY, or South Yemen). Although Soviet-PDRY ties had been close before, Arab hostility to PDRY's aid to the Soviet involvement in Ethiopia had caused this alignment to be questioned internally. The new regime moved to consolidate its ties to the USSR by requesting membership in COMECON, increasing its supplies of Soviet arms, and signing a Soviet-PDRY Friendship Treaty (December 1979).

Iran. Iran had been solidly in the Western camp, although it had maintained significant commercial relations with the USSR, which borders Iran to the north. Shah Reza Pahlavi had used oil wealth earnings to build up the Iranian military and promote huge projects to modernize the country so that it could play the role of a major regional power. The shah's rule was repressive and corrupt, while conditions of the Iranian people remained poor, and in the winter of 1978-1979, his regime was brought down by a massive revolt. Although many sectors of the Iranian polity welcomed the fall of the shah, the momentum of the revolution put in the forefront fundamentalist Islamic leaders, who took the Iranian revolution forward on a wave of anti-Americanism and anti-Westernism.

The loss of an ally was a bad blow for the United States. Moreover, when a group of armed radicals seized the U.S. embassy in Tehran and took its personnel hostage, a nightmare of embarrassment began for the United States. (These hostages were released in January 1981 after a rescue effort failed and after lengthy indirect negotiations.) Yet although the new Islamic republic set up under the spiritual guidance of the Ayatollah Khomeini was virulently anti-American and deeply critical of Western values, the revolution's course did not favor the East. The West was resented for having supported the shah and imposed its "impurities" on Iranian society, but the East was disliked for being hostile to religion. Although the Soviets tried to be friendly toward this new regime, there was little basis for close ties—in fact, the Iranian communists were soon arrested. Iran's victorious revolutionaries were fundamentalist Shiite Muslims who believed their actions should inspire others. Their appeals to other Muslims to follow their own example added a new and poorly understood factor to the region's volatile politics.

Nicaragua. In Central America, the United States lost another ally, as the dictatorship of Anastasio Somoza in Nicaragua was toppled early in 1979 by a revolution. Like the shah in Iran, Somoza was overthrown by a popular revolution, with many sectors of the polity opposing his repressive dictatorship, fighting for his demise, and welcoming his fall. The momentum of the revolution ultimately favored a strongly nationalistic, anti-imperialist, leftist group, the Sandinista National Liberation Front. Relations between the United States and Somoza had soured in the late 1970s, and President Carter had criticized Somoza's human rights record. Throughout the revolution the United States sought to control the outcome and was deeply involved in negotiations between Somoza and the multiple opposition forces. When it became clear that the Sandinistas would be the dominant political force when the revolution ended, the United States called for an inter-American peacekeeping force (rejected by other Latin American governments) and an alternative interim president. These efforts to prevent a Sandinista political victory were unsuccessful: Nicaraguans and other Latin Americans interpreted the U.S. actions as familiar imperialistic attempts to determine Nicaragua's future. At the same time, the United States feared the left-leaning Sandinistas and became more inclined to see the revolution in East-West rather than North-South terms. It is important to note, however, that not all the members of the West agreed with the U.S. view of Nicaragua.

The Soviet Invasion of Afghanistan and Its Ramifications

In December 1979, the event that definitively killed détente occurred: the Soviet invasion of Afghanistan. The communist regime there was a troubled one, and its radical policies attempting rapid social engineering had alienated the population and produced widespread revolt. Soviet attempts to tone down the regime or move in a more tractable leader had failed. During the Soviet invasion the radical Afghan leader Hafizullah Amin was killed, and a new leader, Babrak Karmal, returned from exile to take his place. He announced that the Soviet troops had been invited in because of "foreign assistance to counterrevolution."

Overnight, world politics had changed, or so it certainly seemed to President Carter, who pronounced the Soviet invasion of Afghanistan "an extremely serious threat to peace." It would no longer be possible simply to do "business as usual" with the USSR.[5] With Iran already in turmoil and still seeking its political way as an Islamic state in the modern era, U.S. officials determined that the security of the oil flow from the Persian Gulf was at risk. In what became known as the Carter Doctrine, the government announced that any attempt by an outside power to gain control of the Persian Gulf would be regarded as an attack on Western and U.S. interests. The Soviets were warned that should they move toward the gulf, that "would mean war."[6] The trappings of détente were dropped. The SALT II treaty was withdrawn from the U.S. Senate (where bilateral agreements with the USSR were already under heavy criticism), and a variety of sanctions was imposed on the USSR (including an embargo on grain sales, cancellations of cultural and educational exchanges, and a boycott of the Olympic Games in Moscow).

The U.S. government ordered the upgrading of its military capabilities for operations in and around the Persian Gulf. Creation of a Rapid Deployment Force, negotiation of new military basing agreements with friendly African and Middle Eastern states, and joint military exercises in the Middle Eastern region were components of this new approach.

Western and Southern Responses to Third World Crises

Western responses to these crises were increasingly mixed. The Europeans had a significant stake in the economic benefits of détente and were inclined to be less alarmist than the United States about political changes in the Third World. But there was also a perception, manifested most clearly in the United States, that the problem was both Soviet aggressiveness and Western inaction. Even for those who were more willing to credit internal political problems for the situations of opportunity that were opening up for the socialist camp, the overall impact of all these developments was disquieting and seemed to call for a more assertive Western stance against the East.

For the most part, Southern states resisted efforts to interpret these situations as East-West agenda items, on the grounds that this invited superpower meddling, competition, more violence, and an escalation of conflict. In some cases it proved possible to secure broad agreement on multilateral conflict-resolution approaches. However, partisan divisions meant that many of these problems rested as issues on several agendas at once.

THE NORTH-SOUTH AGENDA

The North-South agenda during the period from 1975 to 1980 was focused on efforts to implement the New International Economic Order. The Nonaligned Movement and the Group of 77 coordinated their efforts to negotiate with the Northern states in several forums on a number of specific economic issues. These included the general system of preferences, the Common Fund and Integrated Program for Commodities, and debt relief. Several North-South meetings that focused on the NIEO goals were held during these years: the Conference on International Economic Cooperation (CIEC), UNCTAD IV (1976), and UNCTAD V (1979). Southern unity and mutual cooperation reemerged as important objectives as North-South economic dialogue failed to produce significant results and as Third World crises exposed Southern political diversity. Back-burner issues on the North-

South agenda included OPEC's unity and impact on the world economy and human rights.

Implementing NIEO

North-South negotiations in several important meetings from 1975 to 1980 exemplified the old adage: You can lead a horse to water, but you can't make him drink. Agenda battles characterized every proposed negotiation, precisely because there were so many differences of opinion about how to define the issues. North and South disagreed both about the nature of international economic problems and about Southern needs. Even where North and South agreed that a problem existed, fundamental clashes that inhibited cooperative action occurred over appropriate mechanisms and the scope of and techniques for solving the problem. The Southern countries' convictions about the necessity for cooperative action were based on perceptions that the North had both an interest in their problems and an obligation to assist in their solution. Very much aware also of their own weakness in negotiations with the North, the Southern states relied upon solidarity to achieve their aims, with the additional weight of OPEC support for the NIEO.

The Conference on International Economic Cooperation

The Conference on International Economic Cooperation (CIEC) was a diplomatic improvisation intended to provide a forum for North-South dialogue less threatening to the North than a United Nations forum. Organizationally, the CIEC was actually a West-South body. In negotiation style and in outcome it typified the differences in purpose and goals that divided the North and South, and it reflected fundamental internal divisions within both the North and the South. Twenty-seven representatives attended, including nineteen from the South and the rest from Western-Northern states (including a single representative for the EEC). The CIEC meetings began with a preliminary planning session in October 1975 and moved to full negotiation strength in December 1975. Additional meetings occurred periodically until June 1977.

Not surprisingly, it proved difficult to agree upon an agenda: The Third World states attending CIEC were divided over how hard to press the North; the North had internal divisions as well; some European states were inclined to be sympathetic to the Southern complaints about inequities in the world economy as presently managed; however, most Western states were opposed to discussion of measures that could reduce the openness of the free market and permit international regulation or other kinds of interference with its mechanisms. To the United States, OPEC's coercive management of the oil cartel represented such interference. U.S. interest in discussing the need for access to supplies (which would permit criticism and correction of OPEC) was in sharp contrast to Southern interest in discussing the need for access to markets (which would permit criticism and correction of the trade policies of the industrial states). By and large, the major economic powers defended existing international economic institutions and mechanisms. Because Northern states did not wish to discuss any major overhaul of the entire international economic system, they focused instead on hard bargaining over smaller, specific issues.

The CIEC managed to establish four commissions to examine producer-consumer problems in the areas of energy, raw materials, development, and monetary issues. The specific issues of debt, indexation, and commodity-pricing agreements became major areas of dispute during the sessions. The meetings went well until April 1976 when the South began to insist that the delegates move from studying problems to formulating solutions. CIEC recessed while UNCTAD IV took place in May 1976.[7]

The final series of meetings in 1977 were disappointing for the South; nevertheless, the conferees reached agreement in three areas: increases in aid to Southern states, special assistance to the poorest countries, and discussions of schemes for commodity price stabilization. A pledge by Northern states to contribute 0.7 percent of their gross national product (GNP) to economic aid for Southern states was an important symbolic victory, since most of the Northern states (including Eastern Europe and the USSR) had been reducing their levels of aid. Establishment of a special $1 billion fund for aid to the very poorest Southern countries was encouraging, but not so generous as many Southern states thought necessary. Although commodity price fluctuations were recognized as a serious problem, the Northern states would agree only to further talks on this problem—certainly a disappointing result after two years of negotiations.

UNCTADs IV and V

North-South negotiations in UNCTAD IV (1976) and UNCTAD V (1979) were similarly disappointing for the South. These were much larger meetings, held under UN auspices. Once again, the Group of 77 met ahead of time to formulate a Southern plan. When UNCTAD IV assembled in Nairobi, Kenya, the South pressed the North for the establishment of an Integrated Program of Commodities (IPC) financed through an associated Common Fund. Many Southern states were suffering from worldwide economic trends in the 1970s that had inflated prices of Northern manufactured goods and depressed prices for most primary products. The Integrated Program of Commodities was designed to alleviate some of this economic distress by regulating the supply and price of primary commodities through producer-consumer agreements. Certain commodities would be stockpiled when in plentiful supply and released to international markets during times of shortages to help keep supplies and prices steady. The IPC would rectify supply and price fluctuations with the backing of a Common Fund as a source of cash to buy and sell buffer stocks.

The North entered UNCTAD IV with obvious internal divisions centered around differences of policy toward the Common Fund idea. The United States, West Germany, Japan, and Great Britain opposed seventeen other Northern states by objecting even to Common Fund negotiations. An important source of this split was the South's desire to take commodity production, marketing, and transport out of the control of private investors, particularly multinational corporations, and give control of these areas to local producers and state governments.[8] The Netherlands led the Northern faction that insisted on a clear agreement on the fund. Although the Eastern states applauded some Southern positions, they were accused by the South of being unwilling to help rectify the Southern economic problems. Eventually compromises were reached on the IPC and Common Fund issues. Common Fund negotiations were scheduled to begin the following March (1977), and eighteen commodities were selected for a limited IPC. Another two years of negotiations were necessary before an agreement was finally reached in March 1979 on a fund with two "lending windows": The first set of funds— $400 million from government contributions—would be used to finance buffer stocks; the second "window"—$350 million, all but $70 million of it to be provided by voluntary contributions—was a fund for commodity marketing and research in the South. The South had wanted a much larger Common Fund capable of financing a much stronger regulatory program.

Frustration with lack of progress led to a renewed emphasis on mutual economic cooperation among Southern states, but also to some ideas for new instruments. In December 1977 Southern countries secured UNGA approval for a new body, a Committee of the Whole (COW) to deal with international economic matters. A new UNCTAD post was also created: a deputy general for development and international cooperation.

The Group of 77 put together a set of common positions on trade, commodities, and finance for UNCTAD V (scheduled for May 1979) but also assembled a proposal to give UNCTAD authority to review economic policies of Northern states in light of the NIEO objectives and principles. UNCTAD V endorsed the Common Fund agreement that had been worked out in the wake of the CIEC, but made little progress on other issues. Although Northern countries went along with measures to facilitate South-South regional economic cooperation, they resisted any suggestion for multinational regulation of trade policies unless such moves would include intrusions into the OPEC system. Soviet efforts to redefine the problem in terms of general nondiscriminatory economic coexistence were ignored.[9]

Factors Inhibiting Progress on the NIEO

Global Economic Problems. Northern resistance to Southern demands was only one factor inhibiting progress toward realization of the NIEO. Global economic problems were affecting states unevenly, making it more difficult to reach agreement on common approaches to particular questions. Northern protectionism against Southern imports was a growing source of conflict despite the ameliorative measures taken by Western European states. (The Lomé Convention between the EEC and the ACP countries was revised in 1979 to raise aid levels and increase compensatory finances available for commodity exporters.)

International Indebtedness. Another problem was increasing levels of international indebtedness, a phenomenon related to high energy prices, extremely high interest rates, and increased borrowing. This problem was so serious that in 1978 Sweden, the Netherlands, Canada, and Switzerland permitted cancellation of the debts of some Southern states. The price of oil jumped again in 1979 (partly because of the sudden halt in production of Iranian oil), feeding the international recession and compounding the problems of all energy-importing states, and as a result, the working alliance between OPEC and the South was shaken.

Political Disunity. Political divisions caused problems too, despite the priority given to Southern unity on international economic issues. Intrusion of East-West alignments were especially apparent within the Nonaligned Movement, which had achieved recognition during this period as the political agent for the South on many issues. Cuba's obvious pro-Soviet position was a special problem when Cuba hosted the nonaligned summit in 1979. The Cuban military interventions in Angola and Ethiopia had drawn heavy criticism within the South. Resentments over Cuba's pro-Soviet international stance crystallized when Cuba defended the Soviet invasion of Afghanistan and sought to identify the socialist countries as "natural allies" of the nonaligned. The Cuban move was rejected in favor of less partisan formulations.

Southern states were also split on the question of Kampuchea, and ultimately no Kampuchean delegation was seated at the nonaligned summit. (At the United Nations, the Pol Pot delegates were able to retain their seat.) The radical Arab states brought their dispute with Egypt over its peace treaty with Israel into the nonaligned meetings too. The Nonaligned Movement was already on record in favor of Palestinian rights (for most Southern states, this was a national liberation question) and criticized the Egypt-Israeli peace treaty for interfering with the achievement of these rights. Nonetheless the nonaligned summit managed to subdue its political disputes and reaffirmed its traditional position of "equidistance" between East and West.

Global Negotiations

Thus, at the end of the 1970s, attempts to seek solutions appropriate to international economic problems as defined by the NIEO had reached an apparent stalemate. There were suggestions for new approaches, however. The nonaligned summit in June 1979 passed a resolution suggesting "global negotiations" with an integrated approach in a forum broader than CIEC, but narrower than the UN. This resolution proposed that the Group of 77 present this idea to the UN's new Committee of the Whole. The UNGA did pass a resolution to this effect in December 1979, and the COW began work on specific proposals for such negotiations in March 1980.

The idea of global negotiations as a fresh start on North-South dialogue was also endorsed by an independent international commission chaired by former West German Chancellor Willy Brandt. The report of this commission, *North-South: A Programme for Survival*,[10] called for a summit of world leaders that would not itself negotiate North-South issues but would set a framework and mandate for such negotiations.

OPEC as a North-South Issue

OPEC Loses Southern Support

In Chapter 4 OPEC was discussed as an example of the use of producer associations as a Southern weapon and as a symbol of Southern determination. In the 1975–1980 period OPEC was once again an issue on the North-South agenda, but this time OPEC was not so controlled in its management of the oil commodity nor was it so universally supported by the rest of the South as it had been in the earlier period. In addition, its own internal cohesion began to loosen.

A Divided OPEC Loses Control of Prices

From 1973 to 1978 OPEC states met regularly and controlled the international price of petroleum. Internal divisions existed in OPEC that were ideological, political, and economic and that affected its deliberations as a result of the very different economies of its members and the varied importance of oil for them. Nevertheless, one member, Saudi Arabia, stood out as exceptionally important: Its oil supplies were enormous, much larger than those of other OPEC members; in fact, its oil accounted for nearly one-third of OPEC's production. Saudi Arabia often acted to reduce production during periods of excess supply in order to maintain the price of oil and to increase production when supplies were low in order to prevent the price of oil from rising too high.[11]

After the initial shock of the 1974 price rises, the international economic system adjusted to the price of oil and also reduced consumption to a considerable extent. But by 1978 several changes had occurred that made the system vulnerable to another crisis. Consumption of oil was up as economies recovered from the 1974-1975 recession and supplies were tight. During the Iranian revolution in the fall of 1978, Iranian oil production was suddenly halted, and world oil supplies dropped very quickly. In December 1978, the OPEC ministers met and raised prices by 5 percent and announced an increase of 14.5 percent for 1979. Prices rose even higher than OPEC had planned, however, and continued to climb in 1979. From 1973 to 1979, the average price of a barrel of oil was $12; from 1979 to 1984, it was $28.[12] Saudi Arabia and some other members of OPEC were eager to control prices to prevent serious disruptions of the international economic system. They tried to regain control of the price increase during 1979, but this was very difficult with such high potential profits at stake.

These oil price rises disrupted the economies of the North and the South, contributed to the recession of 1979, and in addition, indicated trouble brewing within OPEC. Few of the poorest Southern states had actually benefited from the OPEC offer to contribute funds to relieve their economic stresses resulting from the global recession. Moreover, increasing numbers of Southern states expressed resentment that OPEC's power had not yet produced the economic policy changes in the North that they had hoped for.

Human Rights

U.S. Concern with Human Rights

We have already seen that human rights became a live issue on the East-West agenda as détente replaced the Cold War. The Final Act of the CSCE at Helsinki had formalized this interest in human rights for East-West relations. However, human rights was also a North-South issue. For a number of reasons during the 1975-1980 period, the United States highlighted human rights in its foreign policy; this was a response to critiques of U.S. policy in Vietnam as well as to increased publicity about human rights abuses in communist states and dictatorial Third World regimes. Activities of private international human rights groups, such as Amnesty International, were important in raising the public's awareness of this issue. The concern with human rights was institutionalized in the United States by linking foreign aid to annual assessments of human rights performance in the eligible countries.

U.S. criticisms of human rights abuses in communist countries were familiar, but open criticism of governments friendly to the United States like Brazil, Guatemala, Argentina, and Chile was new. The assessments of countries' records were not entirely evenhanded, and the policy was not applied consistently, but the emphasis was welcome to local political forces in many countries. However, the U.S. human rights policy met with considerable hostility from Southern states accused of violations: It was regarded as an interference in their domestic affairs and as an effort to divert attention from international inequalities. Guatemala was so angered by the U.S. insistence that military aid would be withdrawn unless its treatment of political prisoners improved that for a time it simply turned down future aid and went elsewhere for weapons.

The Basic Human Needs Idea

A different approach to human rights focused on "basic human needs"— the elements necessary for survival, the world over. Advocates of this perspective argued that the North and South should concentrate upon supplying these needs and that minimum standards should be set and met for food, nutrition, health services, and education.[13] The basic human needs concept received support from some international organizations such as the Dag Hammarskjold Foundation, the World Employment Conference, the World Bank, and some governments, including that of the United States. The South tended to be suspicious of the basic human needs approach, however, seeing it as a Northern attempt to replace the NIEO considerations with something that did not require fundamental transformation of the system and that made an issue of Southern political institutions and performance.

In many ways the conceptualization of North-South relations that had produced the NIEO and all the related agenda items was a fundamentally confrontational one. As Southern states struggled to achieve their aims on these issues, the asymmetry of relative power confirmed the perception even as it intensified frustration. Failing any basic realignment of effective power, it was clear that real progress toward NIEO was unlikely and that modification of international economic structures would come only with slow and painstaking negotiation.

THE GLOBAL AGENDA

With so much attention to the newly enlarged scope of the North-South and East-West agendas, the global agenda was in some ways in the shadows during this period although it was growing in scope and importance. During the years 1975 to 1980, the global agenda included economic and political issues that paralleled similar issues on the East-West and North-South agendas.

Political Issues

The global agenda included political issues related to decolonization and racism in Rhodesia, Namibia, and South Africa. Although none of these situations was entirely new, developments in this period underlined a broad consensus on the legitimacy of intervention by the larger international political community in internal affairs—at least in circumstances where those internal political systems were racist.

The End of White Rule in Rhodesia

It was in this period that the long struggle of Rhodesia (which since 1965 had defied Britain and survived UN-authorized international sanctions) to retain white minority government in the face of international disapproval finally ended. For a long time the Rhodesian government's willingness to engage in a series of negotiations with the British over various political reform proposals had helped encourage those who argued for patient and peaceful international approaches to the Rhodesian situation, but this patience ran out. The emergence of independent black majority governments in the former Portuguese colonies of Angola and Mozambique deprived Rhodesia of nearby allies and racially altered the regional environment (most significantly, by reducing South Africa's willingness to support Rhodesia).

Meanwhile, Rhodesia's neighbors helped to foster unity among the black opposition forces, who cooperated in an increasingly effective guerrilla war against the Rhodesian regime. International disapproval was important in discrediting an internal political settlement in 1978 that offered some concessions to Rhodesia's blacks. Finally, the Rhodesian government agreed to British-mediated negotiations with all opposition groups (beginning in December 1979). These discussions finally produced an agreement for a transition to majority rule, which would permit internationally recognized independence at last. In elections to set up the new government of Zimbabwe, Robert Mugabe, a Marxist guerrilla leader who had enjoyed Chinese rather than Soviet support, was the winner. Mugabe's government promised racial peace and reconciliation with a rival, Soviet-affiliated guerrilla group.

South Africa and Namibia

The departure of the Portuguese increased direct and indirect pressures on South Africa. Independence for Namibia and changes in South Africa's internal system of apartheid became highly visible global issues. A shift in U.S. policy toward greater support for political change in southern Africa was also an important factor in this pressure. Indications of this change were the UN Security Council's imposition of a mandatory arms embargo on South Africa in 1977 and a new set of diplomatic initiatives designed to pressure South Africa to relinquish Namibia as demanded by the United Nations and the International Court of Justice (ICJ, often referred to as the World Court). Formation of the Western Contact Group in 1978 may have represented an attempt by the Western countries to find a way to engineer a peaceful solution for Namibia that, as we have seen, might benefit the West, but this new effort to negotiate specific conditions for a cease-fire in South Africa's war with SWAPO guerrillas and a transition to self-government for Namibia reflected a consensus on a global approach to this problem. An important part of this new effort was a threat of Western sanctions against South Africa should the negotiated solution for Namibian independence fall through.

Wars and Armed Interventions

In the second half of the 1970s, there were several wars and armed interventions, each of which some states sought to put on the global agenda. Soviet-assisted Cuban interventions in Angola and Ethiopia angered some pro-Western African states and worried many small countries; however, the Organization of African Unity eventually accepted these as legitimate responses to invitations. Syria's intervention in Lebanon, Somalia's invasion of Ethiopia, Vietnam's invasion of Kampuchea, and China's subsequent invasion of Vietnam all brought protests about the unacceptability of coercive uses of force. But partisan splits on these disputes prevented consensus on how to label these events, nor was agreement possible on multilateral responses by regional or international bodies.

The Soviet invasion of Afghanistan in December 1979 was an exception, however. All but a few of the USSR's closest socialist allies voted to condemn the action at the United Nations and in organizations like the Islamic Conference. Although there was little that could be done to dislodge the Soviets, the legitimacy of the Soviet presence, the credentials of the client government, and the cause of the indigenous opposition that developed became new global issues.

Economic Problems

In Chapter 4 we saw that OPEC price increases posed a significant challenge to the international economy. However, the international effects of OPEC's price increases moderated in the late 1970s. International trade expanded and it seemed that the international economy was adjusting to the changes of the early 1970s. In fact, the adjustment was an illusion.

A number of patterns developed that posed ominous prospects for the future. The U.S. trade deficit continued, and the Western economic powers had difficulty reaching agreements on economic reforms. Squabbles occurred among the United States, Western Europe, and Japan concerning the value of currencies and trade practices. A summit of the major industrial states in 1978 failed to achieve meaningful coordination of economic policies. The United States tried to persuade its allies to follow more expansionistic economic policies; some agreements were reached to that effect. However, these agreements could not be put into effect before the dollar experienced another crisis as its value began another precipitous decline.

Meanwhile, the debt of non-oil-exporting developing countries had risen dramatically, from $48 billion in 1970 to more than $301 billion in 1980.[14] Until 1979 they had been able to borrow money to finance their debts, the poorest countries relying upon the IMF, and the Third World countries with larger and wealthier economies borrowing increasingly large amounts from private banks and bank consortiums. For a time, increased exports covered debt service, but in 1979 the global economy was hit with another major increase in the price of oil, and the illusion of prosperity began to crack. Along with the increase in the price of oil, inflation and interest rates soared, and the Northern capitalist states began to restrict their internal economic activities. This, in turn, caused a decline in revenues for Southern exports even as interest payments due on Southern debts rose sharply. Still, little was done. Debt was a simmering problem that would heat up in the 1980s.

Food

Food was a back-burner global issue from 1975 to 1980. Efforts had been made during this time to establish a grain reserve, and several negotiating sessions concerning food occurred. During the mid-1970s the food crisis was in remission as production increased in the South and progress was made in negotiations. But in the late 1970s the problem of food shortages began to inch its way onto the agenda again as the international recession caused a deterioration in the living conditions in the South. Food production did not keep up with population increases, particularly in sub-Saharan Africa and South Asia.

By 1980, the need for broad international cooperation to increase food production was recognized by the Brandt commission and discussed in its report. A similar recognition of the global nature of the food problem was presented in *Global 2000*, a massive document produced by the U.S. government to assess world economic trends. The U.S. report echoed the Brandt report in its call for "unprecedented cooperation and commitment" and "vigorous, determined initiatives" to solve problems of world poverty, hunger, overpopulation, and pollution.[15] After nearly six years of unproductive North-South negotiations, however, this summons was not received with optimism.

*   *   *

Conclusions

Although all three agendas overlapped in this period, each raised distinctive issues appropriate to very different perceptions about the important problems in world politics. The East-West agenda was dominated by questions about the nature of East-West relations and by conflicts that affected assessments of the merits and mechanisms of détente. Interest in détente weakened in the West as East-West competition and mistrust persisted, while new concerns about the Eastern military threat challenged ideas about the mutual benefits of détente, even in the realm of arms control.

The North-South agenda was clear, but still not acceptable to the North. Accordingly, the prospects for the South's achieving its ambitious goals seemed slim.

The global agenda contained a diversity of political and economic topics and shared many issues with the North-South and East-West agendas during this period. The most remarkable feature of the global agenda was the contrast between the strength of the perceptions that issues required global solutions and the weakness of actual international responses to these problems.

Notes

1. A Carter-Brezhnev summit in Vienna in June 1979 reaffirmed these principles of parity and restraint in the interest of avoiding nuclear war. World war was described as a "disaster for all mankind." Text of the joint communiqué appears in *U.S. State Department Bulletin*, July 1979.

2. For details of the treaties, see *Arms Control and Disarmament Agreements: Texts and Histories of Negotiations*, 1982 ed. (Washington, D.C.: U.S. Arms Control and Disarmament Agency, 1982).

3. David N. Schwartz, *NATO's Nuclear Dilemmas* (Washington, D.C.: Brookings Institution, 1983), Chapter 7.

4. See Banning Garrett, "China Policy and the Strategic Triangle," in Kenneth Oye et al., eds., *Eagle Entangled: U.S. Foreign Policy in a Complex World* (New York: Longman, 1979), pp. 228–263.

5. Jimmy Carter, "Soviet Military Intervention in Afghanistan," Speech to the Nation, January 4, 1980, in *Vital Speeches of the Day*, vol. 46, no. 7, January 15, 1980, pp. 194–195.

6. President Carter's State of the Union Address of January 23, 1980, is in *Facts on File*, 1980, p. 41. Clark Clifford's warning to the Soviet Union on January 31 is available in *Facts on File*, 1980, p. 83.

7. On these North-South meetings, see Robert A. Mortimer, *The Third World Coalition in International Politics*, 2d updated ed. (Boulder, Colo.: Westview Press,

1984); and Joan Spero, *The Politics of International Economic Relations*, 2d ed. (New York: St. Martins, 1981), Chapter 7.

8. Karl Sauvant, "The NIEO Program: Reasons, Proposals, and Progress," in Karl P. Sauvant, ed., *Changing Priorities on the International Agenda: The New International Economic Order* (New York: Pergamon Press, 1979), p. 90.

9. Although we have been using the phrase "North-South," we must note that important negotiations on the NIEO are really West-South. Eastern bloc states do not participate in controlling certainly key institutions (such as the IMF), nor are their national markets open or their currencies convertible. The Eastern states often trade on the basis of barter agreements, with prices negotiated on a bilateral basis. Moreover, although East-South trade has increased, the South's major export and import markets are still in the advanced economies of the Western part of the North.

Although the USSR initially endorsed the NIEO for its attacks on imperialism, by the 1976 UNGA session the Soviet bloc was criticizing several aspects of the Southern position. Specifically, the communist states objected to suggestions that they shared any responsibility for Southern problems, or were part of the North. The Soviets also sought to enlarge the North-South agenda to include their own grievances against the Western states for discriminatory treatment in trade and finance. See Elizabeth K. Valkenier, *The Soviet Union and the Third World: An Economic Bind* (New York: Praeger, 1983), Chapter 4.

10. *North-South: A Programme for Survival*, Report of the Independent Commission on International Development Issues (Cambridge, Mass.: The MIT Press, 1980).

11. The change in OPEC cohesion and the causes of the second oil crisis are explained in detail in Spero, *The Politics of International Economic Relations*, pp. 306-338.

12. Lester R. Brown et al., *The State of the World, 1985* (New York: Random House, 1986).

13. Roger Hansen, *Beyond the North-South Stalemate* (New York: McGraw-Hill, 1979), p. 79.

14. David Blake and Robert Walters, *The Politics of Global Economic Relations*, 2d ed. (Englewood Cliffs, N.J.: Prentice-Hall, 1983), p. 78.

15. Council on Environmental Quality and Department of State, *The Global 2000 Report to the President* (Washington, D.C.: Government Printing Office, 1980), vol. 1, p. 5.

1980s

Six / FORWARD TO THE PAST

By the 1980s the three international agendas had become strikingly similar to those of the 1950s. Each superpower approached issues on the East-West agenda with deep suspicion and hostility, reminiscent of the tension of the 1950s. As in the 1950s, the South found itself speaking to a partially deaf North with many members unwilling to acknowledge Southern demands. The South had to struggle to keep Southern unity and the North-South agenda alive. Meanwhile, issues on the global agenda reflected increasingly ominous world trends but received little attention from the dominant international actors in the 1980s. By 1987 there were encouraging signs of a greater willingness to seek cooperative solutions to world problems.

• **EAST-WEST AGENDA** A contentious East-West agenda took the central place in world politics after 1980. References to détente and the need for mutual restraint were replaced by more confrontational themes reminiscent of the Cold War. Security issues rose in importance, as each superpower intensified its efforts to assure its own power through careful attention to military capacities. The advent of the Reagan administration in the United States had serious consequences for both the East-West and North-South agendas: The new U.S. administration rejected the concept of a North-South agenda and defined major international issues and events largely in East-West terms.

• **NORTH-SOUTH AGENDA** For many reasons, the North-South agenda entered the 1980s in disarray. The Southern coalition lost momentum and direction, partly as a consequence of repeated failures in Southern efforts to win concessions from the North. Southern debt and trade problems dominated the agenda, although attempts to view Third World crises and instability in East-West terms affected North-South issues and drew new attention to ideological differences.

• **GLOBAL AGENDA** The global agenda remained very limited, as global approaches to world problems were generally neglected or rejected in favor of more nationalistic ones. Although several serious armed conflicts occurred in this period, cooperative international actions did not contribute to their resolution. A few political and environmental issues did receive global attention; however, the most important global issues were economic ones.

THE EAST-WEST AGENDA

Whereas détente had sought to reduce tensions and emphasize the need for superpower communication, tensions dominated East-West relationships in the early 1980s. In the aftermath of Afghanistan, the emphasis shifted to ideological differences, fundamental hostilities, and competing spheres of influence. For the West, increased Soviet power and objectionable Soviet behavior were the major issues, and for the East, Western rejections of détente were the problem.

The U.S. leadership revived Cold War themes, including the need to secure the West against the dangers of communism. Although East-West tensions did increase generally, they increased most between the two superpowers themselves rather than in Europe, where détente and East-West interaction remained fairly intense. In fact, both superpowers experienced difficulties in their relationships with allies during this period. Direct contact between the United States and the USSR initially contracted during this period (President Reagan did not meet with his Soviet counterpart until November 1985), while superpower competition and involvement in the internal politics of third-party countries took an important position on the East-West agenda.

The United States sought to exercise leadership in mounting a Western response to increases in Soviet political influence, an effort that did not have the support of all the Western states (or even of all the NATO allies). Nonetheless, it was important in defining the shape of East-West relations and agenda issues, the most fundamental being the balance of power between the two camps. The U.S. focus was on action to meet the Soviet challenge and to restrain or perhaps even reduce the Soviet sphere of influence.

Although the shift to more explicitly confrontational attitudes toward the USSR began under President Carter, the inauguration of President Ronald Reagan in 1981 brought a new energy to anti-Sovietism. Reagan characterized the Soviet Union as an "evil empire"[1] and called for a global campaign to enlarge the family of democratic states and for concrete assistance to armed groups resisting communist rule.[2] Official references to Soviet immorality and atheism, to its alleged promotion of totalitarianism, and to its association with terrorism and subversion emphasized East-West differences and helped to justify a new U.S. foreign policy activism. The United States intervened in several Third World conflicts, sought to bolster states that were perceived to be targets or potential targets of communist expansion, and supported insurgencies against Marxist-Leninist regimes. The USSR held its positions in the Third World but found itself on the defensive in several important sites.

Arms control remained the single substantive area in which East and West recognized common interests and where dialogue did occur. But even though both sides professed interest in arms control, the tense, competitive atmosphere made the purposes and scope of arms control agreements more problematic than before. Important developments in defensive weaponry challenged the concept of deterrence and altered the terms of arms control discussions dramatically. Doubts about the value of arms control also operated to inhibit agreement.

The East sought to defend its own political system and accused the West of abandoning détente in favor of militarist policies. The Soviets tried to make U.S. imperial behavior and rejection of détente an issue, stressing, by contrast, their own reasonableness; they sought to capitalize on the European interest in détente by presenting the case for continued normal commercial relations and highlighting their own professed interest in arms control. The USSR also launched a vigorous but unsuccessful campaign in Europe to encourage opposition to the deployment of U.S. intermediate-range nuclear missiles.

In this period, three Soviet leaders died in office. (Yuri Andropov succeeded Leonid Brezhnev in 1982, but died in 1984 after a serious illness and was replaced by the elderly Konstantin Chernenko, who died in 1985 and was succeeded by Mikhail Gorbachev.) This factor may help explain the professed Soviet interest in perpetuating détente, since all three new leaders stressed the Soviet Union's need to attend to domestic economic priorities. Gorbachev's ascendancy in 1985 brought an even more striking emphasis on reform (perestroika, or restructuring) and pledges of greater openness (glasnost). The Soviet leaders made clear their belief that the campaign to improve Soviet economic performance required a halt in the arms race and stable international relationships. Soviet diplomacy accordingly acquired a new look, with initiatives to cultivate West European governments, seek new overseas markets for Soviet goods, promote economic cooperation with a variety of states, and defuse the threats being perceived by the United States.

The East also tried to shift some East-West issues to the global or the North-South agendas: For example, in 1980, the USSR urged nonaligned states to make an issue of the "colonial" status of the Indian Ocean island of Diego Garcia, which the United States had leased from Great Britain and fortified as a naval support base; the USSR associated itself with proposals for nuclear-free zones;[3] and in 1987, Soviet leaders sought to globalize arms control issues by suggesting that the superpowers pledge that expenditures saved by arms reductions be dedicated to Third World development aid.

Arms Control

Although many other kinds of East-West contact declined, the superpowers conducted a number of negotiations on arms control matters. In fact, both sides publicly proclaimed their dedication to arms control in the interests of peace and in the service of a legitimate and lasting military balance. However, these East-West arms control negotiations at first took on a fundamentally competitive flavor. The proposals and counterproposals that were exchanged in the early 1980s established very little common ground, so attuned was each side to the competing military aspirations of the other.

Background of Distrust

The impact and purposes of arms control were important issues. New developments in weaponry had complicated old assumptions about arms control, whereas additional deployments of multiple-warhead weapons and increasingly diverse arsenals had changed calculations of the overall balance and the practical context of specific proposals (see Fig. 6.1). The value of arms control became an issue too: Doubts about the level of compliance with existing agreements led many Westerners to question the wisdom of new ones and stimulated greater interest in verification procedures and enforcement mechanisms. The nature of proposals exchanged raised questions about each side's motives and purposes. Each side mistrusted the other's acceptance of the principle of parity. And although both superpowers claimed to be interested in the stability of the strategic balance, each put forward proposals that could be criticized for promoting a relative advantage. The arms control environment was thus more complicated conceptually and practically.

Superpower arms control negotiations resumed in 1981 in a somewhat frosty atmosphere. Delegates discussed a great variety of arms control proposals, including qualitative and quantitative arms limitations, reductions in strategic weapons, testing restrictions, weapons policy restrictions, and prohibitions on development and research. Between 1981 and 1983, there were discussions on strategic arms and intermediate-range nuclear forces (INF), with the need for reductions as the primary focus of both sets of negotiations.

Intermediate-Range Nuclear Missiles

Intermediate-range nuclear weapons were the key issue in Europe, where the West was very concerned about Soviet numerical weapons advantages. The NATO alliance was following its "two-track policy" by taking steps to match existing Soviet deployments while simultaneously negotiating for Soviet reductions. NATO deployment of its own IRBMs was scheduled to

THE IMPACT OF MIRV TECHNOLOGY ON THE MILITARY BALANCE

**US and Soviet ICBM Launcher and Reentry
Vehicle (RV) Deployment 1971-1987**

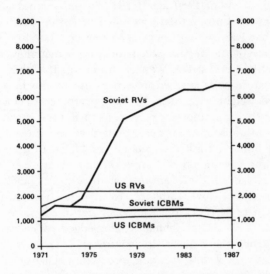

**US and Soviet SLBM Launcher and Reentry
Vehicle (RV) Deployment 1971-1987**

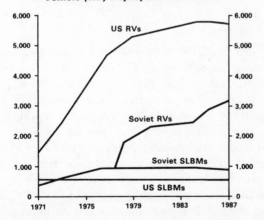

FIGURE 6.1   Source: *Soviet Military Power, 1987* (Washington, D.C.: U.S. Government Printing Office, 1987), pp. 29, 31.

begin in 1982 unless the Soviets could be persuaded to cut back or remove theirs. An initial U.S. proposal for a "zero-zero" option (wherein both sides would forgo IRBMs in Europe) ran into disputes over how to calculate strategic equivalence. The Soviets tried to challenge the view that they had numerical advantages when all weapons systems were counted and denounced NATO's deployment plans as provocative.

Actual deployment of Pershing II IRBMs and ground-launched cruise missiles in Western Europe then proceeded with the approval of the host governments but with strong opposition from the USSR. The speed and relative accuracy of the Pershings led to charges that they were offensive weapons useful in a first strike. Western arguments that these missiles were defensive in nature and designed as a response to the buildup of Soviet IRBMs carried weight with most NATO governments. However, spokespersons of the strong antinuclear movement in Europe expressed fears that the Pershing and cruise missiles were so effective and threatening that they would become important initial targets for the USSR in the event of war—thus assuring the devastation of Europe in any superpower confrontation. The USSR applauded these antinuclear movements and attempted to manipulate them; but Soviet attempts to influence the German elections toward rejection of NATO's nuclear policy backfired, since the new government under Chancellor Helmut Kohl pledged to cooperate with the plans for deploying the missiles. In November 1983, once it had become clear the Pershing deployments would proceed, a stalemate developed and the Soviet delegation walked out of both sets of East-West arms control talks.

Talks on Intercontinental Missiles

Intercontinental missiles were the main subject of superpower negotiations on strategic arms. Although SALT II remained unratified, both the United States and USSR had pledged not to subvert it. Nonetheless, the new discussions were referred to as Strategic Arms Reduction Talks (START), with the new acronym emphasizing the interest in quantitative cuts as well as the desire for a break with the past discussions. Both sides proposed reductions that would prevent unfavorable developments in their respective areas of vulnerability. All the proposals had important implications for the strategic arsenals of each side.

The United States was particularly interested in cutting the number of Soviet SS-18 ICBMs. These large missiles carried multiple warheads and were powerful enough to be thought capable of destroying hardened U.S. missile emplacements (they were called silo busters). The USSR had installed so many of them that it looked as if the Soviets might be planning for a saturation attack against U.S. weapons.

U.S. arms control proposals suggested reductions primarily in land-based missile launchers, precisely the area in which the Soviet advantage was most marked. (Land-based missiles constitute about two-thirds of the Soviet strategic forces.) Other proposals covered reductions in the total number of warheads permitted each side and limits on total throw-weight (the size of the load that can be carried by a missile, often used as a measure of the power of its rockets).

The United States had no exact equivalent of the Soviet SS-18 missile but was planning a new, more accurate ICBM called the MX. In 1980, the United States began to introduce a fleet of large new missile-carrying submarines (the Trident class) that could strike at Soviet territory from much greater distances than was previously possible and that would carry new and more powerful missiles capable of delivering as many as fourteen warheads each. Cruise missiles represented another important area of U.S. weapons development. These "flying bombs," which carried small warheads, could travel close to the ground, evading radar. Soviet arms control proposals sought to make an issue of the quantity and quality of U.S. missile-carrying submarines and bombers and suggested a freeze on new weapons (such as cruise missiles and the intermediate-range missiles being developed for Europe). The Soviets also displayed interest in arms control measures by declaring a halt to their own nuclear tests, by promoting the idea of nuclear-free zones, and by advocating "no first use" declarations.[4]

The Strategic Defense Initiative

Arms control discussions took a new direction in 1983, after President Reagan announced a program to explore the feasibility of space-based defense systems. The Strategic Defense Initiative, or SDI (also known as Star Wars because it would use beam and laser technology based on orbiting devices), proposed to discard *deterrence*, the premise of which was that fear of damaging retaliation would prevent nuclear attack. The SDI, in contrast, was supposed to prevent war by providing invulnerability to attack, and thus making victory impossible. A defensive shield would remove the need to rely on an enemy's rationality or on a generalized fear of war. Such a shield also would take care of the problem of accidental missile launches or provocative acts by small states.

Pro-SDI Arguments. Advocates of SDI argued that deterrence was failing: The balance of forces was changing in ways that actually might encourage the Soviets to attack. If the Soviets could expect to destroy a great many U.S. weapons in a first strike, with many of their own available for another blow against U.S. cities, it might be the U.S. retaliation, not the first strike, that would be deterred. This kind of scenario was even more probable if Soviet defenses could be trusted to absorb much of the potential impact of U.S. retaliation. SDI also offered an attractive alternative to negotiations with the USSR because agreements to control nuclear weapons would not be necessary if a shield existed to nullify them. It could also be argued that a shield would effectively disarm the USSR and permit the United States either to strike the USSR or to threaten to do so without fear of damage in return.

Anti-SDI Arguments. Arguments against SDI included warnings of a new arms race in new technological areas and new physical realms where competition would be both expensive and dangerous. The prospect of armed orbiting devices was disquieting; moreover, since these devices would become targets themselves, they would need to be defended or armed. Orbiting defensive weapons might also have offensive uses. Because the technology to produce such a space shield did not yet exist, the project would be both costly and prolonged. It could be expected that the Soviets would seek ways to counter such a system or to build one of their own, but in the meantime, the prospect of imminent U.S. invulnerability to Soviet weapons could motivate the USSR to strike first.

Plans for strategic defenses threatened the established consensus on strategic stability that had been expressed in the SALT agreements and the ABM treaty and that had confirmed the basic premises of deterrence: Neither side could overwhelm the other in an attack, and fear of significant damage from a retaliatory second strike would inhibit the first strike. Weapons should be protected, but for deterrence to work, both sides had to fear war. According to this logic, it was not only undesirable but also dangerous for one side to be invulnerable.

SDI Versus ABM Treaty. Ballistic missile defense had been discarded and restricted in 1972 because it was expensive, did not work well, and was believed to be destabilizing to the strategic balance. The SDI proposals not only contravened these ideas but also came in conflict with the ABM treaty. Although the treaty had been reaffirmed at the prescribed five-year intervals by both sides, it had lost favor in the United States—both because it included a commitment to equality of strategic arsenals and because it appeared to preclude further development of defenses against ballistic missiles. In 1986 and 1987, the United States and USSR publicly quarreled about correct interpretations of the ABM treaty's prohibitions on testing "new technologies." Although the Soviets advocated strengthening the treaty, the United States charged that the Soviets themselves were violating it to develop their own defensive technology. The Soviets protested the U.S. SDI proposal as an attempt to "militarize space" and pressed for testing and development restrictions that could inhibit progress toward the space shield weaponry. Meanwhile, both continued their efforts to proceed with upgrading existing weapons systems and experimented with various kinds of defensive technologies.

The European Perspective. The SDI proposal also changed the attitude of many Europeans to intermediate-range missiles because the prospect of U.S. invulnerability brought the Europeans new doubts about whether the United States would come to their defense. Although U.S. leaders denied that strategic defenses would dampen U.S. interest in European security, many Europeans were not convinced. They shifted their attention to the need to keep the intermediate-range nuclear missiles in Europe and thereby to couple European and U.S. security interests in a concrete way.

Steps Toward Arms Control

All these problems complicated the arms control environment. Nonetheless, both the United States and the Soviet Union repeatedly affirmed their desire to conclude arms agreements, no doubt spurred on by spiraling costs, the need for balance, and apprehensions about the impact of continued technological competition and a new, defensive arms race. Both U.S. and Soviet leaders became more receptive to negotiations in 1985 and affirmed their interest in arms control at a summit conference. In September 1986, a set of negotiations among the CSCE states concluded a symbolically valuable agreement on confidence-building measures (CBMs) in Europe, which comprised some specific rules to govern notification and verification of military activities in the region.

The Reykjavik Meetings. In October 1986, the Soviet and U.S. leaders met at Reykjavik, Iceland, where they discussed a comprehensive arms control agreement. Essentially, this proposal would have eliminated all strategic nuclear weapons and all intermediate-range nuclear weapons in Europe and would have included major restrictions on the Star Wars project.[5] Reagan was unwilling to accept such a package deal, and the talks broke off without agreement. However, both sides continued to profess interest in some form of arms reductions.

Intermediate-Range Nuclear Force Reduction. In 1987, the arms control focus shifted from strategic weapons like ICBMs to "theater" weapons. In September, the United States and the USSR agreed to prepare a treaty to eliminate intermediate- and medium-range nuclear missiles in Europe. The West had originally proposed IRBM reduction in 1981—the zero-zero option. At that time, since the Western alliance had no intermediate-range missiles in Europe and the Soviets did, this was a request for a Soviet withdrawal. By 1987, NATO deployments had changed this situation so that both sides would be removing missiles. Inclusion of medium-range missiles raised some controversy because many in the NATO alliance had long believed that the Warsaw Pact's overwhelming superiority in conventional military forces in Europe had to be offset by nuclear weapons, even if only of a type with very restricted range. In a nuclear-free Europe, they argued, the Eastern bloc would be more militarily powerful than the NATO countries; hence many questioned the wisdom of disarmament proposals that would expose these disparities without conventional reductions to offset them. The INF treaty, signed in December 1987, actually affected only about 4 percent of nuclear weapons. However, the treaty represented a major diplomatic break-through and raised hopes that progress could be made in other areas. One new feature was the treaty's provision for inspection teams resident on each other's territory near weapons facilities.

Nuclear Proliferation. Proliferation of nuclear weapons arose as a trou-blesome back-burner arms control issue. In 1981, Israel directed an air attack on an Iraqi nuclear reactor, alleged to be part of an Iraqi program to build nuclear weapons. Israel itself had long been suspected of nuclear weapons capability, and charges in 1986 that it had secretly stockpiled large numbers of nuclear weapons were unsettling. India had achieved nuclear weapons capability in 1974; in 1987, neighboring Pakistan appeared on the verge of doing likewise, despite the risk that U.S. aid would be cut off as a result.

Competition for Influence and the Use of Coercion

Each superpower accused the other of interfering in the affairs of other countries and of attempting to encroach upon each other's interests. Whereas in the 1970s the USSR had openly used force to advance its interests, in the 1980s it was the United States, Britain, and France that did so. The new U.S. aggressiveness in searching for means to reduce Soviet international influence included the use of sanctions and various forms of economic and military intervention. In the Third World, the United States made a concerted effort to identify strong allies and to support them while at the same time targeting neutral or nonaligned countries, as well as Soviet allies, as opponents.

The Soviet-European Gas Pipeline

The United States imposed sanctions several times during the 1980s. Domestic political pressure on Reagan's administration secured a lifting of the embargo on grain sales to the USSR, but the government maintained other restrictions. Although détente continued to be valued by the West European states, the United States launched an active campaign against it and, with sharply confrontational rhetoric, tried to break some of the links already established across the iron curtain. Attempts to enforce a ban on high technology sales to the Eastern bloc caused some problems with regard to a Soviet-European natural gas pipeline project that would bring natural gas from the USSR to Europe. Specifically, the United States sought to halt Western cooperation in the pipeline project by preventing the export of machinery or work contracts that would help build it—even sales by foreign-owned subsidiaries of U.S. companies. The United States worried that this pipeline could someday make Western Europe dependent on the USSR for its energy needs. The European states, however, generally viewed the pipeline as a mutually beneficial arrangement that would reduce their dependence on Middle Eastern fuel. Western Europeans also believed that the pipeline project would increase the USSR's vested interest in peaceful relations with the West.

The Polish Crisis

An economic and political crisis in Poland was one occasion for these Western differences to surface. When Polish workers defied their government in 1981 to create a revolutionary-minded independent national union, "Solidarity," they aroused Western sympathies. This time the Soviet Union did not invade its satellite but was responsible for the imposition of martial law. The United States led a campaign for sanctions against the Soviet Union—and against Poland's new, repressive military government, but other states refused to cooperate, on the grounds that sanctions against Poland would hurt the whole Polish people and would damage Poland's creditors in the West.

The Reagan Doctrine

The Reagan administration, particularly eager to compete with the USSR in the Third World, challenged established Soviet positions. In February 1986, President Reagan announced a determination to "enlarge the family of free nations," which came to be called the Reagan Doctrine:

> To those imprisoned in regimes held captive, to those beaten for daring to fight for freedom and democracy . . . we say to you tonight you are not alone freedom fighters. American will support . . . with moral and material assistance your right not just to fight and die for freedom but to fight and win freedom— to win freedom in Afghanistan, in Angola, in Cambodia, and in Nicaragua.[6]

The regimes Reagan referred to were Marxist-Leninist and were in fact all faced with armed opposition movements.[7] The United States did become involved in these struggles, although its involvement proceeded indirectly and cautiously, without clear military commitments of a kind that could lead to a U.S.-Soviet confrontation. The United States sent arms to the Afghan rebels, primarily through Pakistan; U.S. military aid reached the Angolan rebel movement UNITA, whose leader, Jonas Savimbi, has traveled widely in search of assistance; some U.S. aid went to the Kampuchean resistance.

Some U.S. politicians advocated U.S. aid to the Mozambican rebel group (known by the acronym RENAMO or the initials MNR—both meaning Mozambican National Resistance), which operates against the Marxist government of Mozambique. South Africa had been supporting this group for many years but in 1984 agreed to stop doing so in a treaty with Mozambique called the Nkomati accords. In return, Mozambique pledged not to harbor guerrillas of the African National Congress. (RENAMO is still active, and the Mozambican government has charged that South Africa still supports this armed force.)

U.S. Policy Toward Nicaragua. In the case of Nicaragua, U.S. policy was much more confrontational because what happened in Central America was deemed to be of great strategic importance to the United States. Reagan made his opposition to the government of Nicaragua clear during the 1979 presidential election campaign; after entering office, he accused Nicaragua of spreading subversion in Central America, denounced its government as undemocratic, and sought to mobilize local and international pressures against the Sandinista government. The Reagan administration criticized Nicaragua's warm relations with Cuba and growing dependence on the USSR for economic aid and military supplies. The United States warned the USSR against sending advanced fighter aircraft (MIG-23s) to Nicaragua, but other types of military aid continue to reach the Sandinistas. The United States also undermined efforts by Mexico, Venezuela, Colombia, and Panama (known as the Contadora group) to forge a negotiated settlement to conflict in the region. Instead, the United States undertook overt and covert measures to destabilize the Nicaraguan government by imposing an economic blockade on Nicaragua, sending military aid to its neighbors, conducting military maneuvers close to its borders, and mining its harbors. In an application of the Reagan Doctrine, the United States also financed and assisted armed opposition groups (known as the Contras, loosely grouped as the United Nicaraguan Opposition). This policy was controversial within the United States, but assistance to the Contras was continued under semiofficial and private auspices even when Congress had prohibited official military assistance.

The Nicaraguan Position. The Nicaraguans, however, denied spreading subversion (and the Reagan administration has had difficulty providing reliable evidence of such activity) and repeatedly stated that they believe in democracy (elections were held in 1984). The government has also declared that it will follow a nonaligned foreign policy and have ties with both East and West. U.S. policies have been very costly to the Nicaraguans, both in terms of lives and economic resources; Nicaragua has turned not only to the Soviet Union but also to Western European countries for economic and humanitarian aid.

Arias Peace Plan. Attempts by the local governments to promote peace resulted in the acceptance of a proposal of Costa Rican President Oscar Arias in August 1987. The plan, known as the Arias Plan or Guatemala Accords (because it was signed in Guatemala), called for cease-fires, the termination of foreign support for rebels, amnesty for all rebels, and pledges by signatory governments to move toward democratization. U.S. reaction was mixed: President Reagan publicly criticized the plan but became less critical after President Arias received the 1987 Nobel Peace prize; many in Congress were prepared to adjust U.S. policy to support the plan's implementation.

Efforts to implement the plan have proved to be very difficult. El Salvador and Guatemala opened negotiations with rebels, but those talks had not achieved success by January 1988. The government of Guatemala refused to agree to a cease-fire, while fighting in El Salvador continued despite a cease-fire there.

Nicaraguan implementation of the agreements was also partial. Some political prisoners were released, the opposition press was permitted to resume publication, and indirect talks were held with the Contras. However, the Contras ignored a Nicaraguan offer of a cease-fire, and the Reagan administration continued to demand aid for the Contras from Congress, a request with which Congress complied. The Sandinistas refused to lift the state of emergency, which would have restored full constitutional liberties, until U.S. support for the Contras was terminated. In January 1988, the deadline for the peace plan approached and it appeared that the plan would die. At the last minute, the Nicaraguans made major concessions, agreeing to lift the state of emergency, enter into direct talks with the Contras, and release more political prisoners. Thus the peace plan had a reprieve, but peace was still not at hand in Central America.

The Grenada Invasion. In October 1983, U.S. forces invaded the tiny Caribbean island of Grenada. A leftist, pro-Cuban regime there had been destabilized by a coup brought about by an even more radical group. The public disorder that followed provided the United States with a pretext for an attempt to put a pro-Western government into power. The invasion of Grenada also served to demonstrate U.S. willingness to use force in the region, especially where such action could forestall gains for the East and was evidently meant as a warning to the Nicaraguans.

Soviet Activities in the Third World

The Soviets also took steps to reinforce their own areas of influence in the Third World. In Southeast Asia, the USSR continued its military support of Vietnam, which made the occupation of Kampuchea possible. In return, the Soviet Union acquired access rights to Cam Ranh Bay in

Vietnam, thus extending its naval patrol areas south of China. Soviet arms shipments to Syria replaced losses incurred during fighting with Israel in 1982 and justified a Soviet personnel presence in sensitive areas. Soviet naval installations at the Dahlak islands off Ethiopia provided a Soviet military presence near the Indian Ocean, a supplement to its presence in Aden in South Yemen. Military and economic aid to Angola demonstrated Soviet determination to sustain the Marxist government there; however, the Soviets were cautious about risking military encounters with the South Africans, and Cuban troops in Angola reportedly kept away from border regions where South Africans were active. By contrast, the Soviets did not commit themselves to the defense of Mozambique, which was beleaguered by an armed rebel group supported by South Africa and suffered South African air attacks on several occasions in this period.

The Libyan Provocations and the U.S. Response

Greater U.S. willingness to use force was also demonstrated in its confrontational relations with Libya. The regime of Muamar Khaddafi was stridently anti-American, supportive of the most radical Palestinians, and widely implicated in sponsorship of various terrorist groups. Libya was also a major customer for Soviet arms, and its military expansionism was grounds for concern within Africa. Libyan troops were active in neighboring Chad, where they supported a rebel force against Hissein Habre's French-backed central government. Libyan forces invaded in 1971 to help the rebels take temporary control of the country and again in 1983, but then the United States sent military and economic assistance to Habre's government and pressed France to step in.

Libya's association with radical groups and its unorthodox diplomacy provoked many states (including Britain and a number of African countries) to break off diplomatic relations. The United States withdrew its ambassador in 1981, invoked economic sanctions, and took the lead in challenging Libya politically and militarily. In 1981, the U.S. navy, during exercises off the Libyan coast, shot down two intruding Libyan jets. Additional encounters occurred in 1983, and in 1986, U.S. airplanes conducted a surprise bombing raid on Libya's capital after a terrorist attack in Europe was traced to Libyan agents.

Constructive Engagement in Africa

An active U.S. approach to Africa also had an East-West emphasis. The United States lowered the priority of the effort to promote independence for Namibia and instead, under a policy known as constructive engagement, sought to emphasize the value of a positive relationship with South Africa, claiming that this position offered greater opportunities to influence and change its racial policies. Some people justified this position because of South Africa's value as a source of strategic minerals and as an anti-Soviet power in command of key shipping routes. The United States also tried to act as a mediator between South Africa and its Marxist neighbors, Mozambique and Angola. In Angola, both South Africa and the United States were supporting antigovernment forces of UNITA and made attempts to arrange a cease-fire that would link Namibian independence to withdrawal of Cuban forces from Angola.

Middle East Conflict

Conflict in the Middle East continued to frustrate both superpowers, which nonetheless sought to influence developments in the region. In 1982, Israel invaded Lebanon, once again attempting to quell the Palestinian military actions against Israel, which originated in camps and bases in southern Lebanon. When the Israeli army went all the way to Beirut, it created a major dilemma. Soviet-armed Syrian forces were poised nearby but had been hit hard before by the Israelis and chose not to engage them. However, Syrian units became actively involved in the fighting in Lebanon, where they attacked Palestinian groups loyal to Yasser Arafat. Lebanon's factions were warring among themselves but eventually permitted an evacuation of Arafat's PLO fighters by sea. U.S. military units joined British and French forces in an international peacekeeping force in Lebanon in 1983 that sought to shore up the Christian-dominated national government. The U.S. contingent became entangled in the fighting between local ethnic groups and was withdrawn when it became the object of terrorist attacks. (More than two hundred Americans were killed when a bomb destroyed a Marine barracks.)

Yet to a large extent the efforts to find East-West conflict axes everywhere were not fruitful. The revolutionary political change in Iran had produced a number of policy problems for the superpowers within the Persian Gulf region. The Iranian government aligned itself with the most extreme of the Palestinians and worked with Libya to organize other Arab states against Egypt. Iran's efforts to incite Islamic fundamentalists elsewhere against conservative Arab governments, its affiliation with terrorists and radical factions in Lebanon, and its territorial and political ambitions in Iraq and Kuwait split the Arab world and raised new issues that cut across familiar alignments.

The Iran-Iraq War

The Iran-Iraq war presented several dilemmas: Victory for either protagonist could threaten the interests of major states, but continued war interfered with oil production and could hamper the flow of energy resources to Western Europe and Japan. The United States was especially uneasy about political instability in the Persian Gulf because of the Soviet military presence in Afghanistan. Both the United States and the USSR remained officially neutral in the Iran-Iraq war that broke out in 1980, and both also gave strong support to UN efforts to secure a cease-fire between the warring parties. At the same time, each superpower took some steps to multiply its diplomatic options within the area.

The U.S. Response and Irangate. The United States initially stepped up its military and economic assistance to Pakistan, where several million Afghan refugees posed a major drain on the economy, and funneled increasing amounts of small arms aid to the Afghan resistance fighters (generally referred to as *mujahedin*). The United States also strove to build its ties with the states that were potential Iranian targets and took a strong public stance against arms sales to Iran by others. U.S.-Iranian hostility was also related to increased instances of terrorism and hostage-taking by groups affiliated with or supported by Iran; nevertheless, some in the U.S. government who were worried about the regional balance were interested in opening some channels to the Iranian regime. In 1986 it was revealed that President Reagan had authorized secret arms sales to Iran—first through Israeli mediation and then directly. These arms sales in 1985 and 1986 had violated official U.S. policy and been kept secret from Congress. Moreover, White House officials (National Security Adviser John Poindexter and his assistant, Lt. Col. Oliver North) produced as a byproduct a scheme to use profits from the Iranian arms sales to provide military aid to the Contras in Nicaragua—a type of aid that Congress had prohibited. The resulting scandal, dubbed Irangate by the media, discredited U.S. policy abroad and raised doubts about the competence and coherence of the Reagan administration at home.

The Soviet Response. The Soviet Union also sought ways to protect itself against unfavorable changes in the Persian Gulf. Although condemning U.S. policies in the area, the Soviet Union distanced itself from Libya, sought improved ties with conservative Arab regimes, and opened discussions with Israel in 1986 about reestablishing consular relations (the USSR had broken full diplomatic relations with Israel in 1967). At the same time, the Soviets also responded to Iranian interest in exporting petroleum products, by means of a pipeline from Iran through the Soviet Union to West Europe (the pipeline had originally been constructed for natural gas in an agreement with the shah).

Competition Between the Superpowers. Within the Persian Gulf area, the United States and the USSR competed for influence among the small oil-rich nations affected by the war. In 1987, against a background of Iranian attacks on shipping in the Gulf, both superpowers offered the protection of their flags to Kuwaiti tankers. The war between Iran and Iraq served as a reminder that local conflicts have their own logic and are not always susceptible to external solutions.

THE NORTH-SOUTH AGENDA

Trade, debt, and revolution were the major issues on the North-South agenda during the 1980s. The legitimacy of the agenda received new challenges due to the swing to the right of important members of the Northern coalition, expanding the North's ideological spectrum and causing more acute controversy over the definition and relative importance of the Southern issues.

Economic Problems

Northern criticisms centered on the Southern states' responsibility for their own economic problems and on the political character of many economic issues. Rejection of the kind of multilateral international solutions most often proposed by the South was a central feature of these Northern criticisms. Although the North-South agenda in many ways became very important in world politics in the 1980s, little action was taken to address its issues except where Northern interests were directly and seriously threatened.

Global Negotiations

Southern states, despite some major splits on trade and energy matters, continued to defend an agenda for North-South discussions that included few new issues but that was presented in a new and less confrontational form: "global negotiations" between the North and South to explore the nature of international economic problems in general ways, rather than negotiations designed to secure agreements on specific remedies. This represented a new strategy of discussing all issues, ranging from trade to energy, under the rubric of an examination of the entire structure of the international economic system. The emphasis shifted from the need for a New International Economic Order to an argument that Southern and Northern economies were inextricably linked, that greater international economic efficiency could only come from "greater equity" and Southern growth. This Southern growth would help alleviate export slumps in the North, thereby contributing to the revitalization of Northern economies.[8] The South offered this argument most strongly as a justification for commodity price stabilization and for regulations which would stimulate trade.

The Group of 77's proposals for global negotiations, as modified by the United Nations Committee of the Whole in July 1980, included recommendations for changes in international economic institutions and practices as steps to improve global economic health. Southern states sought concessions that would facilitate access to Northern markets and still permit some protection of new industries in the South. However, trends in the international economy and in international politics were not favorable for increased Northern receptivity.

The South Loses the Sympathy of the North

On the one hand, the very serious problems afflicting Southern states were attracting more attention. On the other hand, these problems also highlighted Southern management and development failures that reduced the sympathy for Southern difficulties and made an issue of Southern capacity for improvement. Critics could blame the mounting debts of Third World states on poor planning or incompetence. Their repayment difficulties led in many cases to interventions by the World Bank and International Monetary Fund, which entailed austerity programs and internationally supervised financial management. These arrangements were humiliating for many states and often inflamed nationalist resentments. At the same time, drought, famine, and food shortages produced an emphasis on charitable emergency reflief rather than structural assistance directed at export development.

Several developments contributed to a deterioration in the South's ability to trade: Prices of raw materials declined, while the prices earned for manufactured products the South exported rose far less than the prices of imported products from the North. For non-oil-producing Southern states, the years from 1980 to 1987 generally saw a decline in net trade earnings, and as export earnings declined, Third World countries used up currency reserves and went further and further into debt. Ironically, economic successes in the South reduced the chances for Northern trade concessions. Several Southern newly industrialized countries (NICs) were emerging as vigorous competitors with advanced countries in certain areas, particularly in textiles.

The North Moves to the Right

Political shifts in some important Northern countries have also intensified criticism of the Southern states. The Reagan administration came into office rejecting the very notion of a South, opposing multilateral institutions and negotiations, and asserting that its economic concern lay primarily in improving the economy of the United States. Furthermore, the administration at first accused the Soviet Union of being responsible for instability in the South and rejected the idea that internal economic, social, and political conditions produced discontent. Both the United States and Great Britain rejected plans for global economic management, pressing instead for freer markets and greater scope for private investment in Southern states.

At the same time, economic troubles in the major industrial states of the North meant that fewer resources would be available for aid or for development loan funds. Economic relationships with Southern states were more closely scrutinized for direct benefits for Northern economies. In the United States and Great Britain, official economic policies emphasized the "trickle-down" principle: Promoting growth in the Northern economies would eventually benefit the poorer states. A number of U.S. initiatives sought to shift the emphasis within the South to the need for economic growth and hence to private-sector initiatives and a better climate for private investment in Southern countries. Moreover, the Western part of the North (especially the United States and to some extent also Great Britain and West Germany) firmly resisted any effort to replace existing international economic institutions with United Nations institutions, where voting could give great weight to the more numerous Southern states.

The Eastern Bloc Looks Inward

The socialist countries also displayed concern for their own domestic economic development. The three leaders who succeeded Leonid Brezhnev as head of the Party in the USSR each stressed the primacy of the Soviet Union's own economic needs. Soviet statements advised Third World states that the USSR had a limited ability to help them and that they would have to rely on their own resources to build socialism. Although Soviet bloc aid to Southern countries continued, many prospective clients have been disappointed in the 1980s with its volume. For example, in 1977 the USSR had signed a Friendship and Cooperation Treaty with desperately poor Mozambique but in 1981 refused this self-described Marxist-Leninist country admission to COMECON, the Warsaw Pact's economic coordinating body. The USSR has also emphasized the principle of mutual profitability in its economic relations with Southern states and has relaxed its central economic controls to permit joint projects between Soviet trade associations and private foreign capital.

The Cancun Meeting

Global negotiations got off to a shaky start with an informal North-South summit in Cancun, Mexico, in October 1981. The Group of 77 sent a delegation of thirteen; nine Northern states completed the group. President Reagan decided to attend, provided there be no effort to discuss substantive issues, no final statement, and no Cuban presence. No progress was achieved on specific issues although support was expressed for global negotiations in the United Nations. Support for those negotiations ultimately broke down due to attempts to preempt any agreement introducing new international economic regulatory bodies.

Trade

By 1983, the Group of 77 had altered its strategy somewhat by pressing for negotiations on specific urgent problems. Thus structural reform of the international economic system fell in priority, as attention shifted to the need for immediate action on trade and debt issues. Nonetheless, UNCTAD VI, held in June 1983, proved another disappointing confrontation: The conferees rejected Southern proposals for increases in development financing from the International Monetary Fund and for an international conference on development funding, and all the discussion on trade problems for commodity exporters did not stipulate final acceptance of the commodity fund.

Commodities

The Common Fund program for commodity price stabilization had been designed to help remedy one source of Third World economic difficulties. Prolonged negotiations on this issue had produced an agreement in 1980, but as of 1987, this agreement had still not been ratified. Although the deadline was extended twice, the ninety state ratifications required had still not been obtained by 1987. The United States was a conspicuous abstainer, although several large industrialized countries did join the fund. Inflation, poor trade balances of Third World states, and price uncertainties discouraged many important members of the United Nations.

Many Northern states were important commodity producers and shared an interest, in some cases, in price stabilization with Southern countries. However, given uneasiness about the new regulatory bodies, many of these Northern commodity producers preferred to rely on their own economic strength and traditional trading mechanisms and institutions to protect their interests, rather than join in the Southern plan. For example, although the International Tin Agreement (ITA) came into force in 1982 to regulate the tin market in order to cushion consumers and producers against price and production swings, the absence of the major tin market countries has made this agreement ineffective. The world's largest tin consumer (the United States) and two major producers (Bolivia and the USSR) have refused to join.

Trade: Liberalization or Protectionism

The North addressed the South's general trade problems at GATT. The United States advocated trade liberalization as a solution to international trade problems. However, the Northern states (including the United States) experienced increasing domestic pressures for protectionism that conflicted with liberalized trade practices. The 1982 GATT meeting revealed fairly deep disagreements between the United States and the EEC concerning the concept of "graduation" (whereby certain Southern states are judged to have improved economically so that they no longer need special economic benefits) and about textiles and steel. Conflict within GATT was particularly intense between the European Economic Community and several Southern producers (including South Korea, Brazil, Malaysia, India, and Hong Kong) concerning textiles: Problems arose over competition between Northern and Southern textile producers and demands by these Southern producer states for access to Northern markets.

Southern states are caught in a dilemma on trade liberalization issues. The South's interest in access to Northern markets is in harmony with free-trade principles, but its desire to protect or subsidize its fledgling local industries against Northern competition is not.

Lomé III

Trade problems were confronted more successfully in a more limited forum. Relations between the EEC and the countries of the ACP (African, Caribbean, and Pacific) group presented a condensed version of the North-South agenda. In 1983 and 1984, these two groups negotiated a third time on the Lomé Convention, which regulated their economic relations. The major issues negotiated included market access, commodity prices, and the terms and targets of development assistance. The previous Lomé conventions had eliminated duties for nearly all ACP products exported to Europe, although some were subject to quotas or could be restricted where they came into damaging competition with European products. Lomé III registered some small improvements for the Southern states: It raised some important quotas and added some new products to the commodity-price-stabilization program. The aid fund did not increase as much as the ACP countries had hoped, but a broader variety of projects were made eligible for assistance. The convention added some compromise political declarations that responded to ACP requests by denouncing apartheid and pledging protection for immigrant workers in Europe. ACP countries satisfied European positions by pledging to respect human rights and to encourage and protect private investment. All told, Lomé III represented marginal improvements in an agreement that already had established a structure for accommodating Southern interests through negotiations.[9]

Changes in Trade Policy

A final trade issue involved changes in Northern policy toward development financing and multilateral financial institutions. The World Bank has drawn heavy Northern criticism and been accused of excessive lending for public-sector projects to the neglect of private initiatives. In fact, its lending has long been designated for traditional public-sector concerns such as improvements in roads and railways. By the early 1980s the bank also devoted considerable resources to energy development projects. The Reagan administration called upon the development banks to emphasize funding that would promote private investment as the source of capital for development projects. At the same time, the administration planned to reduce U.S. contributions both to development "soft loan" programs by up to 45 percent and to the International Development Association (IDA). Not all members of the North agreed with these policies.

Debt

The 1982 Debt Crisis

Causes of the Crisis. Southern debt became a very serious issue in the 1980s. By 1982, the debt of Third World countries had reached such magnitude that remedial action was vital.[10] A number of factors provided the elements of the crisis that exploded in 1982. The circumstances vary for each country and there are significant regional differences as well, but several general factors were at work. First, the oil price increase of 1979 hurt the ability of major oil-importing borrowers to achieve the growth necessary to finance their debts. Second, a significant proportion of the debt was tied to floating interest rates; thus, as interest rates rose internationally, so did the interest payments demanded of international borrowers. High interest rates were part of the larger recession that had hit the North in the late 1970s. Northern imports from the South declined, as did Southern profits from trading. Oil-importing states were hurt first by the declining profitability of trade, but in the early 1980s, a drop in oil prices hurt the financial status of oil-producer states as well. Southern states thus became less and less able to manage their debts, as income declined and interest charges soared.

Austerity Programs. Eventually, indebted states were forced to adopt domestic economic austerity programs as they fought to make payments while still meeting basic domestic economic needs. Additional loans were available to states in economic difficulties, but these tended to be short-term, high interest loans. Increases in short-term indebtedness together with austerity programs contributed to further declines in domestic productivity, as exhibited in the case of Mexico. When that government announced in August 1982 that it would not be able to meet its debt obligations, North and South agreed that something needed to be done.

The Role of the IMF. For a number of reasons, the policies and approaches for dealing with the debt problem have become a major North-South issue. Despite many differences over the proper role and policy of the International Monetary Fund, the Northern states moved to seek solutions to the debt problem through this Northern-dominated institution. At the same time, individual governments and private banks were persuaded to support the IMF's approach rather than suffer the consequences of multiple defaults. In 1983, the International Monetary Fund's Special Drawing Rights quota available to Third World debtors was increased and emergency funds made available for debtors. In addition, the IMF applied pressure to commercial banks to continue to make loans to their Southern debtors to prevent total default. The IMF took on the role of rescuer and, together with major Northern governments, devised individual financial packages for Southern debtors.

The bulk of this debt was actually owed to commercial banks, which had become increasingly active as international creditors in the late 1970s, as the income expansion associated with oil revenues made Third World countries seem attractive credit risks. However, because Third World debts were also owed to public creditors, negotiations for debt rescheduling and refinancing became quite complicated. Generally, private creditors (banks) negotiated debts in the so-called New York or London clubs, while public debts were negotiated at the Paris club. Meanwhile, the IMF would negotiate a general debt reorganization agreement, and at some point these separate negotiations had to be reconciled.[11]

The Mexican crisis was followed by more than thirty additional cases in which debtor states were unable to meet loan and interest payments. The IMF took a major role in renegotiating debt-payment schedules for these countries, providing additional funds, and setting terms for Southern economic performance to ensure progress in meeting loan obligations.

The Reaction of the South

The reaction of Southern debtors to their financial crises and to IMF conditions for debt relief have varied. Mexico has been commonly regarded as the model debtor by the North. It has accepted and implemented IMF requirements, despite the sacrifices this has forced upon the Mexican people. However, many Southern states resented the tutelage of this essentially Northern institution. Peru, under President Alan Garcia, has simply announced that it will not utilize more than 10 percent of its export earnings for debt payments. Argentina has been quite aggressive in response to IMF requirements, refusing to impose on the Argentinean people the required costs of reduced wages and social programs. Some countries, such as Nigeria, have simply refused IMF debt relief completely, finding the conditions totally unacceptable. In a few instances, austerity programs imposed by the IMF and foreign banks have precipitated political unrest (in Sudan, rioting in 1985 that eventually brought down the pro-American government was at least partly related to price increases produced by such programs).

The Reaction of the North

Northern states have not been in agreement about the solutions to the debt problem. Neither Northern states nor their commercial banks are equally exposed, and they have different regional concerns. The Southern states have argued that the causes of the debt crisis did not lie solely in Southern economic policies. They saw the origins of the problem in larger global economic conditions and in the economies of certain Northern states, particularly the United States. The North, however, has assumed that with proper domestic policies in the South and growth in the North, the debt problem would diminish. The United States moved away from this position marginally after yet another downturn in Southern economic conditions in 1985. In the Baker Plan, named after U.S. Treasury Secretary James Baker, the United States called for commercial bank lending of $20 billion over three years, increased private investment in the South, and more World Bank loans.

By the end of 1987 the United States recognized that some of the South's debt would never be repaid. In January 1988, a new idea was proposed that was designed to help Mexico repay some of its debt and that conceivably could be applied to other debtors. Banks to whom Mexico owed money agreed to exchange the old debt for a new debt of lower value paid for with Mexican bonds backed by the U.S. Treasury. This innovative plan represents a new effort by public and private financial institutions to reduce the debt burden.

Whatever the position of the North on the debt crisis, the fact remains that the international institutions called upon to alleviate the crisis, the IMF in particular, were not designed to manage a debt crisis of such magnitude. The IMF was established to ensure international liquidity and correct occasional balance-of-payments problems. The debt crisis reveals the extent to which the international economic system lacks leadership today. The response to the crisis has been piecemeal and has produced no general systemwide program for debt alleviation.

Revolution

A final item on the North-South agenda throughout the 1980s was the persistence of political instability in the South. Its causes and the appropriate responses to it have been contentious issues within the North and between the North and the South.

Causes of Political Instability

The North has split in identifying the causes of political instability. The United States, Great Britain, and West Germany have seen it as an East-West issue and accused the East of fomenting or benefiting from conflict. This position has been opposed by France, Holland, Spain, Portugal, and the Scandinavian countries. They have identified internal causes of political instability and have seen it as an issue that most properly belonged on the North-South agenda. The South has been divided: Many in the South have seen instability and revolution to be a result of North-South problems. Others, particularly those tightly allied with the United States (such as El Salvador), have identified the problem in East-West terms.

Responses to Political Instability

United States: Military Aid. Responses to political instability have differed as well: The policy approach advocated and followed by the United States was essentially a military one—the increased use of intervention. The Reagan administration has also shifted its aid policy to favor military aid (direct and indirect) over developmental aid, and bilateral aid over multilateral aid (bilateral aid having the advantage of giving the United States more leverage). In 1981, U.S. security assistance constituted 55 percent of total U.S. aid, and development aid amounted to 45 percent. By 1985, security assistance constituted 67 percent of the total; development aid, 33 percent.[12]

The Dilemma of South Africa. The preoccupation of the administration with the East-West conflict was one reason for its reluctance to support the struggle of the African National Congress against the government of South Africa. Worries about the Eastern affiliations of antigovernment groups (including the ANC) were responsible in part for the U.S. support of the South African government's plans for gradual reform and U.S. opposition to international action against the regime. However, many states took the position that the South African government's racism and its reluctance to risk loss of its power were the problems. Meanwhile, there were internal disorders associated with the introduction of a new constitution (which failed to give voting power to the black population). Domestic U.S. political pressure in 1985 and 1986 ultimately led the United States to join many other Northern and Southern countries in imposing sanctions on South Africa. Although international sanctions against South Africa have indicated strong global condemnation of the regime, so far it has not been clear how effective such sanctions will be in ending apartheid.

European Views. Other Northern states have disagreed with the Reagan administration in its response to revolution and instability. Many have opposed the U.S. campaign to overthrow the government of Nicaragua. In general, European opponents of the Reagan administration's policies toward Central America have interpreted the crises there as Western Hemispheric manifestations of North-South differences that reflected the history of injustice in the region. These critics would have preferred a policy to transform the social, political, and economic structures in the region that caused such conflict: massive reforms in agriculture, land distribution, tax laws, and income distribution to prevent radical forces from taking control.

One must be careful not to oversimplify Western divisions concerning the causes of Third World instability. In general, the United States, Great Britain, and West Germany have often seen demands for change in the Third World as a challenge to the West and victory for the East. Other Western states, such as France, Spain, Greece, and Sweden, have been less suspicious of change and argue that it is inconsequential for the East-West conflict. However, even these states have resisted change in some cases: France, for example, has been exceptionally protective of its ties to African states and has had continuous conflicts with Libya concerning Libya's intrusion into Chad. Furthermore, not even the Reagan administration has opposed all instability and political change in the Third World. The decline and fall of the Ferdinand Marcos dictatorship in the Philippines and of the "Baby Doc" Duvalier dictatorship in Haiti were welcomed throughout the North, including the United States.

The Southern View. The Southern view of political instability has also been complicated, since Southern states have varied greatly in ideology and in policies toward their local neighbors. Nevertheless, in general, revolutionary movements were more likely to be seen as responses to internal problems than as a result of externally driven subversion. Southern states also have tended to oppose superpower intervention in the affairs of Third World states. Thus, even as radically antileftist a government as that in Guatemala under the military (pre-1986) publicly refused to support U.S. efforts to depose the government of Nicaragua. African states opposed support for insurgencies against the government of Angola; however, there has been strong and consistent Southern opposition to the South African government and at least verbal support for opposition groups like ANC and SWAPO. In 1986, the entire British Commonwealth reached a point of possible dissolution over Great Britain's reluctance to impose sanctions on South Africa.

In short, the issue of political instability appeared on the North-South agenda as well as on the East-West agenda and demonstrated how the definition of the issue, the policy preferences supported by different governments, and the solutions advocated to resolve problems could vary depending upon the perceptions of leaders in different states. When a great deal of disagreement over an issue has existed, it has been difficult to determine the proper agenda for it.

THE GLOBAL AGENDA

The global agenda during the 1980s was full: The most important issues were economic problems, unresolved conflicts, and ideological controversies over globalism. A variety of general issues received attention, including terrorism, population control, housing problems, health, the status of women, education, and energy. There was a fair amount of contention over community issues like the law of the sea, nuclear-free zones, and refugee rights. Despite the fact that little meaningful action was taken on these issues, international conferences, exchanges, and agreements established some rough consensus on their importance for the whole global community.

Disarray in the International Economic System
Tops the Agenda

The global issue of highest priority in the 1980s was the need for order in the international economy. Trade and currency problems were of special importance. The dominant economies in the capitalist system suffered from a variety of ills including inflation, slow growth, unemployment, and in some cases (including the United States and Britain), severe trade deficits. Protectionist inclinations increased generally: Almost every country had a particular product or sector where weakness relative to international competition made protectionist policies attractive. Domestic political pressures for relief from foreign competition drove many governments to institute barriers to foreign goods or to seek voluntary reductions in imports; states also made adjustments to currency exchange values to manage trade flows. In the United States, protectionism was a response to the dramatic increase in the trade deficit (between 1982 and 1986 it had risen from $36 to $175 billion).

A GATT ministerial meeting in 1982 reflected the global economic problems. The meeting did not go well: The participants had hoped that protectionism could be halted, but they reached only a weak agreement to "resist" further protectionism and "study" agricultural trade and industries negatively affected by import fluctuations. Disputes have continued among the industrialized countries regarding acceptable measures for alleviating global economic problems and, in many instances, have pitted the United States against Europe and Japan. On several occasions the United States has attempted to press other countries to help it cut its trade deficit.

Causes of the U.S. Trade Deficit

A Strong Dollar. One of the major reasons, according to conventional wisdom, for the U.S. trade deficit has been a strong dollar, with a value high relative to other currencies. This has permitted Americans to buy easily in foreign markets, but it has made it difficult for U.S. goods to be sold abroad. In September 1985, the so-called Group of Five (the United States, Japan, West Germany, Britain, and France) met to consider techniques for lowering the value of the dollar. Although they succeeded in making the dollar decline, it was not clear that this was entirely beneficial because the prospect of a rapid and uncontrolled decline in the value of the dollar caused concern and economic problems for others. In fact, by 1987, the *decline* in the value of the dollar had become a serious problem, threatening to contribute to another worldwide recession. The issues of currency value and trade restrictions became interlaced and affected the entire international political economy.[13]

The U.S. Budget Deficit. Although the position of individual countries has varied, a stalemate has existed for the international political economy since 1986, making corrections for chronic economic problems difficult to achieve and consensus on overall reform of the system impossible. The Europeans and Japanese have accused the United States of causing the global problems through its enormous budget deficits. (In 1986, the United States became the world's largest debtor-nation.) Although the United States has pledged to reduce its deficit, it has not yet done so.

The stalemate regarding reform of the international economic system and adjustments in the economic policies of the individual members of that system was manifested again in October 1987 when the U.S. stock market "crashed." On October 19 the market fell a total of 508 points, or 22.6 percent. This was followed by dramatic declines in the stock markets of other countries. Although there was considerable debate about the causes of the crash, the state of the U.S. economy and in particular its budget and trade deficits were blamed by economists and political leaders worldwide. The Reagan administration pledged to meet with Congress and devise a plan for immediate deficit reduction, but by early 1988 there was no major change of policy. By the beginning of 1988 the value of the dollar had declined. Although this improved U.S. exports, the decline was precarious, and the United States, Japan, and West Germany struggled to keep the value of the dollar from slipping too low. Other economic problems, such as the Japanese and West German trade surpluses, continued to be contentious issues in the West during the early days of 1988.

Unfair Trading Practices. The United States, for its part, has accused its OECD trading partners of unfair trade practices and an unwillingness to accept their share of the responsibility for putting the world economy back in order.[14] In 1985, the United States even filed suit against the EEC, Japan, Korea, and Brazil to recover damages attributed to alleged government subsidies of exports. In 1987, the United States imposed sanctions on some Japanese products to protest Japanese import restrictions and unfair competitive practices.

GATT Responses

In September 1986, GATT members agreed to an ambitious agenda for trade talks, including agricultural subsidies, foreign investment restrictions, and trade in service areas such as banking. GATT sought to address trade restraints of various kinds, such as subsidies and finance and investment restrictions. However, its actions have not dissuaded its members from these occasional resorts to punitive measures or threats of trade reprisals.

International Violence

Invasions and Wars

Conflicts presented a different sort of global issue. Invasions and wars that occurred in the period from 1980 to 1987 were of interest to most states, but no effective methods for asserting a global interest against violence were found.

The war between Iran and Iraq, which began in 1980, proved destructive not only to the two countries involved but also to the oil industry, to shipping in nearby areas, and to the populations and territory of neighboring states. Yet international mediation efforts proved unable to halt the fighting, and arms continued to flow to each of the belligerents, with no end in sight in 1987. Iran's fundamentalist Islam was explicitly hostile to the established order in most of the Middle East, and many governments in the region feared this fundamentalism could be used to weaken or topple their own regimes from within.

A short war in Latin America centered on an old territorial dispute. In 1982, Argentina occupied and claimed the Falkland Islands (known to the Argentines as the Malvinas Islands), which are located in the Atlantic Ocean, several hundred miles from the coast of Argentina. Great Britain, which had administered the islands as a colony, sent a naval task force that retook the islands by force. In September 1982, Israel invaded Lebanon, producing a short-term occupation marked by excesses of communal violence and massacres of Palestinians by their local Lebanese enemies. Disorder in Lebanon has continued to attract military interventions by outsiders: In 1987, Syrian forces moved in to the capital city, Beirut, where rival armed groups had destroyed order and where hostage taking was rampant. The South African government has conducted armed raids or bombing attacks on its neighboring states, primarily Mozambique and Angola. These raids were allegedly directed at leaders or assets of groups dedicated to the liberation of Namibia or of the blacks within South Africa.

In Afghanistan, Soviet troops and the Afghan army continued fighting against a popular insurrection. The Soviets insisted that the problem was external intervention and promised that their troops would leave when order was restored. Nonetheless the Soviets took some steps to defuse international criticism of their military presence in Afghanistan, including offers to form a coalition Afghan government that would include some rebels and token troop withdrawals. "Proximity talks" also took place between Afghan and Pakistani representatives through the agency of a UN mediator, but these talks did not have any real effect on the fighting in Afghanistan.

Neither the international (UN) condemnations of some of these actions nor internationally brokered solutions had impact on the belligerents. Increasingly it seemed that international bodies were irrelevant to conflict. Clearly, the parties involved in these conflicts preferred to trust in the use of force to advance their own interests.

Terrorism

Terrorism was a difficult issue for the international community in the 1980s. Western citizens and government officials were the object of terrorist attacks in France, West Germany, Greece, Turkey, Italy, and Lebanon. European terrorists came from a variety of radical as well as some ethnically defined extremist groups (like the Basques and the Armenians), but Middle Eastern terrorists drew most attention internationally. These terrorists were responsible for assassinations, plane bombings, hijackings, and hostage takings. In some cases, they demanded release of other terrorists or Arabs imprisoned by Israel during its sorties into Lebanon. Some of the groups involved were not identified with a particular state, although Libya, Iran, and Syria have been implicated in official sponsorship or encouragement of terrorism.

Many Southern states have resisted international efforts to combat terrorism because of their sympathy for national liberation groups. These states have complained that the terrorist label is often used unfairly to justify repressing such groups, and they have condemned armed reprisals against terrorists (for example, Israeli air strikes against the PLO headquarters in Tunis in 1985 and a U.S. air strike against Khaddafi's headquarters in Libya in 1986). Terrorism remains extremely difficult to control.

Refugees

In modern times refugees have posed delicate political problems in world politics. Between 1980 and 1987 natural disasters, wars, and politics lent great urgency to the problems of refugee rights and refugee relief. Drought and war in Africa produced millions of refugees in several countries, for example, Ethiopia, Sudan, and Chad. The war in Afghanistan has driven approximately three million refugees into neighboring Pakistan; Vietnam's presence in Kampuchea drove about one million into Thailand. Because large groups of refugees have created enormous logistical problems regarding food, housing, and repatriation, host countries have desperately sought international aid in assuming the burden of caring for such people.

Globalism as an Ideological Issue on the Agenda

Ideology had become an issue between East and West, and ideological conflicts spilled over onto the global agenda in the 1980s as well. One manifestation of this was the controversy over the UN's regulatory role. Many smaller states believed that the UN should regulate the use of environmental resources and establish rules and standards for international trade and commerce. Controversy over global regulations was a political issue with important philosophical aspects. To be sure, regulation of world economic activity by UN bodies in which all states have one vote puts the wealthy industrial states at a disadvantage. But because most of the wealthy states also have free-market economies, they resented the socialist inclinations of many advocates of global regulation and were reluctant to accept the principle of economic regulation by international political agencies. Several issues illustrate these practical and philosophical conflicts.

The Law of the Sea treaty represented twelve years of painstaking international negotiations. A U.S. decision in 1982 to reject the treaty was a major defeat for globalism. Specifically, the United States, Britain, and West Germany objected to provisions for deep seabed mining, which presumed that the resources found in the deep seabed were planetary property. According to the proposed treaty, private exploitation could proceed only if some mining sites were set aside to generate revenues that would flow to an international body, as a kind of global tax. Mining technology was also to be shared. This degree of international political control over private economic activity was not tolerable to many economically powerful states.

The failure of the treaty has served to symbolize other discontents over global regulation within the United Nations. A similar controversy developed over proposals to introduce UN supervision over the Antarctic. A treaty setting up a cooperative arrangement among various states that conducted scientific experiments in Antarctica or had territorial claims there was already in effect. The Antarctic Treaty signatories firmly resisted proposals to impose UN oversight on their activities.

Discontent with the United Nations itself as an organization was reflected in disputes over budget and over wasteful and politicized management of UN funds. One such squabble led to U.S. and British withdrawal from the United Nations Educational, Scientific, and Cultural Organization (UNESCO) in 1986. Replacement of UNESCO's controversial director in 1987 offered hope that UNESCO could re-earn Western support. A decision by the United States to cut its contributions to the overall UN budget was particularly serious, since the United States alone accounted for 25 percent of the organization's regular funding. By 1987, a special UN commission had proposed a number of organizational and financial reforms to trim costs and improve efficiency.

*   *   *

Conclusions

East-West tensions rose in the 1980s, although the nuclear standoff kept the superpowers talking about arms control and careful about risking direct encounters. The United States took a confrontational position, challenging rhetorically, physically, and politically the Soviet Union's presence and influence. The use of force was common between 1980 and 1987. Soviet troops fought to subdue the Afghan population, the United States used force against Grenada and Libya, and Britain went to war with Argentina. France fought against Libyan-backed rebels in Chad; South Africa against Angola and Mozambique; Israel and Syria in Lebanon. Iran and Iraq fought a protracted war, and insurgencies persisted in Kampuchea, Angola, Mozambique, Ethiopia, and Nicaragua.

The world economy was in disarray, as key industrial states found it difficult to cooperate on common means of stabilization. Trade deficits and heavy indebtedness in the South elicited pleas for help that may yet provoke globally cooperative economic action. At the end of 1987, rejection of cooperative solutions to both political and economic problems meant that simmering conflicts persisted on all three agendas.

Notes

1. See excerpts from a speech by President Ronald Reagan on March 8, 1983, in *Facts on File*, March 11, 1983, pp. 165–166.

2. President Reagan's State of the Union Address, February 4, 1986, in *Facts on File*, February 7, 1986, pp. 76–77.

3. Both the USSR (1986) and the People's Republic of China (1987) signed the protocols of the South Pacific Nuclear Free Zone Convention (an agreement known as SPNFZ or "spinfiz"), but the United States had not done so as of late 1987. A

major issue behind this convention was a protest against port visits by nuclear-powered or nuclear-armed ships. In fact, in 1986 New Zealand was viewed as having suspended its participation in its military alliance with the United States and Australia (the ANZUS pact) over this issue. (As a matter of policy, both superpowers have refused to acknowledge whether or not their warships were carrying nuclear weapons.)

4. The USSR had announced that it would not be the first to use nuclear weapons in a war and challenged the United States to make a similar "no first use" declaration. However, the United States has not done so because it has believed that if the Soviets worried that even a conventional attack could provoke a nuclear response they would be deterred from attacking Europe.

5. Confusion persisted about the precise terms of the package proposal discussed. U.S. participants have insisted that only intercontinental and intermediate-range missiles were to be eliminated. See James Schlesinger, "Reykjavik and Revelations: A Turn of the Tide?" and Michael Mandelbaum and Strobe Talbott, "Reykjavik and Beyond," both in Foreign Affairs, Winter, 1986-87, pp. 426–446, and pp. 215–234.

6. Facts on File, February 7, 1986, p. 77.

7. Marxist Ethiopia faced an insurgency by separatists in the province of Eritrea. Some of these were leftists who had previously enjoyed the support of the socialist bloc. However, after the emergence of a leftist central government in Ethiopia, the Soviets abandoned the Eritreans.

8. John Ruggie, "Another Round, Another Requiem? Prospects for the Global Negotiations," in Jagdish N. Bhagwati and John G. Ruggie, eds., Power, Passions and Purpose: Prospects for North-South Negotiations (Cambridge: MIT Press, 1984), p. 34.

9. Tony Hill, "Africa and the European Community: The Third Lomé Convention," in Africa South of the Sahara, 1985-86 (London: Europa, 1986), pp. 60–69.

10. Cynthia Bogdanowicz-Bindert, "World Debt: The U.S. Reconsiders," Foreign Affairs, Winter, 1985-86, p. 261. Overall debt grew from $134 billion in 1974 to $830 billion in 1984.

11. Charles Lipson, "The International Organization of Third World Debt," in Jeffry Frieden and David Lake, eds., International Political Economy (New York: St. Martin's, 1987), pp. 327–328.

12. United States Agency for International Development, Summary Tables, FY 1985.

13. For a detailed account of current trade problems see I. M. Destler, American Trade Politics: System Under Stress (Washington, D.C.: Institute for International Economics, 1986).

14. See Leonard Silk, "The U.S. and the World Economy," Foreign Affairs: America and the World, 1986, pp. 458–476; and Lester Thurow, "America, Europe and Japan: A Time to Dismantle the World Economy," in Frieden and Lake, International Political Economy.

CONCLUSION

This survey of world politics from 1945 to 1987 was designed to help the reader achieve an orderly understanding of complex events by focusing on three changing agendas. The East-West, North-South, and global agendas each represent clusters of issues that have reflected dominant but distinctive perspectives on international problems. When we identified these changing sets of issues we have had to provide some details about circumstances and outcomes. However, our purpose was to provide a guide to recent history, not a condensed narrative. We have attempted to convey contemporary priorities without pretending to offer definitive analysis. We hoped that the reader would see that issues arise in world politics not only because states have different interests, not only because states differ about appropriate solutions for problems, but also because there is controversy about what the problems are. Because action to resolve a problem is unlikely to be widely accepted or successful so long as problems are perceived differently, the definition of a problem is an area of very real conflict. It can be a battlefield for proponents of opposing interests who wish to prevent action by other states or to preserve a free hand for themselves.

For each of the three agendas, distinct impressions have emerged: The importance of each agenda for world politics as a whole and the world's population has differed. Policymakers and citizens in the East and the West have tended to believe that the East-West agenda has been dominant. In many ways this agenda has powerfully shaped all our lives, although both the reasons for the prominence of this agenda and the nature of its leading issues have changed significantly. At first, East-West issues reflected the ideological antagonisms and political rivalry associated with the rise of the Soviet Union to the position of a major European power. Over time, many of the issues surrounding the formation of the Eastern bloc in Europe were resolved or faded. The USSR and its allies are still adversaries for the West, and their socialist political systems are still resented; but attention has shifted somewhat to the activities and capacities of the Eastern states in areas outside Europe.

The East-West agenda continues to be the agenda wherein the world's most dangerous issues of war and peace are debated. At this writing, early 1988, the position of the United States and the USSR as antagonists with nuclear military capabilities of approximately equal strength is the central reason for the significance attributed to the East-West agenda, whatever specific disagreements and conflicts of interest may arise otherwise. Their competitive relationship has been a troubling backdrop for conflicts everywhere, even though it has become clear that both superpowers have found it increasingly difficult to control the actions of other states. Arms control has remained a tense but active sphere for limited cooperation and continual dialogue between the superpowers.

Whereas the success of the East and West in controlling the nuclear contest and preventing nuclear war determines the destiny of the planet as a whole, the North-South agenda involves life and death struggles on a daily basis for the majority of the world's population. Over two-thirds of the world's population lives in the South, and for these people the East-West agenda is clearly secondary to the items debated on the North-South agenda. This agenda has had a fundamentally antagonistic quality, reflecting deeply divergent interests between states that are basically powerful and affluent, and those that are not. Issues on the North-South agenda express frustrations of the weak and the many grievances of those who believe themselves to have been unjustly deprived of the possibility of a decent standard of living and condemned to lives of endless poverty, due to the legacy of colonialism and the ongoing policies of the politically and economically powerful. Many North-South issues are in the area of political economy, and economic problems are at the heart of the political and ideological debates they generate.

The articulation of a highly visible North-South agenda itself has represented a victory of sorts for the South, since a major complaint has been the refusal of wealthier states to recognize the problems of the poorer, Southern ones. Real disparities of power have made it easier for the North to refuse to accept and work with the issues as the South has defined them. Yet it is also the relative weakness of the Southern states that has encouraged them to work together to make demands and to force the North to take notice of them within institutions where their greater numbers have made a difference; thus their appeals for justice might receive more sympathy.

In the immediate postwar years, the global agenda was of great importance, but over time the attractiveness of global cooperative approaches to world problems has diminished. Initially, this cluster of issues was related to ambitious plans for restructuring international relations, that is, setting up multinational institutions to keep the peace, establish rules and norms to guide international behavior of states, and solve common problems. All of these purposes require a considerable degree of cooperation, but East-West and North-South tensions have reduced the common ground available for such cooperation. It is apparent that even the most fundamental consensus (against aggression) can dissolve in controversies over what constitutes a legitimate use of force. Armed conflict between states is still a global agenda item, but there has been very little concerted international action to control or moderate such conflict.

Political issues such as decolonization, racism, and terrorism have appeared regularly on the global agenda, although there have been many disagreements about the cases where these labels are appropriate and few occasions for truly international action on these issues. Definition of issues as global ones has clearly been controversial probably because doing so implies exposure of individual state actions to possible censure and coercion in the name of the whole international community. A variety of social issues has also appeared regularly on the global agenda but has had low priority. In recent years, economic issues have dominated the global agenda, not because economic interdependence is a new idea, but because the international economic arrangements established after World War II have been unable to manage contemporary economic problems or have managed them in ways unsatisfactory to a great many states.

The decline of the global agenda in comparison with the more conflict-laden East-West and North-South agendas is discouraging when measured against the postwar aspirations for a new kind of world politics. Yet in some essential ways, the waning of the global agenda reflects its potential power. That is, states have tried to "globalize" issues in the hope that action by the community of states would follow. However faithful such community action may be to group ideals and standards, mistrust about community standards and reluctance to compromise individual state autonomy can promote self-reliance instead. When states see themselves as fundamentally split on appropriate values and standards of behavior, and unequally equipped to defend these preferences, uncertainty about the effect of community judgment on their affairs can produce rejection of a global agenda in principle. Where diversity is low or perceived to be at tolerable levels and trust in community standards is high, framing issues in global terms may yet be attractive and prudent. Whereas the existence of a large global agenda in itself has neither eliminated conflict nor assured cooperative community action to solve common problems, the agenda's existence has legitimized and reinforced the possibilities for such action.

The record of the changing agendas leaves us with both pessimistic and optimistic conclusions. It is hardly encouraging to observe the extent to which political actors have debated, redefined, and continually failed to resolve some of the most dangerous and pressing international conflicts. Nevertheless, perceptions of common interests have emerged, even in situations where hostility and suspicion were strong. Assumptions, perceptions, and interests can change through debate and dialogue: The possibility of this change makes conflict resolution a realistic and attainable goal.

ILLUSTRATIONS

184

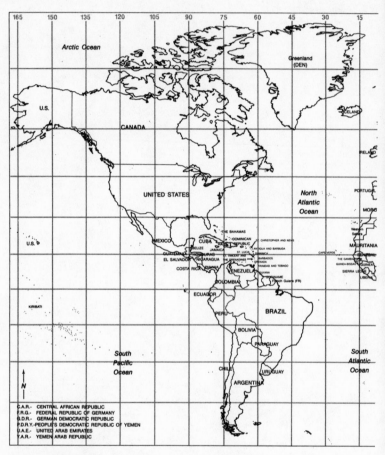

The world (country names are as of April 1986)

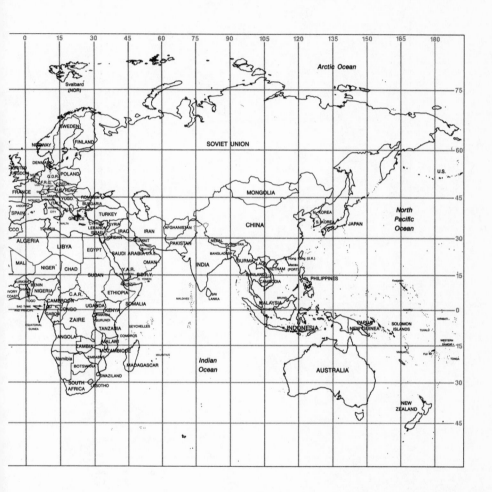

186

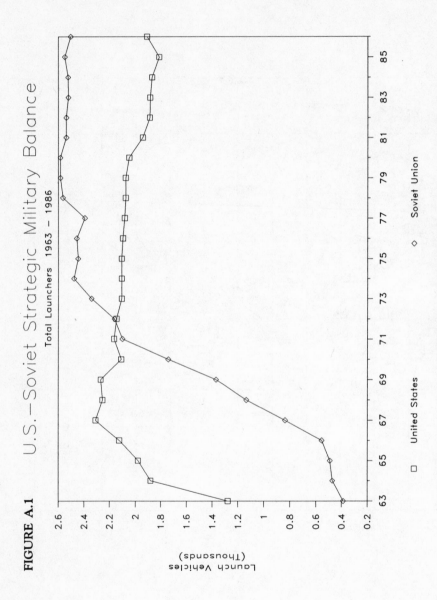

FIGURE A.1 U.S.–Soviet Strategic Military Balance

Total Launchers 1963 – 1986

☐ United States   ◇ Soviet Union

Source: Data from *The Military Balance* (London: Institute for Strategic Studies, relevant years).

FIGURE A.2 U.S.—Soviet Strategic Military Balance

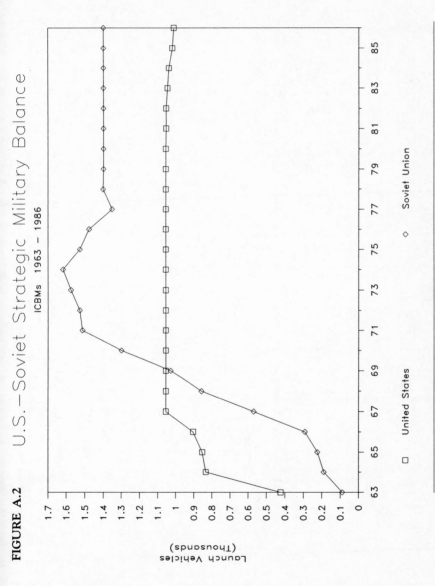

ICBMs 1963 – 1986

□ United States   ◇ Soviet Union

Source: Data from *The Military Balance* (London, Institute for Strategic Studies, relevant years).

188

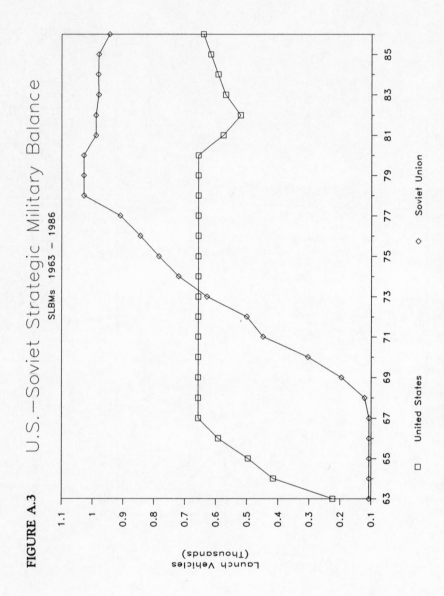

FIGURE A.3   U.S.–Soviet Strategic Military Balance

SLBMs 1963 – 1986

□ United States   ◇ Soviet Union

Source: Data from *The Military Balance* (London, Institute for Strategic Studies, relevant years).

FIGURE A.4 U.S.—Soviet Strategic Military Balance

Bombers 1963 – 1986

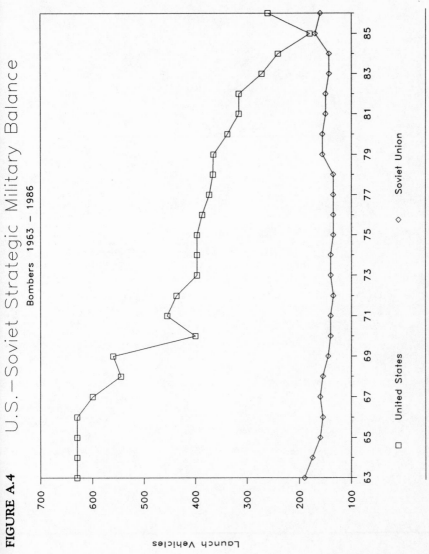

□ United States   ◇ Soviet Union

Source: Data from *The Military Balance* (London: Institute for Strategic Studies, relevant years).

ACRONYMS

AAPSO	Afro-Asian People's Solidarity Organization
ABM	Antiballistic missile
ACP	African, Caribbean, and Pacific countries
ALCM	Air-launched cruise missile
ANC	African National Congress
ANZUS	Australia–New Zealand–U.S. Pact
BPA	Basic Principles Agreement
CBM	Confidence-building measure
CCD	Conference of the Committee on Disarmament
CENTO	Central Treaty Organization
CIEC	Conference on International Economic Cooperation
CMEA, COMECON	Council for Mutual Economic Assistance
COW	Committee of the Whole
CSCE	Conference on Security and Cooperation in Europe
ECOSOC	Economic and Social Council
EEC	European Economic Community
ENDC	Eighteen-Nation Disarmament Committee
FNLA	National Front for the Liberation of Angola
FRG	Federal Republic of Germany
GATT	General Agreement on Tariffs and Trade
GDR	German Democratic Republic
GLCM	Ground-launched cruise missile
GNP	Gross national product
GSP	General system of preferences
ICBM	Intercontinental ballistic missile
ICJ	International Court of Justice
IDA	International Development Association
IMF	International Monetary Fund
INF	Intermediate-range nuclear forces
IPC	Integrated Program of Commodities
IRBM	Intermediate-range ballistic missile
ITA	International Tin Agreement
ITO	International Trade Organization
LDC	Less-developed countries
MAD	Mutual Assured Destruction
MBFR	Mutual, balanced force reductions

MFN	Most-favored nation
MIRV	Multiple, independently targeted reentry vehicle
MLF	Multilateral force
MNR	Mozambican National Resistance
MPLA	Popular Movement for the Liberation of Angola
MRBM	Medium range ballistic missile
NATO	North Atlantic Treaty Organization
NIC	Newly industrialized countries
NIEO	New International Economic Order
NPT	Nonproliferation Treaty
OAS	Organization of American States
OAPEC	Organization of Arab Petroleum-Exporting Countries
OAU	Organization of African Unity
OECD	Organization for Economic Cooperation and Development
OPEC	Organization of Petroleum-Exporting Countries
PAC	Pan-African Congress
PDRY	People's Democratic Republic of Yemen
PLO	Palestine Liberation Organization
PNW	Prevention of nuclear war agreement
PRC	People's Republic of China
RENAMO	Mozambique National Resistance
SALT	Strategic arms limitation talks
SAM	Surface-to-air missile
SDI	Strategic Defense Initiative
SEATO	Southeast Asian Treaty Organization
SLBM	Submarine-launched ballistic missile
SPNFZ	South Pacific Nuclear Free Zone
START	Strategic Arms Reduction Talks
SWAPO	South-West African People's Organization
TNF	Theater nuclear forces
UN	United Nations
UNCTAD	United Nations Conference on Trade and Development
UNESCO	United Nations Educational, Scientific, and Cultural Organization
UNGA	United Nations General Assembly
UNITA	Union for the Total Independence of Angola
WTO	Warsaw Treaty Organization

CHRONOLOGY OF EVENTS CITED

1943 Havana Charter produced, ITO proposed

1944 International monetary system discussed at Bretton Woods, New Hampshire

1945 Yalta summit conference; United Nations Charter signed in San Francisco; International Monetary Fund established; German surrender ended war in Europe; Atomic bombs dropped on Japan; Japanese surrender ended war in Asia

1946 United Nations General Assembly's first meeting; United Nations Security Council's first meeting; The Baruch Plan for control of atomic energy proposed; The World Bank began to operate

1947 India divided into two independent countries: India and Pakistan; First unofficial Afro-Asian conference, in India; The Truman Doctrine announced; The Marshall Plan for economic recovery of Europe announced; General Agreement on Tariffs and Trade signed

1948 Israel declares independence; six Arab nations attack; First Arab-Israeli war; Berlin blockade; U.S. airlift to Berlin; Two independent Korean states formed

1949 First official Afro-Asian meeting, in India; NATO charter approved; Berlin blockade ended; Two independent German states formed; communist victory in Chinese civil war, People's Republic of China proclaimed

1950 Indonesian Republic established; Korean War begun after invasion by North Korea

1951 Major Iranian oil company nationalized; U.S. defense pacts with Australia, New Zealand, Philippines, and Japan signed

1952 Nationalist military coup in Egypt; Turkey and Greece joined NATO

1953 Death of Joseph Stalin; Armistice in Korea; Shah of Iran ousted, restored to throne with U.S. assistance

1954 Colombo Conference; Geneva conference to discuss situation in Asia; French defeat at Dien Bien Phu in Vietnam; Guatemalan government overthrown with U.S. assistance

1955 Baghdad Pact formed (initially Turkey and Iraq, later Iran, Pakistan, and Britain); Bandung Conference in Indonesia; Federal Republic of Germany admitted to NATO; Warsaw Treaty Organization formed

1956   Egypt's purchase of arms from Czechoslovakia announced; Khrushchev's denunciations of Stalin; German Democratic Republic admitted to WTO; Israeli-British-French force invaded Sinai; Hungarian uprising; Soviet invasion of Hungary

1957   AAPSO formed; Sputnik launched

1958   U.S. and British forces sent to Lebanon and Jordan; Soviet ultimatum on Berlin

1959   Cuban revolution brought Fidel Castro to power; U.S.-Soviet summit

1960   Soviets withdrew from four-power summit in Paris after U-2 incident; Organization of American States founded; Independence, followed by civil disorders, in the Congo

1961   Sino-Indian border dispute; Unsuccessful U.S. invasion of Cuba (Bay of Pigs); U.S. and USSR agreed to cochair the ENDC; U.S.-Soviet summit in Vienna; Construction of the Berlin wall; Nonaligned conference in Belgrade

1962   China's ambassador withdrawn from the USSR; Cuban Missile Crisis

1963   Organization of African Unity founded; Partial Nuclear Test Ban treaty

1964   UNCTAD established; Cairo nonaligned conference; Gulf of Tonkin resolution permitted U.S. attacks on North Vietnam

1965   Second Afro-Asian Conference failed to open; U.S. troops to Dominican Republic; War between India and Pakistan

1966   France withdrew from NATO's military structure

1967   Nigerian civil war; Six-Day War in the Middle East; Group of 77 formed

1968   UNCTAD II; U.S. President halted escalation in Vietnam; Nuclear nonproliferation agreement submitted to UN; Soviet invasion of Czechoslovakia

1969   U.S.-Vietnamese negotiations began; War of Attrition began along the Suez Canal; Sino-Soviet border clashes; SALT talks began; Four-power talks on Berlin began

1970   FRG signed nonaggression treaties with USSR and Poland; U.S. forces invaded Cambodia; PLO driven out of Jordan

1971   War between India and Pakistan, independence of Bangladesh; Nonaggression treaty between East and West Germany; U.S. off the gold standard; Quadripartite Agreement on Berlin

1972   U.S. president visited China; U.S.-Soviet summit in Moscow: BPA, SALT I, and ABM treaties signed; UNCTAD III

1973   Peace treaty ended the Vietnam war; Conference on Cooperation and Security in Europe opened; Nonaligned summit in Algiers proposed NIEO; Arab-Israeli War; MBFR talks began; OAPEC oil embargo

1974   Israeli-Egyptian disengagement agreement; UNGA Special Session adopted NIEO; PLO recognized by League of Arab States as representative of the Palestinians; Coup in Portugal produced plans for colonial independence; Ethiopian emperor replaced by radical military government; U.S.-Soviet summit at Vladivostok on arms control

1975   Lomé Convention between EEC and ACP countries; CSCE Final Act signed in Helsinki (Helsinki Accord); North Vietnam conquered South Vietnam, formed one country; PLO, SWAPO, ANC, PAC accorded observer status at the UNGA; USSR disavowed U.S.-Soviet trade treaty; Civil war in Angola; Conference on International Economic Cooperation began

1976   Civil war in Lebanon; UNCTAD IV

1977   CSCE follow-up meeting in Belgrade; Committee of the Whole established at the United Nations; Somalia abrogated treaty with USSR, invaded Ethiopia; Egyptian President Sadat visited Jerusalem; Vietnam invaded Cambodia (Kampuchea)

1978   Israeli incursion into Southern Lebanon; Camp David Accords on a framework for Arab-Israeli peace; Revolution in Iran

1979   Sandinistas replaced Somoza in Nicaragua; Shah of Iran fled; U.S. embassy in Iran seized, hostages taken; U.S. and PRC established diplomatic relations; China invaded Vietnam; Israel-Egypt peace treaty; SALT II agreement signed; UNCTAD V; NATO adopted "two-track" policy on IRBMs; USSR invaded Afghanistan

1980   U.S. sanctions imposed on USSR; Common Fund agreement signed; Iran-Iraq war began

1981   U.S. embassy hostages released in Iran; START talks began; Cancun informal North-South summit; Martial law imposed in Poland; Libyan intervention in Chad

1982   Israeli invasion of Lebanon; Mexican debt crisis; War between Britain and Argentina over Falkland/Malvinas Islands; Law of the Sea treaty signed

1983   Strategic Defense Initiative proposed; U.S. invasion of Grenada; UNCTAD VI; Deployment of NATO's IRBMs began, Soviet delegates walked out of arms control negotiations

1984   Nkomati accords between South Africa and Mozambique; Lomé III

1985   U.S. proposed the Baker Plan for international debt relief; U.S. secretly facilitated transfer of arms to Iran from Israel

1986   U.S. and Britain withdrew from UNESCO; Stockholm agreement on Confidence Building Measures; U.S.-Soviet summit in Reykjavik; Irangate scandal surfaced in U.S.

1987   Arias peace plan signed in Central America; U.S.-Soviet treaty to eliminate intermediate-range nuclear missiles in Europe

RECOMMENDED READING

Soviet-American Relations

Bashkina, Nina H., and Trask, David, eds. *United States and Russia.* New York: W. S. Hein, 1982.

Brzezinski, Zbigniew. *Game Plan: How to Conduct the U.S. Soviet Contest.* New York: Atlantic Monthly Press, 1986.

Caldwell, Dan, ed. *Soviet International Behavior and U.S. Policy Options.* Lexington, Mass.: Lexington Books, 1985.

Cockburn, Andrew. *The Threat: Inside the Soviet Military Machine.* New York: Vintage Books, 1983.

Diebel, Terry, and Gaddis, John Lewis, eds. *Containment: Concept and Policy,* 2 vol. Washington, D.C.: National Defense University Press, 1986.

Donovan, John C. *The Cold Warriors: A Policy Making Elite.* Lexington, Mass.: D. C. Heath and Co., 1974.

Freedman, Lawrence. *U.S. Intelligence and the Soviet Strategic Threat.* Princeton: Princeton University Press, 1986.

Gaddis, John Lewis. *Strategies of Containment.* New York: Oxford University Press, 1982.

Garrison, Mark, and Gleason, Abbot, eds. *Shared Destiny: Fifty Years of Soviet-American Relations.* Boston: Beacon Press, 1985.

Garthoff, Raymond L. *Détente and Confrontation: American-Soviet Relations from Nixon to Reagan.* Washington, D.C.: The Brookings Institution, 1986.

George, Alexander L., ed. *Managing U.S.-Soviet Rivalry: Problems of Crisis Prevention.* Boulder, Colo.: Westview Press, 1983.

Hoffmann, Erik P., and Fleron, Frederic J., eds. *The Conduct of Soviet Foreign Policy.* San Jose, Calif.: Alchemist/Light Publishing, 1980.

Hoffmann, Stanley. *Dead Ends: American Foreign Policy in the New Cold War.* Cambridge, Mass.: Ballinger, 1983.

Horelick, Arnold L., ed. *U.S.-Soviet Relations: The Next Phase.* Ithaca, N.Y.: Cornell University Press, 1986.

Hoyt, Ronald E. *Winners and Losers in East-West Trade: A Behavioral Analysis of U.S.-Soviet Détente, 1970–1983.* New York: Praeger, 1983.

Lenczowski, John. *Soviet Perception of U.S. Foreign Policy.* Ithaca, N.Y.: Cornell University Press, 1982.

Melanson, Richard, ed. *Neither Cold War nor Détente: Soviet-American Relations in the 1980's.* Charlottesville: University Press of Virginia, 1982.

Nathan, James A., and Oliver, James K. *United States Foreign Policy and World Order.* 3d ed. Boston: Little, Brown, 1984.

Nogee, Joseph L., and Donaldson, Robert K. *Soviet Foreign Policy Since World War II.* 2d ed. New York: Pergamon Press, 1985.

Stevenson, Richard W. *The Rise and Fall of Détente: Relaxation of Tension in U.S.-Soviet Relations.* Champaign: University of Illinois Press, 1984.

Stoessinger, John. *The United Nations and the Superpowers.* New York: Random House, 1977.

Talbott, Strobe. *The Russians and Reagan.* New York: Vintage Books, 1984.

Ulam, Adam. *Dangerous Relations: The Soviet Union in World Politics, 1970-1982.* New York: Oxford, 1982.

Weihmiller, Gordon R., and Doder, Dusko. *U.S.-Soviet Summits: An Account of East-West Diplomacy at the Top.* Washington, D.C.: Georgetown University Press, 1986.

Whelan, Joseph. *Soviet Diplomacy and Negotiating Behavior: The Emerging New Context for U.S. Diplomacy.* Boulder, Colo.: Westview Press, 1982.

White, Ralph K. *Fearful Warriors: A Psychological Profile of U.S.-Soviet Relations.* New York: Free Press, 1984.

Arms Control

Betts, Richard. *Nuclear Blackmail and Nuclear Balance.* Washington, D.C.: The Brookings Institution, 1987.

Bhaduri, Amit. *Domination, Deterrence and Counterforce: An Analysis of Strategic Objectives and Doctrines in the Superpower Arms Race.* New York: Apt Books, 1986.

Bracken, Paul. *The Commands and Control of Nuclear Forces.* New Haven: Yale University Press, 1985.

Carter, Ashton B., ed. *Managing Nuclear Operations.* Washington, D.C.: The Brookings Institution, 1987.

Dahl, Robert A. *Controlling Nuclear Weapons.* Syracuse, N.Y.: Syracuse University Press, 1985.

Dougherty, James E. *JCS Reorganization and U.S. Arms Control Policy.* Cambridge, Mass.: Institute for Foreign Policy Analysis, 1986.

Ehrlich, Paul; Sagan, Carl; Kennedy, Donald; and Roberts, Walter. *The Cold and the Dark: The World After Nuclear War.* New York: Norton, 1984.

Freedman, Lawrence. *The Evolution of Nuclear Strategy.* New York: St. Martin's Press, 1983.

Goldblat, Jozef. *Arms Control Agreements: A Handbook.* New York: Taylor and Francis, 1983.

Harrison, Roger. *Verifying a Nuclear Freeze.* Wolfeboro, N.H.: Longwood Publishing Group, 1986.

Harvard Nuclear Study Group. *Living with Nuclear Weapons.* New York: Bantam, 1983.

Holloway, David. *The Soviet Union and the Arms Race.* 2d ed. New Haven: Yale University Press, 1984.

Jervis, Robert. *The Illogic of American Nuclear Strategy.* Ithaca, N.Y.: Cornell Univ. Press, 1984.

Jordan, Amos, and Taylor, William. *American National Security.* 2d ed., Baltimore: Johns Hopkins University Press, 1984.

Kaplan, Fred. *The Wizards of Armageddon.* New York: Simon and Schuster, 1983.

Kegley, Charles, and Wittkopf, Eugene, eds. *The Nuclear Reader: Strategy, Weapons, War.* New York: St. Martin's, 1985.

Miller, Steven E., ed. *Strategy and Nuclear Deterrence.* Princeton: Princeton University Press, 1984.

Scientific American Staff. *Arms Control and the Arms Race.* New York: W. H. Freeman, 1985.

Smoke, Richard. *National Security and the Nuclear Dilemma.* New York: Random House, 1984.

Talbott, Strobe. *Deadly Gambits: The Reagan Administration and the Stalemate in Nuclear Arms Control.* New York: Vintage Books, 1985.

Union of Concerned Scientists. *The Fallacy of Star Wars.* New York: Vintage Books, 1984.

The Nonaligned Movement

Banerjee, Malabika. *The Nonaligned Movement.* Columbia, Mo.: South Asia Books, 1983.

Bhagwati, Jagdish N., and Ruggie, John G., eds. *Power, Passions and Purpose: Prospects for North-South Negotiations.* Cambridge: The MIT Press, 1984.

Chand, Attar. *Non-Aligned Nations: Challenges of the Eighties.* Flushing, N.Y.: Asia Book Corp. of America, 1983.

Goyal, D. R. *Non-Alignment: Concepts and Concerns.* Columbia, Mo.: South Asia Books, 1983.

Hansen, Roger D. *Beyond the North-South Stalemate.* New York: McGraw-Hill, 1979.

Jaipal, Rikhi. *Non-Alignment: Origins, Growth and Potential for World Peace.* Columbia, Mo.: South Asia Books, 1983.

Kardel, Edvard. *The Historical Roots of Non-Alignment.* Lanham, Mass.: University Press of America, 1985.

Kimche, David. *The Afro-Asian Movement.* New York: Halsted Press, 1973.

Misra, K. P., ed. *Non Alignment: Frontiers and Dynamics.* New York: Advent Books, 1982.

Mortimer, Robert A. *The Third World Coalition in International Politics.* 2d, updated ed. Boulder, Colo.: Westview Press, 1984.

Neuhold, Hanspete, and Thalberg, Hans. *The European Neutrals in International Affairs.* Boulder, Colo.: Westview Press, 1985.

Sauvant, Karl P., ed. *Changing Priorities on the International Agenda: The New International Economic Order.* New York: Pergamon Press, 1981.

Sundelius, Bengt, ed. *The Neutral Democracies and the New Cold War.* Boulder, Colo.: Westview Press, 1986.

International Political Economy

Ansari, Javed. *The Political Economy of International Economic Organization.* Boulder, Colo.: Lynne Rienner, 1986.

Barnet, Richard, and Muller, Ronald. *Global Reach.* New York: Simon and Schuster, 1974.

Bergesen, Albert, ed. *Crises in the World-System.* Beverly Hills, Calif.: Sage, 1983.

Bergsten, C. Fred, ed. *The United States in the World Economy: Selected Papers of C. Fred Bergsten 1981–82.* Lexington, Mass.: Lexington Books, 1983.

————. *Global Economic Imbalances.* Washington, D.C.: Institute of International Economy, 1986.

Bergsten, C. Fred, and Krause, Lawrence B., eds. *World Politics and International Economics.* Ann Arbor, Mich.: Books on Demand UMI, 1984.

Blake, David H., and Walters, Robert H. *The Politics of Global Economic Relations.* 2d ed. Englewood Cliffs, N.J.: Prentice-Hall, 1983.

Destler, I. M. *American Trade Politics: System Under Stress.* Washington, D.C.: Institute for International Politics, 1986.

Didsbury, Howard F., ed. *The Global Economy: Today, Tomorrow and the Transition.* Bethesda, Md.: World Future Society, 1985.

Donaldson, John. *International Economic Relations: A Treatise on World Economy and World Politics.* New York: Garland Publishing, 1983.

Ellsworth, P. T., and Leith, J. Clark. *The International Economy.* New York: Macmillan Information, 1984.

Feinberg, Richard E. *The Intemperate Zone: The Third World Challenge to U.S. Foreign Policy.* New York: Norton, 1983.

Freiden, Jeffry, and Lake, David, eds. *International Political Economy: Perspectives on Global Power and Wealth.* New York: St. Martin's, 1987.

Frey, Bruno S. *International Political Economics.* New York: Basil Blackwell, 1985.

Grassman, Sven, and Lundberg, Erik, eds. *World Economic Order: Past and Prospects.* New York: St. Martin's, 1980.

Hinshaw, Randall, ed. *Global Economic Priorities.* New Brunswick, N.J.: Transaction Books, 1984.

Keohane, Robert, and Nye, Joseph. *Power and Interdependence.* Boston: Little, Brown, 1977.

Krasner, Stephen. *Defending the National Interest.* Princeton: Princeton University Press, 1978.

Spero, Joan. *The Politics of International Economic Relations.* 3d ed. New York: St. Martin's Press, 1985.

Regional Issues

Africa

Akagha, Fidelis S. *Strategies for Economic Development in Africa.* New York: Vantage, 1985.

Ake, Claude. *A Political Economy of Africa.* White Plains, N.Y.: Longman, 1982.

Calvocoressi, Peter. *Independent Africa and the World.* White Plains, N.Y.: Longman, 1985.

Delancey, Mark W., ed. *Aspects of International Relations in Africa.* Bloomington: Indiana University Press, 1980.

Fieldhouse, David K. *Black Africa, 1945-80.* Winchester, Mass.: Allen and Unwin, 1986.

Ghosh, Pradip K., ed. *Developing Africa: A Modernization Perspective.* Westport, Conn.: Greenwood Press, 1984.

Gutkind, Peter, and Wallerstein, Immanuel, eds. *Political Economy of Contemporary Africa.* Beverly Hills, Calif.: Sage, 1985.

Ungar, Stanford J. *Africa: The People and Politics of an Emerging Continent.* New York: Simon and Schuster, 1985.

Zartman, I. William. *Ripe for Resolution: Conflict and Intervention in Africa.* New York: Oxford University Press, 1985.

Asia

Chawla, Sudershan, and SarDesai, D. R., eds. *Changing Patterns of Security and Stability in Asia.* New York: Praeger, 1980.

Darling, Frank C. *The Westernization of Asia: A Comparative Political Analysis.* Cambridge, Mass.: Schenkman Books, 1980.

Downen, Robert, ed. *Northeast Asia in the Nineteen Eighties.* Washington, D.C.: Center for Strategic and International Studies, 1982.

Jeffrey, Robin, ed. *Asia: The Winning of Independence.* New York: St. Martin's, 1981.

Karnow, Stanley. *Vietnam: A History.* New York: Penguin, 1984.

Pye, Lucian W. *Asian Power and Politics: The Cultural Dimensions of Authority.* Cambridge: Harvard University Press, 1985.

Research Institute for Peace and Security, ed. *Asian Security.* New York: Pergamon, 1985.

Solomon, Richard H., ed. *Asian Security in the Nineteen Eighties: Problems and Politics for a Time of Transition.* Boston: Oelgeschlager, 1980.

Young, Hum Kim. *American Frontier Activities in Asia.* Chicago: Nelson-Hall, 1981.

Central America

Alonso, Marcelo. *Crisis in Central America.* New York: Paragon House, 1984.

Barry, Tom. *Low Intensity Conflict: The New Battlefield in Central America.* Albuquerque, N.M.: Inter-Hemispheric Education Resource Center, 1986.

Camarda, Renato. *Forced to Move.* San Francisco: Solidarity, 1985.

Chace, James. *Endless War: How We Got Involved in Central America and What Can Be Done.* New York: Random, 1984.

Child, Jack, ed. *Conflict in Central America.* New York: International Peace Academy, 1986.

Dominguez, Jorge, and Lindenberg, Marc. *Central America: Current Crisis and Future Prospects.* New York: Foreign Policy, 1984.

Feinberg, Richard E., ed. *Central America: International Dimensions of the Crisis.* New York: Holmes and Meier, 1982.

Gettleman, Marvin E. *El Salvador: Central America in the New Cold War.* New York: Grove Press, 1987.

Kissinger, Henry. *Report of the National Bipartisan Commission on Central America.* Washington, D.C.: Government Printing Office, 1984.

LaFeber, Walter. *Inevitable Revolutions: The United States in Central America.* New York: Norton, 1984.

China

Arendrup, Birthe, ed. *China in the 1980's and Beyond.* Atlantic Highlands, N.J.: Humanities Press, 1986.

Fife, Joy L. *China's Foreign Policy: Apparent Contradictions.* New York: Carlton, 1981.

Garside, Roger. *Coming Alive: China After Mao.* New York: McGraw-Hill Books, 1981.

Gladue, Ted E. *China's Perceptions of Global Issues.* New York: Associated Faculty Press, 1981.

Harding, Harry, ed. *China's Foreign Relations in the Nineteen Eighties.* New Haven: Yale University Press, 1986.

Pye, Lucian W. *The Dynamics of Chinese Politics.* Boston: Oelgeschlager, 1981.

Shaw, Yu-ming. *Power and Policy in the PRC.* Boulder, Colo.: Westview Press, 1985.

Townsend, James R., and Womack, Brantly. *Politics in China.* Boston: Little, Brown, 1985.

Wang, James C. *Contemporary Chinese Politics.* Englewood Cliffs, N.J.: Prentice-Hall, 1985.

Yahuda, Michael. *Towards the End of Isolationism: China's Foreign Policy After Mao.* New York: St. Martin's, 1985.

Eastern Europe

Bahro, Rudolph. *The Alternatives in Eastern Europe.* New York: Schocken Books, 1981.

Hazan, Baruch. *The East European Political System.* Boulder, Colo.: Westview Press, 1985.

Lewis, Paul, ed. *Eastern Europe: Political Crisis and Legitimation.* New York: St. Martin's, 1984.

McCrea, Barbara P. *The Soviet and East European Political Dictionary.* Santa Barbara, Calif.: ABC-Clio, 1984.

Narkiewicz, Olga. *Eastern Europe Nineteen Sixty-Eight to Nineteen Eighty-Four.* Totowa, N.J.: Barnes and Noble, 1986.

Simon, Jeffrey. *Cohesion and Dissension in Eastern Europe: Six Crises.* New York: Praeger, 1983.

————. *Security Implications of Nationalism in Eastern Europe.* Boulder, Colo.: Westview Press, 1985.

Subtelny, Orest. *Domination of Eastern Europe Native Nobilities and Foreign Absolutism.* Kingston, Ont.: McGill–Queens University Press, 1985.

Latin America

Brown, Janet, and Maguire, Andrew, eds. *Bordering on Trouble: Resources and Politics in Latin America.* Bethesda, Md.: Adler & Adler, 1986.

Falcoff, Mark. *The Crisis in Latin America: Strategic, Economic and Political Dimensions.* Washington, D.C.: American Enterprise, 1984.

Ferris, Elizabeth, and Lincoln, Jennie, eds. *Latin American Foreign Policies: Global and Regional Dimensions.* Boulder, Colo.: Westview Press, 1981.

Finan, John, and Child, John, eds. *Latin America: International Relations.* Detroit: Gale, 1981.

Kryzanck, Michael. *U.S.–Latin American Relations.* New York: Praeger, 1985.

Lincoln, Jennie, and Ferris, Elizabeth, eds. *The Dynamics of Latin American Foreign Policies.* Boulder, Colo.: Westview Press, 1984.

Lozoya, Jorge, and Estevez, Jaime, eds. *Latin America and the New International Economic Order.* New York: Pergamon, 1980.

Novak, Michael, and Jackson, Michael P., eds. *Latin America: Dependency or Interdependence?* Washington, D.C.: American Enterprise, 1985.

Perry, Williams, and Wehner, Peter, eds. *The Latin American Policies of U.S. Allies: Balancing Global Interests and Regional Concerns.* New York: Praeger, 1985.

Wionczek, Miguel S. *Politics and Economics of External Debt Crisis.* Boulder, Colo.: Westview Press, 1985.

Middle East

American Friends Service Committee. *A Compassionate Peace: A Future for the Middle East.* Philadelphia: American Friends Service Committee, 1981.

Ayoob, Mohammed, ed. *The Middle East in World Politics.* New York: St. Martin's, 1981.

Heller, Mark A. *The Middle East Military Balance, 1984.* Boulder, Colo.: Westview Press, 1985.

Ismael, Tareq Y. *International Relations of the Contemporary Middle East.* Syracuse, N.Y.: Syracuse University Press, 1986.

Khouri, Fred J. *The Arab-Israeli Dilemma.* 3d ed. Syracuse, N.Y.: Syracuse University Press, 1985.

McLaurin, Ron D. *Middle East Foreign Policy: Issues and Processes.* New York: Praeger, 1982.

Marantz, Paul, and Stein, Janice, eds. *Peace-Making in the Middle East: Problems and Prospects.* Totowa, N.J.: Barnes and Noble, 1985.

Martin, Lenore. *The Unstable Gulf: Threats from Within.* Lexington, Mass.: Lexington Books, 1984.

Pajak, Roger F. *Nuclear Proliferation in the Middle East: Implications for the Superpowers.* Washington, D.C.: Government Printing Office, 1982.

Safran, Nadav. *Israel, the Embattled Ally.* Cambridge: Harvard University Press, 1982.

Shwadran, Benjamin. *The Middle East Oil and the Great Powers.* Boulder, Colo.: Westview Press, 1985.

Spiegel, Steven, ed. *The Middle East and the Western Alliance.* Winchester, Mass.: Allen and Unwin, 1982.

Wells, Samuel F., and Bruzonsky, Mark, eds. *Security in the Middle East: Regional Change and Great Power Strategies.* Boulder, Colo.: Westview Press, 1986.

Western Europe

Aron, Raymond. *In Defense of Decadent Europe*. Lanham, Md.: University Press of America, 1984.

Bethlen, Steven, and Volgyes, Ivan. *Europe and the Superpowers: Economic, Political and Military Policies in the 1980's*. Boulder, Colo.: Westview Press, 1985.

DePorte, Anton W. *Europe Between the Super Powers*. New Haven: Yale University Press, 1984.

Grosser, Alfred. *The Western Alliance: European-American Relations Since 1945*. New York: Random, 1982.

Jordan, Robert S., and Feld, Werner J. *Europe in the Balance*. Boston: Faber and Faber, 1986.

Knudsen, Baard B. *Europe Versus America: Foreign Policy in the 1980's*. Totowa, N.J.: Rowman, 1985.

Mendl, Wolf. *Western Europe and Japan Between the Superpowers*. New York: St. Martin's, 1984.

Tindemans, Leo C. *Europe and the United States: The Balance After Ten Years*. Washington, D.C.: Center for Strategic and International Studies, 1984.

Zinner, Paul E. *East-West Relations in Europe*. Boulder, Colo.: Westview Press, 1983.

INDEX

AAPSO. *See* Afro-Asian People's Solidarity Organization
ABM. *See* Antiballistic missiles
ACP countries. *See* African, Caribbean, and Pacific countries
Aden, Soviet presence in, 158
Afghanistan, 31, 86(n4), 125
anti-communist insurrection in, 140, 160, 174
communist coup in, 128–129
Mujahedin, 160
and Persian Gulf stability, 160
proximity talks with Pakistan, 174
refugees from, 175
Soviet invasion of, 130, 140
and the Soviet Union, 128–129, 130
and the U.S., 155, 160
African, Caribbean, and Pacific (ACP) countries
and the European Economic Community, 108, 135, 165
Lomé Convention, 108, 135, 165
African National Congress (ANC), 113, 126
Southern support for, 169
and U.S. policy, 169
Afro-Asian movement, 30, 84, 93
conferences, 31–32, 85
disunity of, 85
and Sino-Soviet conflict, 85
Afro-Asian People's Solidarity Organization (AAPSO), 57
Agenda, concept of, 1, 2. *See also* East-West agenda; Global agenda; North-South agenda
Albania, 46, 86(n4)
Algeria, 29, 82, 84
and Afro-Asian conference (1965), 85
and Soviet Union, 49
Algiers Charter, 82, 103
Allied Powers, 7, 34(n1)

Amin, Hafizullah, 130
ANC. *See* African National Congress
Andropov, Yuri, 147
Angola (People's Republic of Angola), 86(n4), 126
decolonization of, 125, 126, 139
external aid to insurgents in, 170
national liberation movements in, 126. *See also* National Front for the Liberation of Angola; Popular Movement for the Liberation of Angola; Union for the Total Independence of Angola
South African attacks on, 174
Soviet-Cuban intervention in, 126
Antarctic Treaty, 175
Antiballistic missiles (ABM), 71–72, 94
and the arms race, 71
U.S. and Soviet competition in, 72
See also Arms control agreements, Antiballistic missile treaty
ANZUS. *See* Australia–New Zealand–U.S. pact
Apartheid, 43, 107
as a global issue, 66, 113, 139
international sanctions against, 169, 170
Arab-Israeli conflict
and African states, 112
cease-fires, 98, 99
disengagement agreements, 105
Geneva peace conference, 105, 122
Israeli-Egyptian treaty (1979), 123
and OAPEC oil embargo, 104–105
October War (1973), 100–101, 104
shuttle diplomacy, 105
Six-Day war (1967), 66, 67(map), 68
Soviet involvement in, 99, 100–101, 122, 123
and the U.S., 99, 100, 101, 122, 123
War of Attrition (1969–1970), 98, 99

war of 1948, 11, 27, 28
Arab nationalism, 47
Arafat, Yasser, 112, 124
  and disunity in the PLO, 159
  in Lebanon, 159
Argentina, 138
  claim to Falkland/Malvinas Islands,
    173
  as debtor, 167
  war with Britain, 173
Arias, Oscar, 157. See also Nobel Peace
  Prize
Arias Plan, 157
Arms control, 41, 43, 52–53, 118
  and Cuban Missile Crisis, 52, 53
  and détente, 70–71, 93, 95, 96
  in Europe, 119–120. See also
    European security
  qualitative, 118, 119
  quantitative, 118
  and the UN, 65–66
  and the U.S.-Soviet military balance,
    94
  value of, 120, 148, 153
  and weapons technology, 118, 119,
    147, 148, 149(fig.)
  See also Arms control agreements;
    Arms control issues; Arms race;
    Nuclear weapons
Arms control agreements
  Antiballistic Missile treaty (ABM
    treaty), 95, 96, 118
  ban on biological and toxic weapons,
    96
  ban on nuclear weapons in outer
    space, 65
  ban on nuclear weapons on seabed,
    65, 114(n5)
  hot-line agreement, 53
  NPT, 65
  Partial Nuclear Test Ban Treaty
    (1963), 53, 76
  on prevention of accidental war,
    114(n5)
  prevention of nuclear war (PNW)
    agreement, 96
  SALT I treaty, 95, 118
  SALT II treaty, 95, 119
  Treaty of Tlateloco, 65
  underground test ban, 96

Arms control issues
  INF, 148, 150
  no-first-use declarations, 41, 151,
    177(n4)
  nuclear-free zones, 151, 176(n3)
  parity, 96, 118, 148
  verification, 96, 148
  zero-zero option, 150, 153
Arms race, 39, 40
  and ABMs, 71, 94
  and détente, 93
  and weapons technology, 94
Article 19 crisis, 68
Atomic energy, 11. See also Nuclear
  weapons
Australia, 3, 4, 31
  and ANZUS pact, 36(n19)
  and SEATO, 36(n19)
Australia-New Zealand-U.S. pact
  (ANZUS), 36(n19), 176–177(n3)
Austria, 6(n1)
  peace treaty (1955), 22
Axis powers, 7, 14. See also Germany;
  Italy; Japan

Baghdad Pact, 32–33, 36(n19), 47
Baker Plan, 168. See also Debt
Balance of terror, 40, 41, 45
Bandung conference (1955), 34, 55
  attendance, 55, 56, 62(n6)
  British support for, 55
  and nonalignment, 55
  and peaceful coexistence, 55
  U.S. suspicion of, 55
Bangladesh, 100
Baruch Plan (Atomic Development
  Authority), 11
Basic Principles Agreement (BPA), 96–
  97. See also Détente
Batista, Fulgencio, 48
Bay of Pigs invasion, 48
Begin, Menachem, 123. See also Nobel
  Peace Prize
Beirut, 159, 173. See also Lebanon
Belgium, 6(n1), 8
  and the Congo, 42
  and decolonization, 25
Belgrade nonaligned conference (1961),
  59–60
  appeal for U.S.-Soviet contacts, 60
  attendance, 59, 62(n12)

Cairo preparatory meeting, 58
definition of nonalignment for, 58–59
importance of, 60
protest of nuclear weapons tests, 60
Ben Bella, Ahmed, 84, 85
Berlin
blockade of, 18–19
crisis of 1958, 50
crisis of 1961, 50–51
Quadripartite Agreement (1971), 93
Berlin Wall, 51
Bipolarity, 31, 48
dangers of, 52
and small states, 49
Black September, 114(n9)
Bolivia
and Cairo economic conference, 60
and ITA, 164
BPA. See Basic Principles Agreement
Brandt, Willy
and détente, 92, 93
and North-South dialogue, 136, 141
Brandt Commission. See Brandt, Willy,
and North-South dialogue
Brazil, 4, 165
and Cairo economic conference, 60
and nuclear nonproliferation, 71
and the U.S., 138
Bretton Woods, 12, 111
Brezhnev, Leonid, 95, 147, 163
Brezhnev Doctrine, 77, 91
Brinkmanship, 49
Britain
and arms control, 53
and Austria, 22
and Baghdad Pact, 32, 36(n19)
and commodity trade regulation, 134
and decolonization, 10, 25, 27, 28
and Egypt, 28, 47
and Falkland/Malvinas Islands, 173
and Geneva conference on Asia, 22
and Germany, 16
and globalism, 162, 163
and India, 27
and Indonesia, 28
and international sanctions on South
Africa, 170
and Malaya, 28
and NATO, 6(n1)
opposition to UN economic role,
163

and Palestine, 27–28
and political instability in the South,
170
and SEATO, 36(n19)
and Suez crisis, 47
and the Third World, 125
and UNSC, 35(n7)
war with Argentina, 173
British Guiana, 28
Bulgaria, 6(n1), 86(n4)
Burma, 14, 26, 28, 31, 32, 33

Cairo economic conference (1962), 60
Cambodia, 23, 125
competing claims to govern, 128, 135
and the U.S., 90, 155
Vietnamese invasion, 128, 140
Camp David Israeli-Egyptian
negotiations, 123
Cam Ranh Bay, 158
Canada, 3, 5
and NATO, 6(n1), 8, 19
and Southern debt, 135
Cancun summit. See Global
negotiations
Carter, Jimmy
and Africa, 127
and Israeli-Egyptian negotiations, 123
and SALT II, 120, 130
and Soviet invasion of Afghanistan,
130
Vienna summit with Brezhnev,
142(n1)
Carter Doctrine, 130
Castro, Fidel, 48
CBMs. See Conference on Security
and Cooperation in Europe,
Confidence Building Measures
agreement
CCD. See Conference of the
Committee on Disarmament
CENTO. See Central Treaty
Organization
Central American conflict, 129–130,
170
Contadora peace plan for, 156
and U.S., 156, 157
See also Arias Plan; Dominican
Republic; El Salvador; Grenada;
Guatemala; Nicaragua

Central Treaty Organization (CENTO),
    36(n19), 47, 100. *See also* Baghdad
    Pact
Ceylon (Sri Lanka), 31, 33, 62(n12)
Chad
    and France, 158, 170, 176
    Libyan military action in, 158
    refugees in, 175
    U.S. aid to, 158
Chernenko, Konstantin, 147
Chiang Kai-shek, 21, 35(n7), 50
Chile
    and Cairo economic conference, 60
    nationalizations in, 109
    and U.S., 138
China, 14, 16, 17
    UN membership for, 35(n7)
    See also People's Republic of China;
        Republic of China; Taiwan
CIEC. *See* Conference on International
    Economic Cooperation
Club of Rome, 112
CMEA. *See* Council for Mutual
    Economic Assistance
Cold War, 4, 8, 18
    and the Afro-Asian movement, 32
    and East-West trade, 101
    and the Korean War, 20
    and nonalignment, 33
    and nuclear weapons, 40
    revival of, 146
    and the South, 29, 31
    and U.S. policy in Vietnam, 29
Colombo Conference (1954), 33
Colonialism, UN Declaration on, 10
COMECON. *See* Council for Mutual
    Economic Assistance
Cominform. *See* Communist
    Information Agency
Comintern. *See* Communist
    International
Committee of the Whole (COW). *See*
    under United Nations General
    Assembly
Commodity trade issues, 82, 106
    and Bolivia, 165
    at CIEC, 133
    Common Fund for, 134, 164
    and GATT, 80
    and global negotiations, 161
    Northern positions on, 134

and the South, 79
and the Soviet Union, 164
at UNCTAD, 82, 103, 107, 133, 134
and U.S., 164
See also European Economic
    Community; General System of
    Preferences; Integrated Program of
    Commodities; International Tin
    Agreement; Lomé Convention
Common Fund. *See* Commodity trade
    issues
Communist Information Agency
    (Cominform), 17–18
Communist International (Comintern),
    17
Communists
    and decolonization, 25
    in Europe, 21–22, 121
    and nationalists, 32
    See also Eurocommunism; Marxism-
        Leninism; Sino-Soviet conflict
Conference of the Committee on
    Disarmament (CCD), 96
Conference on International Economic
    Cooperation (CIEC), 132, 133
Conference on Security and
    Cooperation in Europe (CSCE),
    97, 119, 121
    Confidence Building Measures
        (CBM) agreement, 153
    Final Act. *See* Helsinki Accord
    follow-up meetings, 121
    See also European security
Conflict resolution
    as a global issue, 69, 73
    and the superpowers, 73
    and the UN, 64, 66
    See also Use of force
Congo (Brazzaville), 66
Congo (Zaire), 42, 85. *See also* Congo
    crisis
Congo crisis, 42–43, 48
    and the Third World, 59
    and UN financial crisis, 68
Congress of Oppressed Nationalities,
    30
Contadora peace plan. *See* Central
    American conflict; Nicaragua
Containment, 17, 56, 74
Contras. *See* Nicaragua, United
    Nicaraguan Opposition

Council for Mutual Economic
    Assistance (CMEA or
    COMECON), 86, 163
  in UNCTAD, 86(n4)
  membership, 86(n4)
COW. See United Nations General
    Assembly, Committee of the
    Whole
Cruise missiles. See under Nuclear
    weapons
CSCE. See Conference on Security
    and Cooperation in Europe
Cuba, 48, 86(n4)
  intervention in Angola, 126, 140,
    158
  intervention in Ethiopia, 126, 127,
    140
  and the nonaligned movement, 84,
    135
  and South Africa, 158
  and the Soviet Union, 48, 49, 135
  and the U.S., 48-51
  U.S. military base on, 62(n12)
  See also Cuban Missile Crisis
Cuban Missile Crisis, 51-52
  and arms control, 52, 53, 69
Cyprus, 68, 78
Czechoslovakia, 6(n1), 86(n4)
  domestic political reforms, 77
  invasion of (1968), 72, 77, 84
  and the Soviet Union, 70

Dag Hammarskjold Foundation, 138
Dahlak islands, Soviet use of, 158
Daoud, Mohammed, 128
Debt, 135, 141, 166
  Baker Plan for funding, 168
  causes of, 141, 162, 166
  and the IMF, 141, 167, 168
  Northern response to, 167
  and oil prices, 166
  renegotiating of, 166
Decolonization, 10, 11, 24-26, 31, 41,
    43, 110
  anti-Western outcomes of, 56-57
  of Portuguese Africa, 125. See also
    Angola; Mozambique
  in Rhodesia, 127, 139
  in South Africa and Namibia, 139-
    140
  and the UN, 10, 41, 42

Western response to, 25
  See also Belgium; Britain; France;
    Netherlands; Soviet Union; United
    States
de Gaulle, Charles, 40(n1), 46
  and détente, 69, 70
Deng Xiaoping, 122
Denmark, 6(n1)
Détente, 4, 88
  and arms control, 93
  as code of conduct, 88, 89, 126
  and conventional arms control, 96
  defined, 70, 88, 97, 114(n1)
  East-West differences over, 147
  in Europe, 147
  and human rights, 98, 122
  motives for, 88, 89-90, 99-101, 131
  status of, 118, 126
  and Third World conflicts, 125, 131
  See also Basic Principles Agreement;
    Conference on Security and
    Cooperation in Europe; East-West
    trade; Helsinki Accord; Human
    rights
Deterrence, 53, 147, 151, 152
Diego Garcia, 147
Diem, Ngo Dinh, 74
Dien Bien Phu, 22. See also Indochina;
    Vietnam
Disarmament, 23, 41. See also Arms
    control; Arms control agreements;
    Arms control issues
Dominican Republic, 66, 73
Domino theory, 74
Duvalier, Baby Doc, 170

East
  defined, 3
  and the North, 5, 86(n4), 143(n9)
East Europe, 3, 5
  and the USSR, 16, 45, 70, 76-77
East Germany. See German Democratic
    Republic
East Pakistan. See Bangladesh
East-West agenda
  concept of, 3-4
  general dominance of, 179
  and North-South agenda, 84
  origins, 8, 34
  summary: 1945-1955, 14; 1955-1963,
    44; 1964-1968, 69; 1969-1975, 87;
    1975-1980, 118; 1980s, 146

and Third World conflicts, 125, 131
East-West trade, 12, 101. *See also*
    Détente; U.S.-Soviet trade
Economic Commission on Latin
    America, 86
Economic development, 61, 105–106
Ecopolitical issues, 111. *See also* Club
    of Rome
ECOSOC. *See* United Nations
    Economic and Social Council
Ecuador, 60
EEC. *See* European Economic
    Community
Egypt, 4, 27, 33
    and Israel, 98, 99, 100, 101, 105, 123
    and the League of Arab States, 123
    and Libya, 123
    military coup (1952), 28
    and the October War (1973), 100–
        101
    and the Six Day War (1967), 66, 68,
        73
    and the Soviet Union, 47, 49, 58,
        99, 100, 101
    and the Suez crisis, 46, 47
    and Syria, 47, 123
    and Third World meetings, 31, 33
    See also Arab-Israeli conflict; Suez
        Canal; Suez crisis
Eighteen Nation Disarmament
    Committee (ENDC), 41, 53
    and hot-line agreement, 53
    See also Conference of the
        Committee on Disarmament
Eisenhower, Dwight D., 23
    and U-2 mission, 50
El Salvador, 157, 169
ENDC. *See* Eighteen Nation
    Disarmament Committee
Eritrea. *See* Ethiopia
Escalation, 40
Ethiopia, 4, 31, 86(n4)
    conflict with Somalia, 127–128
    Eritrean secessionists, 127, 177(n7)
    refugees from, 175
    Soviet-Cuban intervention, 126, 127,
        135
    and the U.S., 127
Eurocommunism, 121
Europe
    anti-nuclear movement in, 150

conventional arms balance in. *See*
    Mutual Balanced Force Reductions
East-West strategic balance in, 153
peace movement (1949), 21
postwar, 15
U.S. aid to, 17
See also European security; North
    Atlantic Treaty Organization;
    Warsaw Treaty Organization
European Common Market, 80
European Economic Community (EEC)
    and ACP countries, 108, 135, 165
    and CIEC, 132
    See also Lomé Convention
European security, 23
    and conventional military balance,
        96, 100, 120, 122
    and CSCE, 119
    and IRBMs, 120, 153, 154
    issue definition, 69, 70
    and SDI, 153
    and theater nuclear forces (TNF),
        120
    See also Conference on Security and
        Cooperation in Europe; Mutual
        Balanced Force Reductions; North
        Atlantic Treaty Organization

Falkland Islands. *See* Falkland/Malvinas
    Islands
Falkland/Malvinas Islands, 173. *See also*
    Argentina; Britain
Federal Republic of Germany (FRG),
    6(n1), 19
    admission to UN, 93
    and commodity trade regulation, 134
    and détente, 70, 92
    and the GDR, 93, 114(n4)
    Hallstein Doctrine, 114(n4)
    and NATO, 6(n1), 20
    and nuclear weapons, 71
    opposition to UN economic role,
        163
    Ostpolitik, 92
    and Poland, 93
    and political instability in the South,
        169, 170
    and Romania, 114(n4)
    Soviet attempts to influence, 150
    and the Soviet Union, 92, 93
    and the West, 6(n1), 19, 22

Finland, 6(n1)
First strike capacity, 52. *See also*
    Strategic issues; Strategic policy
FNLA. *See* National Front for the
    Liberation of Angola
Food issues, 141
Ford, Gerald R., 95, 126
France, 6(n1), 7, 8, 34(n1), 127
    and Algeria, 29
    and Arab-Israeli conflict, 21
    and Austria, 22
    and Chad, 158, 170, 176
    Communist party of, 77
    and decolonization, 10, 28–29, 32
    and détente, 70
    and Germany, 16, 22, 23
    and Indochina, 21, 22, 49
    and Libya, 169
    and NATO, 19, 46, 69
    and nuclear nonproliferation, 71
    and nuclear weapons, 46, 71
    and political instability in the South,
        169, 170
    and SEATO, 36(n19)
    and the Suez crisis, 47
    and UN financing, 68
    and UNSC, 36(n19)
    and the U.S., 46
    and Vietnam, 28, 29
Free trade, 12, 80, 164–165. *See also*
    Commodity trade issues;
    International trade issues;
    Protectionism
FRG. *See* Federal Republic of
    Germany

Gandhi, Mahatma, 27
Garcia, Alan, 167
GATT. *See* General Agreement on
    Tariffs and Trade
Gaza Strip, 66, 67(map), 123
GDR. *See* German Democratic
    Republic
General Agreement on Tariffs and
    Trade (GATT), 13, 14
    and North-South trade, 164, 165
    and protectionism, 171
    reforms of, 64, 82
    Southern critique of, 80, 103
    and textiles, 165
    and trade disputes, 173

    U.S.-European differences in, 165,
        171
General System of Preferences (GSP)
    and Group of 77, 103
    and the NIEO, 106
    Northern opposition to, 82, 83
    and UNCTAD, 82, 83
Geneva conference on Asia (1954), 22,
    33
Geneva peace conference on the
    Middle East, 105
Geneva summit conference (1955), 23
German Democratic Republic (GDR),
    6(n1), 19, 23, 86(n4)
    and control over Berlin, 51
    and Czechoslovakia, 77
    and the FRG, 114(n4)
    and the Soviet Union, 44, 70
    status of, 93
Germany
    Allied occupation of, 16, 18–19
    de-Nazification of, 15
    division of, 18
    postwar border changes, 15
    rearmament of, 20, 21, 23
    reunification of, 21
    See also Berlin; Britain; Federal
        Republic of Germany; France;
        German Democratic Republic;
        Soviet Union; United States
Ghana, 27, 78
Glasnost, 147
GLCMs. *See* Nuclear weapons, ground-
    launched cruise missiles
Global agenda
    and East-West rivalry, 72
    concept of, 3
    overall decline of, 80
    summary: 1945–1955, 8; 1955–1963,
        38; 1964–1968, 64; 1969–1975, 110;
        1975–1980, 138; 1980s, 171
Globalism
    as an ideological issue, 175
    and Law of the Sea treaty, 175
    planetary property rights, 68, 75
Global negotiations, 136
    Cancun summit, 163
    and Group of 77, 161, 163
    and the NIEO, 161
    and the UN, 161
Golan Heights, 66, 123

Gorbachev, Mikhail, 147
Great Proletarian Cultural Revolution, 91
Greece, 6(n1), 17
Grenada, 157
Ground-launched cruise missiles. See under Nuclear weapons
Group of Five, 171
Group of 77, 80, 81
  and GSP, 103
  and global negotiations, 163
  and IMF, 103
  and the NIEO, 106, 131, 134
  and nonaligned movement, 102–103
  and UNCTAD, 134, 163
GSP. See General System of Preferences
Guantanamo military base, 62(n12)
Guatemala, 109, 138, 140, 157
  and U.S. policy in Nicaragua, 170
Guatemala Accords. See Arias Plan
Guinea, 27, 66, 78
Guinea-Bissau, 125

Habre, Hissene, 158
Haiti, 170. See also United States
Hammarskjold, Dag, 43
Havana Charter, 13
Helsinki Accord, 97
  compliance with, 121–122
  and détente, 97, 98
  and human rights, 98, 123
  as missing World War II peace treaty, 98
  monitoring groups, 121
  See also Conference on Security and Cooperation in Europe
Heng Samrin, 128
Ho Chi Minh, 22, 27
Holland. See Netherlands
Horn of Africa, 126–127. See also Ethiopia; Somalia
Hot-line agreement, 53, 114(n5). See also Arms control agreements
Human rights
  basic human needs approach, 138
  and CSCE, 98, 121–122
  as North-South issue, 138
  and the UN, 66, 130
  U.S. and, 138
  See also Helsinki Accord

Hungary, 6(n1), 86(n4)
  and the Soviet Union, 45
  and the U.S., 121
Hussein, King, 99, 100
Hydrogen bomb, 21. See also Nuclear weapons

IBRD. See World Bank
ICBMs. See Nuclear weapons, intercontinental ballistic missiles
Iceland, 6(n1)
ICJ. See World Court
IDA. See International Development Association
IMF. See International Monetary Fund
India, 11, 26, 27
  and the Afro-Asian movement, 31, 85
  and Bangladesh, 104
  and nonalignment, 33, 184
  and nuclear nonproliferation, 71
  and Pakistan, 27, 68, 78, 100
  and the Soviet Union, 49, 57, 78, 100
Indochina
  and France, 21, 22, 49
  and Geneva conference (1954), 22
  and the U.S., 49
  U.S. aid to French forces in, 21
  See also Laos; Vietnam
Indonesia, 11, 14, 27
  and the Afro-Asian movement, 31, 84
  independence conflict, 26, 32
  and nonalignment, 32
  and the Soviet Union, 49
INF. See Intermediate range nuclear forces
Integrated Program of Commodities (IPC), 133, 134
Intercontinental ballistic missiles (ICBMs). See under Nuclear weapons
Interdependence, 111
Intermediate range ballistic missiles (IRBMs). See under Nuclear weapons
Intermediate range nuclear forces (INF), 150. See also Arms control issues; Nuclear weapons, intermediate range ballistic missiles

International Bank for Reconstruction and Development. *See* World Bank
International communism, 44
   challenges to Soviet leadership of, 76, 77
   and People's Republic of China, 76
International Development Association (IDA), 166
International economic system
   Northern disagreements over, 171, 172
   postwar construction of, 12, 111
   reform of, 162
   See also Bretton Woods; General Agreement on Tariffs and Trade; International Trade Organization; New International Economic Order
International Monetary Fund (IMF), 12, 13, 103
   and debt payments, 107, 167, 168. *See also* London club; Mexico; New York club; Nigeria; Paris club; Peru; Sudan
   and the East, 143(n9)
   and the NIEO, 106
   at UNCTAD VI, 164
International Tin Agreement (ITA), 164. *See also* Commodity trade issues
International trade agreements. *See* General Agreement on Tariffs and Trade; Havana Charter; International Trade Organization
International trade issues, 13, 81, 82, 106, 131, 164–165, 173. *See also* Commodity trade issues; New International Economic Order; United Nations Conference on Trade and Development
International Trade Organization (ITO), 13, 81
IPC. *See* Integrated Program of Commodities
Iran, 4, 125
   and Afro-Asian movement, 31, 55
   and Baghdad Pact, 33, 36(n19)
   Islamic fundamentalism, 129, 159, 173
   military coup (1953), 21

   and nationalizations, 21, 109
   radical foreign policy of, 159
   revolution (1978), 129
   Soviet troops in, 11, 17
   territorial ambitions of, 159
   and terrorism, 174
   and the U.S., 121, 129, 160
   See also Iran-Iraq war
Irangate scandal, 160
Iran-Iraq war, 159–160
   and the oil industry, 173
   and the Soviet Union, 160
   and the U.S., 160
Iraq
   and the Afro-Asian movement, 31
   and Baghdad Pact, 33, 36(n19), 47
   See also Iran-Iraq war
IRBMs. *See* Nuclear weapons, intermediate range ballistic missiles
Islamic Conference, 140
Islamic fundamentalism, 129, 159, 173
Israel, 3, 4
   and the Afro-Asian movement, 33
   Camp David negotiations with Egypt, 123
   and Egypt, 98, 99, 100, 101, 105, 123
   and Jordan, 99
   and Lebanon, 124, 159
   and nuclear nonproliferation, 71
   and the October War, 100, 101
   origins, 11
   and the Six-Day war, 66, 67(map), 68
   and the Suez crisis, 47
   and Syria, 66, 99, 101, 105, 124, 158, 159
   and terrorism, 175
   and the U.S., 73, 99, 100, 101, 105
   and the War of Attrition, 99
   See also Arab-Israeli conflict
Issue definition, 1, 63–64, 69, 74, 85, 170–171
ITA. *See* International Tin Agreement
Italy, 6(n1), 7
   Communist party of, 77
   peace negotiations with, 16
ITO. *See* International Trade Organization

Jackson-Vanik amendment. *See* U.S.-Soviet trade

Japan
  as Axis power, 7
  and commodity trade regulation, 134
  and East-West trade, 101
  and North-South trade, 108
  and OAPEC oil embargo, 104
  postwar treatment of, 16
  and the U.S., 173
  and the West, 4
Jerusalem, 66, 67(map), 73, 123, 124
Johnson, Lyndon B.
  and détente, 70
  and Kosygin, 72
  and Vietnam, 74–75, 76
Jordan, 28, 47, 66
  expulsion of Palestinians, 99, 114(n9)
  and Israel, 66
  and Syria, 99, 100
  and the U.S., 99

Kampuchea. See Cambodia
Karmal, Babrak, 130
Kashmir, 11, 78. See also India;
  Pakistan
Kennedy, John F.
  and Cuba, 51
  and Europe, 69
  and Khrushchev, 50–51
Kenya, 28
Khadafi, Muamar, 158
Khomeini, Ayatollah, 129
Khrushchev, Nikita, 22
  denunciation of Stalin, 44
  and national liberation wars, 48
  and peaceful coexistence, 45
  and Soviet rocket rattling, 49
Kissinger, Henry
  and China, 91
  and détente, 89
  shuttle diplomacy, 105
Kohl, Helmut, 150
Korea, division of, 19. See also Korean
  People's Democratic Republic;
  Republic of Korea
Korean People's Democratic Republic,
  19
Korean War, 20
  Southern reaction to, 32
  and UN, 11
Kosygin, Aleksy, 72, 75
Kuwait, 14

Laos, 86(n4)
  independence, 23
  neutralization, 49
  and the Soviet Union, 49
  and the U.S., 49
  and Vietnam, 128
  and Vietnam war, 49, 75
Latin American countries
  and the Afro-Asian movement, 31
  at Cairo economic conference, 60
  disinterest in Belgrade conference,
    59
  and nonalignment, 58–59
  nuclear-free zone for, 65
Law of the Sea treaty, 175
  U.S. rejection of, 175
  Western opposition to, 175
  See also Globalism
LDCs. See Less developed countries
League of Nations, 9, 11, 31
Lebanon, 47, 125
  civil strife, 124
  Israeli incursions, 124, 159, 173
  multinational peacekeeping force in,
    159
  Palestinians in, 99, 124, 159
  Syrian intervention, 124, 140, 159,
    173
  UN peacekeeping force in, 124
Less developed countries (LDCs), 14
Libya, 123
  confrontations with U.S., 158
  diplomatic ruptures with, 158
  military action in Chad, 158, 170
  Soviet arms in, 158
  and terrorism, 174
Limits to growth, 112
Lomé Convention, 108, 135, 165
London club, 167
Lumumba, Patrice, 43
Luxembourg, 6(n1)

MacArthur, General Douglas, 20
MAD. See Mutual Assured Destruction
Malaya, 14, 26, 28, 32
Malaysia, 85
Mali, 4, 78, 84
Mao Zedong, 19
Marcos, Ferdinand, 170
Marshall Plan, 17
Marxism-Leninism, 15, 25–26, 45

and Sino-Soviet conflict, 45, 76
  See also Communists;
    Eurocommunism; International
    communism
MBFR. See Mutual Balanced Force
  Reduction
Mexico
  and Cairo economic conference, 60
  as debtor, 166, 167
MIRVs. See Nuclear weapons, multiple
  independently targeted re-entry
  vehicles
MNCs. See Multinational corporations
MNR. See Mozambican National
  Resistance
Mongolia, 36(n14), 86(n4)
Morocco, 62(n12)
Mossadeq, Muhammed, 21
Mozambique, 86(n4), 139
  and African National Congress, 156
  independence of, 125
  and South Africa, 156, 174. See also
    Nkomati Accords
  and the Soviet Union, 163
Mozambican National Resistance (MNR
  or RENAMO), 156
MPLA. See Popular Movement for the
  Liberation of Angola
Mugabe, Robert, 139
Mujahedin, 160
Multinational corporations (MNCs),
  106, 108
Multiple independently targeted re-
  entry vehicles. See under Nuclear
  weapons
Mutual Assured Destruction (MAD)
  definition of, 54
  as U.S. policy, 54
Mutual Balanced Force Reductions
  (MBFR), 96, 119. See also
    European security
MX. See under Nuclear weapons

Namibia (Southwest Africa)
  guerrilla war in, 140
  and South Africa, 140, 174
  and the UN, 113, 139–140
  and the U.S., 127, 139, 140, 158
  See also South Africa; United
    Nations General Assembly; United
    Nations Security Council

Nasser, Gamal Abdel, 27, 28, 33, 47
  and Arab-Israeli conflict, 99
  and nonalignment conferences, 58,
    59, 60, 83, 84
  and the Soviet Union, 49, 59, 99
National Front for the Liberation of
  Angola (FNLA), 126
Nationalizations, 108–109
National liberation struggles
  as legitimate uses of force, 64. See
    also Use of force
  in Portuguese Africa, 126
  in Southern Africa, 126
  and the Soviet Union, 48
NATO. See North Atlantic Treaty
  Organization
Nehru, Jawaharlal, 27
  and the Afro-Asian movement, 31
  and nonalignment conferences, 55,
    57, 58, 60, 83, 84
  and peaceful coexistence, 55
Neocolonialism, 29, 107
Netherlands, 8
  and commodity trade regulation, 134
  and decolonization, 11
  and Indonesia, 11
  and NATO, 6(n1), 19
  and OAPEC oil embargo, 104
  and political instability in the South,
    125, 169
  and Southern debt, 135
New International Economic Order
  (NIEO), 103, 106
  and East-West differences, 108,
    143(n9)
  and global negotiations, 136, 161
  and the Group of 77, 106, 131, 136
  Northern reaction to, 106, 107, 132
  and the North-South agenda, 117,
    131, 138
  progress of, 135
  and Southern political cooperation,
    110
  and the UN, 106, 107
  and UNCTAD negotiations, 131
Newly Industrialized Countries (NICs),
  162
New York club, 166
New Zealand, 3, 4
  and ANZUS pact, 36(n19), 176(n3)
  and SEATO, 36(n19)

Nicaragua, 86(n4), 125, 128
  Arias peace plan for, 156, 157
  Contadora peace plan for, 156
  Sandinista revolution, 129–130
  Soviet military aid to, 156
  and United Nicaraguan Opposition
    (Contras), 156, 157
  and the U.S., 130, 156, 160
NICs. See Newly Industrialized
  Countries
NIEO. See New International
  Economic Order
Nigeria, 4, 28
  as debtor, 167
Nixon, Richard M.
  and China, 91
  and détente, 89
  and Syrian threat to Jordan, 99
  and Vietnam, 89, 90
Nixon Doctrine, 89
Nixon shocks, 111
Nkomati accords, 156. See also
  Mozambique; South Africa
Nkrumah, Kwame, 27, 84
Nobel Peace Prize
  for Anwar Sadat, 124
  for Menachem Begin, 124
  for Oscar Arias, 156
No-first-use declaration, 175(n4). See
  also Arms control issues
Nonaligned Movement
  Algiers summit (1973), 103
  Cuban summit (1979), 135
  disunity within, 135
  and Group of 77, 103, 131
  Lusaka meeting (1970), 102
  and NIEO, 103, 131
  See also Afro-Asian movement;
    Nonalignment
Nonalignment, 32–33
  and Bandung conference, 55
  and Belgrade conference, 59, 60
  Cairo conference (1964), 83, 84
  and the Cold War, 32, 61, 84
  definition of, 58–59
  as moral philosophy, 59
  and Nehru, 57
  relationship to anticolonialism, 59,
    61
  and the Soviet Union, 38, 57
  Third World interest in, 59, 61, 83

  and Vietnam war, 84
  Western suspicion of, 38, 56–57
Nonproliferation of nuclear weapons,
  65, 71, 154. See also
  Nonproliferation Treaty
Nonproliferation Treaty (NPT), 65, 71
Normalization, 88. See also Détente
North, 4, 5
  disunity over economic issues, 105,
    132, 134, 168
  and the East, 143(n9)
  and political instability in the South,
    169, 170
North, Oliver, 160
North Atlantic Treaty Organization
  (NATO), 6(n1), 19, 22, 23, 46
  IRBMs for, 120, 148
  Multilateral Force for, 71
  and nuclear weapons, 40, 69, 120
  two-track policy, 120, 148
  and the Warsaw Treaty
    Organization, 23, 97
  See also European security
North Korea. See Korean People's
  Democratic Republic
North-South agenda
  concept of, 4
  economic issues on, 60, 79, 180
  and global agenda, 55
  summary: 1945–1955, 24; 1955–1963,
    54; 1964–1968, 79; 1969–1975,
    102; 1975–1980, 131; 1980s, 161
  and Third World conflicts, 125, 131
North-South trade, 106, 108, 133, 134,
    162, 164, 165. See also Commodity
    trade issues; European Economic
    Community; International trade
    issues; Lomé Convention; New
    International Economic Order;
    United Nations Conference on
    Trade and Development
North Vietnam, 74
  and Soviet Union, 74
  and the U.S., 74, 75, 90
  See also Vietnam; Vietnam War
Norway, 6(n1)
Novotny, Anton, 77
NPT. See Arms control agreements;
  Nonproliferation Treaty
Nuclear-free zones, 41, 147, 151
  in Africa, 65

in Latin America, 65. *See also*
Tlateloco, Treaty of
in the South Pacific, 176(n3). *See also*
South Pacific Nuclear Free Zone
Convention
Nuclear proliferation. *See* Arms control
agreements; Nonproliferation of
nuclear weapons; Nonproliferation
Treaty
Nuclear strategy. *See* Strategic issues;
Strategic policy
Nuclear weapons
antiballistic missiles (ABMs), 71, 72,
94
cruise missiles, 95, 119, 150, 151
defensive, 39, 71, 72, 94
ground-launched cruise missiles
(GLCMs), 120, 150
hydrogen bomb, 21
impact on security policy, 39
impact on strategic stability, 94, 118–
119
intercontinental ballistic missiles
(ICBMs), 40, 71, 94, 95, 150, 151,
153
intermediate range ballistic missiles
(IRBMs), 120, 147, 150, 153
multiple independently targeted reentry vehicles (MIRVs), 94, 95,
119, 149(fig.)
MX missile, 151
Pershing II, 120, 150
SS-18, 150, 151
SS-20, 120
tactical, 40, 46
threats to use, 49
triad, 52, 94
Trident submarines, 151
See also Arms control; Arms control
issues; Nuclear strategy; Strategic
issues; Strategic policy
Nuclear weapons testing
opposed by Belgrade nonaligned
conference, 60
Soviet resumption of (1961), 51
treaty banning, 53, 76
Nyerere, Julius, 102

OAPEC. *See* Organization of Arab
Petroleum Exporting Countries

OAS. *See* Organization of American
States
OAU. *See* Organization of African
Unity
October War. *See* Arab-Israeli conflict;
Egypt; Israel
OECD. *See* Organization for Economic
Cooperation and Development
Ogaden, 127. *See also* Ethiopia; Somalia
Oil
and Arab-Israeli conflict, 104, 105
and debt, 166
embargo, 104–105
and energy dependence, 105
and global recession, 137
and Iranian revolution, 137
and North-South negotiations, 105
price changes, 104, 137
See also Organization of Arab
Petroleum Exporting Countries;
Organization of Petroleum
Exporting Countries
OPEC. *See* Organization of Petroleum
Exporting Countries
Organization for Economic
Cooperation and Development
(OECD)
membership, 86(n4)
observers, 86(n4)
and trade disputes, 172
Organization of African Unity (OAU)
admission of People's Republic of
Angola, 126
and nuclear-free Africa, 65
and Soviet-Cuban interventions, 140
and UNCTAD, 80
Organization of American States
(OAS), 48
Organization of Arab Petroleum
Exporting Countries (OAPEC),
104, 105. *See also* Organization of
Petroleum Exporting Countries
Organization of Petroleum Exporting
Countries (OPEC), 104, 132, 133
impact on world economy, 104, 109,
136, 137, 140, 141, 142
internal disunity, 136
and the NIEO, 132
oil embargo, 104, 105
Southern support for, 105, 135, 136

stimulus to producer associations,
109
U.S. response to, 105
See also Organization of Arab
Petroleum Exporting Countries

PAC. See Pan African Congress
"Pactomania," 36(n19)
Pahlavi, Shah Reza, 21, 129
Pakistan, 27, 31, 33
and the Afghan insurrection, 174
and Afghan refugees, 174–175
and the Afro-Asian movement, 31,
33
and Baghdad Pact, 33, 36(n19), 100
and Bangladesh, 100
and China, 100
and India, 11, 27, 68, 78, 100
and nuclear nonproliferation, 71
and SEATO, 36(n19), 100
and the Soviet Union, 78
and the U.S., 32
Palestine, 11, 17, 27–28
League of Nations mandate, 11
UN partition plans, 11
war of 1948, 11
See also Arab-Israeli conflict;
Palestinian rights; Palestinians
Palestine Liberation Organization (PLO)
formation of, 99
international recognition of, 112
in Lebanon, 99, 159
and the Soviet Union, 124
U.N. observer status for, 112
See also Arafat, Yasser; Palestine;
Palestinian rights; Palestinians
Palestinian rights, 68, 98, 110, 111–112
and African states, 112
and Camp David agreements, 123
and the League of Arab States, 112,
123
and the Soviet Union, 124
and the U.S., 112
See also Palestine; Palestine
Liberation Organization;
Palestinians
Palestinians
at Geneva peace conference, 112
in Jordan, 99, 114(n9)
in Lebanon, 99, 124, 159
and Syria, 99, 124, 159

terrorism by, 112, 174
See also Palestine; Palestine
Liberation Organization;
Palestinian rights
Pan African Congress (PAC), 113
Pan-African movement, 30
Pan-Arab movement, 30
Pan-Asian movement, 30
Paris club, 167
Paris Peace Conference (1919), 25
Paris summit (1960), 50
PDRY. See People's Democratic
Republic of Yemen
Peaceful coexistence, 88
at Belgrade nonaligned conference,
60
and Khrushchev, 45
Nehru's Five Principles of, 55
People's Democratic Republic of
Yemen (PDRY), 86(n4), 125, 129
and COMECON, 129
and the Soviet Union, 129
People's Republic of Angola, 126. See
also Angola
People's Republic of China (PRC), 11,
20, 41
admission to the UN, 91
and the Afro-Asian movement, 33,
85
attacks on Quemoy and Matsu, 50
and Geneva conference on Asia, 22
and invasion of Cambodia, 128, 130,
140
and invasion of Czechoslovakia, 77–
78
and Laos, 49
and nuclear nonproliferation, 71, 76
and Pakistan, 100
and the Soviet Union, 45, 77, 78,
91, 122. See also Sino-Soviet
conflict
and the U.S., 78, 91, 91–92, 122
and Vietnam, 73, 75, 122, 128
Perestroika, 147
Pershing II. See under Nuclear
weapons
Peru, 109, 167
Philippines, 14, 26
and the Afro-Asian movement, 31,
55
fall of Marcos government, 170

and SEATO, 36(n19)
and the U.S., 21, 170
PLO. See Palestine Liberation
  Organization
PNW agreement. See under Arms
  control agreements
Poindexter, John, 160
Poland, 86(n4)
  borders, 16, 98
  and Czechoslovakia, 77
  and the FRG, 93
  martial law in, 155
  Solidarity political challenge, 155
  and the Soviet Union, 16, 35(n2), 70
  and the UN, 35(n6)
  and the U.S., 121
  and the Warsaw Treaty
    Organization, 6(n1)
Pollution, 111
Pol Pot, 128
Popular Movement for the Liberation
  of Angola (MPLA), 126
Portugal
  and decolonization, 25, 125–126
  military actions in Africa, 66
  and NATO, 6(n1), 19
  and political instability in the South,
    169
Power, diffusion of, 85
Prague Spring, 77. See also
  Czechoslovakia
PRC. See People's Republic of China
Preemptive attack, 40
Producer associations, 108–109
Protectionism, 75, 165, 171
Proxy war, 49

Quadripartite Agreement on Berlin, 93
Quemoy and Matsu crisis, 50

Ramadan war. See October War
Reagan, Ronald, 146
  and anti-Sovietism, 146. See also
    Reagan Doctrine
  and private investment in the South,
    166
  and SDI, 151
Reagan Doctrine, 155, 156
Refugees, 100, 175
Regional trade associations. See
  Council for Mutual Economic

Assistance; European Common
  Market
RENAMO. See Mozambican National
  Resistance
Republic of China, 35(n7), 56, 91
Republic of Korea (ROK), 19
Resolution 242. See United Nations
  Security Council
Rhodesia, 28, 126, 139. See also
  Zambia; Zimbabwe
ROK. See Republic of Korea
Romania, 86(n4)
  and the FRG, 114(n4)
  and invasion of Czechoslovakia, 77
  and the Soviet Union, 70, 77
  and the Warsaw Pact, 6(n1), 77

Sadat, Anwar, 123
SALT. See Strategic Arms Limitation
  Talks; SALT I treaty; SALT II
  treaty
SALT I treaty, 95
SALT II treaty, 95, 132, 156
SAMs. See Surface-to-air missiles
Sandinista National Liberation Front,
  130. See also Nicaragua
São Tomé and Príncipe, 125–126
Saudi Arabia, 31
  in OPEC, 136, 137
Savimbi, Jonas, 126, 155
SDI. See Strategic Defense Initiative
SEATO. See Southeast Asian Treaty
  Organization
Second strike capacity, 52–53
Security dilemma, 38, 40
Selassie, Haile, 127
Senegal, 66
Shanghai Communique, 92
Sinai peninsula, 66, 67(map), 123
Sino-Soviet conflict, 45, 46, 50, 76, 77–
  78
  and the Afro-Asian movement, 85
  border clashes, 91
  and détente, 91
  and international communism, 45, 76
  and the nonaligned movement, 59
  and U.S.-PRC rapprochement, 91,
    122
  and U.S.-Soviet relations, 122
  and Vietnam War, 75

Six-Day War (1967). *See* Arab-Israeli conflict
Somalia, 4
  and the Soviet Union, 126–127
  U.S. aid for, 127
  war with Ethiopia, 127
Somoza, Anastasio, 129, 130
South
  and the Cold War, 32
  defined, 4, 5, 8
  disunity in, 83, 84
  and the East, 83, 103, 163
  East-West rivalry in, 30
  economic independence for, 102, 106
  economic problems of, 79, 105, 106, 162
  and GATT, 80, 82
  and IMF, 107
  and international economic reform, 83, 102
  and nationalizations, 109
  Northern criticism of, 107, 162, 163
  and Palestinian rights, 110
  political instability in, 169
  and Rhodesia, 110
  and South Africa, 110
  and trade issues, 80, 81, 83, 108
  unity of, 30, 31
  See also Third World
South Africa
  and Angola, 126, 173–174
  and Cubans in Angola, 158
  international sanctions on, 139, 169
  and Mozambique, 156, 158, 173–174.
    See also Nkomati accords
  and Namibian independence, 113, 128, 139, 173–174
  and nuclear nonproliferation, 71
  Southern opposition to, 170
  and the UN, 43, 113, 127–128, 139
  and the U.S., 127, 169
  See also African National Congress; Apartheid; Pan African Congress; South-west African People's Organization
Southeast Asian Treaty Organization (SEATO), 36(n19)
South Korea. *See* Republic of Korea
South Pacific Nuclear Free Zone Convention (SPNFZ), 176(n3)
South Vietnam, 74, 90. *See also* Vietnam; Vietnam war

South-west African People's Organization (SWAPO), 113, 126, 170
South Yemen. *See* People's Democratic Republic of Yemen
Soviet Union
  and AAPSO, 57
  and Afghanistan, 128–129, 140, 176
  and the Afro-Asian movement, 57, 85
  and Algeria, 49
  alliances of, 3, 6(n1), 19
  and Angola, 158
  and Arab-Israeli conflict, 73, 99, 101, 123
  and Cuba, 48, 51
  and disarmament, 41
  domestic reforms, 147, 163
  and East Europe, 16, 17, 45, 70, 76–77
  and Egypt, 47, 99, 100, 101
  and Eritrea, 177(n7)
  and Ethiopia, 158, 177(n7)
  and European gas pipeline, 154, 155
  and the FRG, 92, 93, 150
  and Germany, 15, 18–19, 35(n2)
  and India, 49, 57, 78, 100
  and the ITA, 164
  and Iran, 160
  and Israel, 124, 160
  and Japan, 35(n2), 36(n14)
  and Laos, 49
  leadership changes, 147
  and Libya, 160
  and Mozambique, 158, 163
  and nationalizations, 109
  and Nazi Germany, 15, 34(n2)
  and the NIEO, 143(n9)
  and nonalignment, 60, 61
  and nuclear-free zones, 41, 147
  and nuclear threats, 49
  and OAPEC oil embargo, 105
  and Palestinian rights, 124
  and the PDRY, 158
  and the PRC. *See* Sino-Soviet conflict
  and Poland, 16, 35(n2), 40(n2), 44
  and the Quemoy-Matsu crisis, 50
  and the South, 61, 163
  and Syria, 49, 73, 124, 158
  and Taiwan, 50

and the Third World, 37, 78–79,
    163
and the UN, 35(n7), 43, 68
and the U.S. See Superpowers; U.S.-
    Soviet military balance; U.S.-
    Soviet summits; U.S.-Soviet trade
and Vietnam, 73, 75, 157, 158
and West Europe, 77, 150
and Yugoslavia, 35(n10)
Spain, 6(n1)
    and the Third World, 125
    and political instability in the South,
        169, 170
SPNFZ. See South Pacific Nuclear Free
    Zone Convention
Sputnik, 52
SS-18. See under Nuclear weapons
SS-20. See under Nuclear weapons
Stalin, Joseph, 16, 22, 44
START. See Strategic Arms Reduction
    Talks
Strategic Arms Limitation Talks
    (SALT), 93, 94, 95
Strategic Arms Reduction Talks
    (START), 150
Strategic Defense Initiative (SDI)
    and ABM treaty, 152
    and arms race, 152
    and deterrence, 151, 152
    European attitudes toward, 153
    Soviet opposition to, 152
    See also Reagan, Ronald; Strategic
        issues
Strategic issues
    deterrence, 94, 151, 152
    escalation, 93
    parity, 94
    stability, 93, 94
    targeting, 54
Strategic policy
    basic concepts, 40, 52–53
    flexible response, 53
    MAD, 54
    U.S. options for, 54
Sudan
    as debtor, 168
    refugees in, 175
Suez Canal, 28, 47, 98, 99
Suez crisis, 46–47, 49
    and the Third World, 59
Sukarno, 27, 84

Superpowers
    competition of, 52, 78, 146–147,
        160–161
    and détente, 88
    limited control abilities, 72, 85, 146
    mutual interests, 70, 88, 122, 142
    and regional conflicts, 98, 100, 127
    and the Third World, 31, 48–49, 59,
        72, 125
Surface-to-air missiles (SAMs), 99
SWAPO. See South-west African
    People's Organization
Sweden
    neutrality, 6(n1)
    and Southern debt, 135
Switzerland
    neutrality, 6(n1)
    and Southern debt, 137
Syria
    and the Afro-Asian movement, 31
    and Egypt, 47, 123
    and Israel, 66, 101, 105, 124, 158,
        159
    and Jordan, 99, 100
    and Lebanon, 124, 140, 159, 173
    and Palestinians, 99, 124, 159
    and the Soviet Union, 49, 73, 124,
        158
    and terrorism, 174

Taiwan, 50, 56, 92. See also Republic
    of China
Tanzania, 102
Terrorism, 174
Test ban treaty. See Arms control
    agreements
Textile trade issues, 165. See also
    Commodity trade issues
Thailand, 55
    Cambodian refugees in, 175
    and SEATO, 36(n19)
Theater nuclear forces (TNF), 120. See
    also European security;
    Intermediate range nuclear forces;
    North Atlantic Treaty
    Organization; Nuclear weapons
Third World, 4–5
    and the Cold War, 59, 61
    and East-West rivalries. See
        Superpowers, and the Third
        World

and nonalignment, 59, 60
and the Soviet Union, 48–49, 59
See also South
Tibet, 33
Tito, 35(n10)
and nonaligned conferences, 57, 58, 59, 60, 83, 84
Tlateloco, Treaty of, 65
TNF. *See* Theater nuclear forces
Tonkin Gulf Resolution, 74
Touré, Sékou, 27
Triad, 52, 94
Triangular diplomacy, 91
Truman, Harry S., 17
Truman Doctrine, 17
Turkey, 6(n1), 55
and Baghdad Pact, 32, 36(n19)
and Cyprus, 78
and Soviet Union, 16
and the U.S., 17, 78

UAR. *See* United Arab Republic
UK. *See* Britain
UN. *See* United Nations
UNCTAD. *See* United Nations Conference on Trade and Development
UNCTAD I, 81, 82
UNCTAD II, 82, 83
UNCTAD III, 103
UNCTAD IV, 133, 134
UNCTAD V, 134
UNCTAD VI, 164
UNESCO. *See* United Nations Educational, Scientific, and Cultural Organization
UNGA. *See* United Nations General Assembly
Union for the Total Independence of Angola (UNITA), 126
South African support for, 12
UNITA. *See* Union for the Total Independence of Angola
United Arab Republic (UAR), 47. *See also* Egypt; Syria
United Kingdom (UK). *See* Britain
United Nations (UN), 9, 10
and Afghanistan, 174
and Arab-Israeli conflict, 67, 68, 124
and arms control, 65
Article 19 crisis, 68

Charter, 9, 10, 35(n7), 56
and conflict, 64, 66, 68. *See also* Use of force
and the Congo crisis, 42–43
and decolonization, 10, 42, 43
and the Dominican Republic, 66
financial crisis, 68
and human rights, 66
and Korean War, 11, 20
and law of the sea, 68, 175
and Lebanon, 124
and Nigerian civil war, 66
peacekeeping force in Egypt, 66
peacekeeping force in Lebanon, 124
and Portugal, 66
reform of, 175
and the Six-Day War, 66, 67
troika proposal for, 43
trusteeship, 10
and Vietnam, 66
See also United Nations Conference on Trade and Development; United Nations Economic and Social Council; United Nations General Assembly; United Nations Security Council
United Nations Conference on Trade and Development (UNCTAD), 64, 81, 82, 85
and the COMECON countries, 86(n4)
and Common Fund, 134
and GATT, 103
and Group of 77, 80, 81, 103, 133
and IMF, 103
North-South conflict in, 81, 82, 134
and Southern unity, 85
structure of, 82, 134
See also Conference on International Economic Cooperation; International trade issues; UNCTAD I; UNCTAD II; UNCTAD III; UNCTAD IV
United Nations Economic and Social Council (ECOSOC), 81
United Nations Educational, Scientific, and Cultural Organization (UNESCO), 176
United Nations General Assembly (UNGA)
and apartheid, 66, 107, 113

Charter on Economic Rights and
Duties of States, 107
Committee of the Whole (COW),
136, 161
differences with Security Council,
113
and global negotiations, 161
and Namibia, 113
and the NIEO, 106–107
observers: PLO, 112; ANC; 113;
PAC, 113; SWAPO, 113
and South Africa, 113
United Nations Security Council
(UNSC)
and apartheid, 43
differences with General Assembly,
113
and Namibia, 120
Resolution 242, 66, 68, 73
and South Africa, 128
structure, 35(n7)
United States (U.S.)
and the AAPSO, 57
and Afghanistan, 155, 160
and Africa, 127, 158
and the ANC, 169
aid to Greece and Turkey, 17
alliances, 3, 6(n1), 20, 36(n19)
and Angola, 159
and Arab-Israeli conflict, 99, 100–
101, 122, 124
and Argentina, 138
and Brazil, 138, 173
budget deficit, 172
and Cambodia, 90, 155
and Camp David Israeli-Egyptian
negotiations, 124
and Chad, 158
and Chile, 138
and the Congo crisis, 43
and Cuba, 48, 51, 62(n12)
currency devaluation, 111
and the debt crisis, 168
and decolonization, 24, 25, 29
and détente, 89, 90, 126, 130, 131
and disarmament, 41
and the Dominican Republic, 73
economic aid to the Third World,
61
economic problems, 110–111
and Egypt, 47, 104

and Ethiopia, 127
and Europe, 17, 46
and France, 46
and Germany, 16, 18
and globalism, 163, 175
and Greece, 17
and Grenada, 157
and Guatemala, 138, 170
and Haiti, 170
and Hungary, 121
and Indochina, 20–21, 22–23
and ITA, 164
and Iran, 21, 129, 160
and Iran-Iraq war, 160
and Israel, 73, 99, 101, 105, 123
and Japan, 21, 171
and Jerusalem, 124
and Jordan, 99
and the Korean War, 20
and Laos, 49, 90
and Lebanon, 159
and Libya, 123, 158, 173
military aid to Southern countries,
32, 169
military bases abroad, 131
and Mozambique, 156, 159
and Namibia, 127, 128, 141–142
and nationalism, 25, 29–30
and nationalizations, 108–109
and NATO, 6(n1), 19, 23, 46, 69,
120, 148, 150
and neutrality, 32, 61
and Nicaragua, 130, 156, 160
and nonalignment, 55, 61
and North Vietnam, 74, 75, 90
and nuclear threats, 50
and OAPEC oil embargo, 104
and OECD, 172
and OPEC, 104, 105, 133
opposition to UN economic role,
163
and Palestinians, 99
and the PRC, 78, 91, 92, 122
and the Persian Gulf, 131, 160
and the Philippines, 21, 170
and Poland, 121
and political instability in the South,
169
Rapid Deployment Force, 131
and the Republic of China (Taiwan),
55, 96

and Rhodesia, 127
and Romania, 121
and South Africa, 127, 128, 158, 169
and the Soviet Union, 17–18, 52,
    92, 146. *See also* U.S.-Soviet
    military balance; U.S.-Soviet
    summits; U.S.-Soviet trade
and Syria, 101, 105
and terrorism, 174
and the Third World, 147
trade deficit, 110, 140, 171, 172
and Turkey, 17, 78
and the UNSC, 35(n7)
and Vietnam, 73, 74, 75, 76, 89, 90
See also Carter Doctrine; Human
    rights; Nixon Doctrine; North
    Atlantic Treaty Organization;
    Reagan Doctrine; Superpowers;
    U.S.-Soviet military balance
UNSC. *See* United Nations Security
    Council
Uruguay, 60
U.S. dollar, 111, 172
Use of force
and détente, 88
in international relations, 64, 78, 176
legitimacy of, 64, 140, 154, 181
and the UN, 66, 68
U.S.-Soviet military balance
assessing, 52, 94, 118, 148, 149(fig.),
    186(fig.), 187(fig.), 188(fig.), 189(fig.)
asymmetry of, 94
and détente, 89
parity of, 93, 118, 148
stability of, 94, 119
See also Arms control; Arms control
    issues; Nuclear weapons; Strategic
    issues
U.S.-Soviet summits
Glassboro, 72
Moscow, 90, 96
Reykjavik, 153
Vienna, 50, 51, 144(n1)
Vladivostok, 95
U.S.-Soviet trade, 101–102, 121
Jackson-Vanik amendment, 102
and Jewish emigration, 102
treaty, 102, 121
See also East-West trade
USSR. *See* Soviet Union

Venezuela, 60
Vienna summit. *See under* U.S.-Soviet
    summits
Vietcong, 74, 75. *See also* Vietnam war
Vietnam, 4, 11, 27, 32, 86(n4), 125
division of, 22, 74
expansionism, 128
and France, 22, 28, 29, 34
independence of, 28
invasion of Cambodia, 128, 140
and Laos, 128
and PRC, 128
See also Vietnam war
Vietnam war
compared with Korean War, 74
de-Americanizing of, 90
definition of, 74
North Vietnamese involvement, 90
peace treaty (1973), 90
and Sino-Soviet conflict, 75, 96
Soviet involvement, 73, 75, 90
and U.S.-Chinese rapprochement, 90
U.S. involvement, 74, 75, 76, 89, 90
See also Indochina

War of Attrition, 98–99. *See also*
    Arab-Israeli conflict; Egypt; Israel
Warsaw Pact. *See* Warsaw Treaty
    Organization
Warsaw Treaty Organization (WTO)
and the FRG, 114(n4)
and NATO, 6(n1), 19, 97
Romanian independence of, 77
WCG. *See* Western Contact Group
West, defined, 3, 19
West Bank, 66, 67(map), 99
Western Contact Group (WCG), 129
West Europe
energy dependence of, 104
and OAPEC oil embargo, 104
trade with the South. *See* European
    Economic Community; Lomé
    Convention
West Germany. *See* Federal Republic
    of Germany
World Bank (International Bank for
    Reconstruction and Development)
    (IBRD), 13, 83
and economic development, 108
and human rights, 138

and the North, 165
World Court (International Court of
    Justice) (ICJ), 140
World War I, 8, 24
World War II, 7, 34
    and decolonization, 24, 25
    missing peace treaty for. *See* Helsinki
        Accord
    political results of, 8
WTO. *See* Warsaw Treaty Organization

Yalta conference (1945), 15, 16
Yemen, 31. *See also* People's
    Democratic Republic of Yemen

Yom Kippur war. *See* Arab-Israeli
    conflict, October War
Yugoslavia
    and the invasion of Czechoslovakia,
        77
    and the nonaligned movement, 57,
        84
    and the Soviet Union, 35(n10), 57–
        58

Zaire, 42. *See also* Congo (Zaire)
Zambia, 66
Zhou En-lai, 78, 79
Zimbabwe, 139
Zionist imperialism, 124